A BASIC GUIDE TO
Fair Housing Accessibility

A BASIC GUIDE TO
Fair Housing Accessibility

Everything Architects and Builders Need to Know
About the Fair Housing Act Accessibility Guidelines

WRITTEN BY

Peter A. Stratton,

STEVEN WINTER ASSOCIATES, INC.

EDITED BY

Michael J. Crosbie,

STEVEN WINTER ASSOCIATES, INC.

JOHN WILEY & SONS, INC

New York • Chichester • Weinheim • Brisbane • Singapore • Toronto

This publication is designed to provide accurate and authoritative information in regard to the subject matter covered. It is sold with the understanding that the publisher is not engaged in rendering professional services. If professional advice or other expert assistance is required, the services of a competent professional person should be sought.

Library of Congress Cataloging-in-Publication Data:

Stratton, Peter A.
    A basic guide to fair housing accessibility : everything architects and builders need to know about the Fair Housing Act accessibility guidelines / by Peter A. Stratton.
        p. cm.
    Includes index.
    ISBN 0-471-39559-5 (paper : alk. paper)
    1. Architecture and the physically handicapped—United States. 2. Dwellings—Access for the physically handicapped—United States. I. Title.

Printed in the United States of America.

10 9 8 7 6 5 4 3 2 1

Contents

Appendices 125

Index 187

Introduction

WHY SHOULD YOU READ THIS BOOK?

In a 1988 amendment to the Fair Housing Act (FHA), Congress extended protection against discrimination in housing and housing-related transactions to people with disabilities and to families with children. As a result of the 1988 amendment, failure to design and construct covered multifamily housing so that it is accessible to people with disabilities is discriminatory housing practice and a violation of federal law. A complaint for discriminatory housing practice can be filed against anyone involved with the design and construction of a covered project. If you are a designer, architect, builder, developer, contractor, or subcontractor in the multifamily housing industry, you should protect yourself against charges of discriminatory housing practice.

The federal government is stepping up its enforcement of the Fair Housing Act. In an effort to ensure that multifamily housing projects are in compliance with the design and construction requirements of the FHA, and in an effort to increase the availability of accessible housing, disability rights advocacy groups are becoming more active in identifying multifamily housing projects that allegedly are in violation of the FHA. In some cases, the architects and builders of such projects have been required to pay compensation to the litigants, or have been required to pay for alterations to the project to bring them into compliance. Other architects and builders with decisions against them have been required to attend courses, at their expense, which cover the accessibility requirements of the FHA. Our firm, Steven Winter Associates, Inc. (SWA), has presented such courses. SWA has also been retained by the U.S. Department of Justice (DOJ) and the Department of Housing and Urban Development (HUD) to provide expert testimony in legal action against architects and builders of multifamily housing that allegedly does not meet the FHA's accessibility requirements. We are aware of the areas where many architects and builders are most vulnerable in the design and construction of multifamily housing that should comply with the Act. We have designed this book to clearly communicate the facts you need to know to comply with the accessibility requirements of the FHA, with particular attention on those areas where many architects and builders go awry of the law.

JUST THE FACTS

This book is structured according to the accessibility requirements of the FHA. Part 1 focuses on the requirements and how to satisfy them. Part 2 provides a checklist that you can use in the design and construction of multifamily housing, to help make sure that your project is in compliance.

Part 1 tells you exactly what you need to know about conforming with the seven design and construction requirements of the FHA in a simple and clear manner. This section elaborates on technical guidance for FHA compliance, but it does not contain any "recommendations" or "good ideas" that may be beyond the scope of the accessibility requirements of the FHA. This book zeros in on what is required of you as a design and construction professional. If you want to go beyond the requirements of the act, you should develop your own creative solutions for compliance. This book communicates to you only what is required by law.

Part 1 also addresses the subtle differences between several terms defined by the Guidelines, or the regulations that implement the 1988 amendments to the FHA, and the same terms defined by model building codes. We do this because misapplying the commonly understood model-code definition of a term, which is actually defined differently by the Guidelines or the regulations, may be misleading. We also understand that it is a common mistake for those familiar with building codes to assume that other codes or laws define the same terms in the same way. It is extremely important to communicate to you the subtle differences in those definitions, to help you to avoid potential violations of the FHA.

The Checklist

Part 2 includes a comprehensive checklist to be used by multifamily housing industry players to help identify covered multifamily buildings and the dwelling units in them that must comply with the design and construction requirements of the FHA. Once covered projects and units have been identified, the checklist is organized in question format and incorporates the scoping and technical provisions of the Guidelines, including the technical requirements of its referenced standard—ANSI A117.1—beginning with the Guidelines' "Requirement 1: Accessible Building Entrance on an Accessible Route," and ending with "Requirement 7: Usable Kitchens and Bathrooms."

The checklist is a modified version of one that was developed from a survey of nearly 400 multifamily housing projects undertaken by SWA for HUD to study the rates of compliance with the FHA. The original survey was developed by SWA, working closely with HUD. The checklist in this book is a useful tool for architects to use during the preplanning, schematic design, and design development phases of a project, through the production of construction documents to help ensure that covered projects incorporate the accessibility requirements of the FHA. Builders can use the checklist to help ensure that the building construction is also FHA-compliant. The same checklist used by seasoned industry professionals can also benefit students, by helping them become aware of the needs of people with disabilities and of the importance of barrier removal in the built environment to help increase housing opportunities for people with disabilities.

While this book should answer many of your questions about complying with the Fair Housing Act, we realize that every scenario cannot be covered. For those that are not, readers should contact the authors of this book for further professional guidance. They can be reached at Steven Winter Associates, Inc., 50 Washington Street, Norwalk, CT, 06854; through the SWA website at www.swinter.com; or via email to pstratton@swinter.com or mcrosbie@swinter.com.

A BASIC GUIDE TO
Fair Housing Accessibility

PART 1

The Act and the Guidelines

I. THE FAIR HOUSING ACT

Background

The Fair Housing Act (FHA, Title VIII of the Civil Rights Act of 1968, 42 U.S.C. 3601–3619) makes it unlawful to discriminate against people in housing and housing-related transactions based on race, color, religion, national origin, and sex. In 1988, in an amendment to the Fair Housing Act (Pub. L. 100-430, approved September 13,1988), protection against discrimination in housing and housing-related transactions was extended to include families with children and people with disabilities. To ensure that people with and without disabilities have equal access to housing, and to increase the housing stock available to people with disabilities, Congress specified that certain design and construction criteria must be followed in order to make housing accessible to people with disabilities. The Fair Housing Accessibility Guidelines (the Guidelines, 24 CFR Ch. I, Subch. A, App. II) were issued by the Department of Housing and Urban Development (HUD) in response to the Congressional mandate for accessible housing (Appendix A).

In 1989, subsequent to the 1988 amendments to the FHA that extended protection from discrimination in housing and housing-related activities to families with children and people with disabilities, HUD issued the implementing regulations (the regulations, 24 CFR Part 14, et al.) to the Fair Housing Amendments Act. On March 6, 1991, HUD published the Final Fair Housing Accessibility Guidelines, which provide technical assistance for compliance with the design and construction requirements of the FHA. Although the Guidelines are not mandatory, the technical assistance offered provides a "safe harbor" for compliance with accessibility requirements of the FHA.

In 1994, after publication of the Guidelines, HUD published the Supplement to Notice of Fair Housing Accessibility Guidelines: Questions and Answers about the Guidelines (24 CFR Ch. I, Subch. A, App. IV), to clarify the design and construction requirements of the FHA (Appendix B). The Supplement to Notice of Fair Housing Accessibility Guidelines: Questions and Answers about the Guidelines, commonly known as the "Q&As," are an integral part of the accessibility requirements of the FHA. Although much of the information contained in the Q&As does not appear in the regulations or the Guidelines, it was published as a supplement to further clarify and expand on the guidance offered in the Guidelines.

TABLE 1-1 The Act

1968	The Fair Housing Act–Title VIII of the Civil Rights Act of 1968
1988	Fair Housing Amendments Act
1989	The Implementing Regulations to the Fair Housing Amendments Act
1991	The Guidelines
1994	Questions and Answers about the Guidelines
1996	Fair Housing Act Design Manual

Like the Guidelines, compliance with the technical assistance offered in the Q&As is not mandatory. However, the Q&As address many issues in the Guidelines that lack clarity and they are provided as additional technical assistance. Compliance with the technical assistance provided in the Q&As is also a "safe harbor" for compliance with many of the accessibility requirements of the FHA. In this book, reference to "the Act," the "Fair Housing Act," or "FHA," includes the FHA of 1968, the 1988 amendment to the FHA of 1968, the implementing regulations published in 1989, the Guidelines published in 1991, and the 1994 Supplement to Notice of Fair Housing Accessibility Guidelines: Questions and Answers about the Guidelines. Many of the figures contained in this book come from HUD's *Fair Housing Act Design Manual* or from the Guidelines themselves. Original figures were created by Masaki Furukawa of Steven Winter Associates, Inc.

In 1996, HUD published the *Fair Housing Act Design Manual.* The manual offers additional technical guidance to help architects, builders, developers, and others involved with the design and construction of buildings covered by the FHA to comply with its design and construction requirements.

Scope of Coverage

The seven design and construction requirements of the Fair Housing Amendments Act apply only to newly constructed multifamily housing built for first occupancy after March 13, 1991. The requirements do not apply to newly constructed or renovated single-family housing or to renovations or alterations to existing multifamily housing. However, if the renovation or alteration of existing multifamily housing includes the addition of four or more newly constructed dwelling units, only the newly constructed dwelling units are covered by the FHA. Any public or common space newly constructed in addition to the new construction of four or more dwelling units must also comply with the accessibility requirements. Public or common space newly constructed on a site that does not contain multifamily dwellings covered by the FHA is not required to comply with the accessibility requirements.

In addition to public and common areas, such as corridors or recreational facilities, that may be included in newly constructed multifamily housing projects, all of the dwelling units in buildings built for first occupancy after March 13, 1991, with at least four dwelling units and one or more elevators, and only ground-floor dwelling units in buildings built for first occupancy after March 13, 1991, with at least four dwelling units that are not served by elevators, must comply with the design and construction requirements of the FHA.

TABLE 1-2 How to Identify Projects Covered by the FHA

1. Newly Constructed
2. Multifamily housing with at least four attached dwelling units
3. First occupancy after March 13, 1991

TABLE 1-3 Dwelling Units Covered by the FHA	
In Buildings Served by Elevators	In Buildings Not Served by Elevators
All Dwelling Units	Only Ground Floor Dwelling Units

The regulations (24 CFR Part 14, et al.) that implement the FHA define "first occupancy" as "a building that has never before been used for any purpose." For example, an abandoned factory that has been completely gutted and rehabilitated into a new residential condominium complex is not covered by the FHA, because at one time the building functioned as a factory. As a result, although the residential condominium complex is newly constructed, it does not fit the definition of "first occupancy," because at one time the building was used for another purpose, that is, a factory.

Scoping Criteria Versus Technical Criteria

The Guidelines include both "scoping" and "technical" criteria as they apply to covered multifamily dwellings subject to the Fair Housing amendments. Scoping criteria provide the general application of the accessibility requirements, that is, what, where, or when to apply the accessibility provisions of the Act. Technical criteria provide specific guidance on how to comply with scoping criteria. For example, the Guidelines' "Requirement 3: Usable Doors," requires that all doors meant for user passage within a dwelling unit must be "usable." Requirement 3 stipulates the "scope" of doors within dwelling units required to be usable, that is, all doors meant for user passage. Requirement 3 also provides "technical" criteria for doors within dwelling units that are required to be "usable." Technical criteria provide the details, such as how to make an element or space accessible, or, in this case, how to make a door within a dwelling unit "usable." Technical criteria tell us that in order for a door within a dwelling unit to be "usable," it must provide a clear opening width of at least 32 in. nominal measured between the door face and the door stop when the door is open 90 degrees. Compliance with the design and construction requirements of the FHA means compliance with both scoping and technical criteria.

ANSI A117.1 Technical Criteria

Although the Guidelines include technical criteria, where those criteria are not provided the Guidelines and their implementing regulations reference technical criteria contained in the American National Standards Institute (ANSI) A117.1 standard. Compliance with ANSI specifications is a "safe harbor" for compliance with the technical requirements of the FHA. However, full compliance with the ANSI A117.1 standard is not necessary for compliance with the FHA. In many cases, ANSI's technical criteria go beyond what is required by the FHA. In a response to public comments received on the proposed Guidelines, HUD notes

TABLE 1-4   Approved Technical Criteria: A117.1 Standard
1. ANSI A117.1–1986: Providing Accessibility and Usability for Physically Handicapped People
2. CABO/ANSI A117.1–1992: Accessible and Usable Buildings and Facilities
3. ICC/ANSI A117.1–1998: Accessible and Usable Buildings and Facilities

that, "ANSI sections not cited in the Guidelines have been determined by the Department not to be necessary for compliance with the Act's requirements."

Although the regulations reference a specific edition of the ANSI A117.1 standard for compliance with the technical design and construction requirements of the FHA, that is, the 1986 edition—subsequent versions of the ANSI A117.1 standard were published and approved in 2000 by HUD as "safe harbors" for compliance with the technical requirements of the Act (Federal Register, March 23, 2000). Herein, reference to the ANSI A117.1 standard includes the 1986, 1992, and 1998 editions.

Safe Harbors for Compliance with the FHA's Accessibility Requirements

Compliance with the technical assistance provided in the *Fair Housing Act Design Manual*, the Guidelines, and compliance with the appropriate requirements of the 1986, 1992, or 1998 editions of the ANSI A117.1 standard are all "safe harbors" for compliance with the design and construction requirements of the FHA. In addition, the *Code Requirements for Housing Accessibility*, published by the International Code Council (ICC) in the spring of 2000 has been approved as an additional "safe harbor" for compliance with the design and construction requirements of the FHA (see the Q&A on page 12).

TABLE 1-5   "Safe Harbors" for FHA Compliance
1. The Guidelines
2. 1986, 1992, and 1998 editions of the ANSI A117.1 Standard
3. *Fair Housing Act Design Manual*
4. ICC's Code Requirements for Housing Accessibility (CRHA)

Enforcement

Complaints of violations regarding the design and construction requirements of the FHA may be filed with the secretary of HUD at any time and against anyone involved in the design and construction of a building, including, but not limited to, the owner, developer, architect, contractor, builder, subcontractor, and others. Complaint investigations are usually completed within 100 days of the filing of the complaint. After the investigation, the secretary will file a charge or dismiss the complaint. If the secretary files a charge for discrimination, the person who filed the complaint may file a civil action within two years thereafter. According to the *Fair Housing Act Design Manual,* if the judge finds the defendant guilty of discriminatory housing practice, the defendant may be ordered to pay "actual and compensatory damages, injunctive or other equitable relief, attorney's fees and costs, which may also include civil penalties ranging from $10,000 for the first offense to $50,000 for repeated offenses. In addition, in the case of buildings which have been completed, structural changes could be ordered, and an escrow fund might be required to finance future changes."

II. OTHER FEDERAL ACCESSIBILITY LAWS

In addition to the FHA's requirements for accessible multifamily housing, there are other federal requirements designed to ensure that certain types of housing and nonhousing facilities are accessible to people with disabilities. There may also be state and local laws that require housing and nonhousing facilities to be accessible to people with disabilities. In the early planning stages of a project, it is important for the architect and contractor to understand which federal, state, or local requirements for accessibility, if any, apply. If federal, state, and local mandates for accessibility are not adhered to, complaints of discrimination against people with disabilities may be filed against those involved with the design and construction of facilities.

TABLE 1-6 Federal Accessibility Laws That May Apply to Projects:

1. Fair Housing Amendments Act
2. Architectural Barriers Act
3. Section 504 of the Rehabilitation Act
4. Americans with Disabilities Act

According to the preamble to the Guidelines, the FHA's accessibility requirements do not replace those required by the laws of states or local jurisdictions. When differences between federal, state, local, and building code requirements occur, the general rule is to adhere to the more stringent requirement.

The Architectural Barriers Act

The Architectural Barriers Act of 1968 (ABA) requires the removal of barriers in any building built by or on behalf of the United States. Buildings leased or financed by the United States must also provide equal access for people with disabilities by ensuring that barriers to access are removed. The ABA does not apply to privately owned residential facilities; however, any residential facility owned, leased, or financed by the United States must comply with the requirement of the ABA. For example, if the United States government plans to develop a plot of land as a war memorial, it must ensure that all barriers are removed to permit equitable use of the space for people with disabilities. Since the war memorial is "built by" and "on behalf of" the United States, the requirements of the ABA apply. The Uniform Federal Accessibility Standards (UFAS) are the enforceable technical standards for the ABA.

Section 504 of the Rehabilitation Act

According to Section 504 of the Rehabilitation Act of 1973, any program or activity receiving federal financial assistance must be accessible to people with disabilities. Section 504 is intended to prevent discrimination against people with disabilities in any program financed in whole or in part with federal funds. Although Section 504 focuses on program access, housing construction may be part of a program that receives federal funding, and thus must provide access to people with disabilities. The UFAS are the enforceable technical standards for Section 504, although other standards that provide equivalent or greater access may also be used.

The Americans with Disabilities Act

The Americans with Disabilities Act of 1990 (ADA) is a civil rights law that protects people with disabilities from discrimination in the workplace (Title I), in any service provided by state and local governments (Title II), and in places of public accommodations and commercial facilities (Title III). The ADA also requires accessible telecommunication for people with hearing disabilities or speech impairments (Title IV). Title V of the ADA provides instructions to federal enforcement agencies. Title II and III regulations include accessibility standards for the design, construction, and renovation of buildings. The Americans with Disabilities Act Accessibility Guidelines (ADAAG) are the enforceable technical standards for the ADA.

III. BUILDING CODES

Building codes are safety criteria that govern the design and construction of buildings and facilities. Architects, developers, builders, and others plan and develop projects around the requirements of a building code. Many of these codes include accessibility requirements for particular types of facilities, including multifamily housing and nonhousing facilities. However, compliance with the accessibility provisions of a building code may not be enough to satisfy the accessibility requirements of the FHA, or any other federal, state, or local accessibility law.

For the most part, states or local jurisdictions adopt one of four model building codes: The National Building Code, the Standard Building Code, the Uniform Building Code, and the International Building Code. They are called "model codes" because they are provided as a model for adoption by states and local governments in their entirety; or, they are adopted in part with amendments or modifications. A "state-written" code is usually one of the model codes with amendments.

TABLE 1-7 Code Organizations and Their Model Codes

1. Building Officials and Code Administrations (BOCA)	National Building Code (BNBC)
2. International Conference of Building Officials (ICBO)	Uniform Building Code (UBC)
3. Southern Building Code Congress International (SBCCI)	Standard Building Code (SBC)
4. International Code Council (ICC)	International Building Code (IBC)

The International Building Code (IBC) is the newest member of the model code group; its first edition was published in 2000. The International Code Council (ICC), the organization that developed the IBC, was founded by the code organizations that have developed the National, Standard, and Uniform Building Codes. These building code organizations will no longer publish updated editions to those codes. Instead, they will work together toward updating subsequent editions of the IBC only.

Chapter 11 of all of the current editions of the model codes, including the IBC, contain requirements for accessible multifamily housing, many of which are intended to be consistent with the requirements of the FHA and the ADA. However, in a report issued by HUD (Final Report of "HUD Review of Model Building Codes," Federal Register, March 23, 2000), all of the model codes include provisions that do not meet the accessibility requirements of the FHA. As a result, following the accessibility requirements of the building code alone will not satisfy the accessibility requirements of the FHA. HUD recommended to the model code groups how the code provisions that do not meet the requirements of the FHA may be modified to reflect the requirements of the Act. The ICC has responded to HUD's recommendations, and intends to incorporate them in subsequent editions of the IBC to ensure consistency with the requirements of the FHA. In the meantime, the ICC has published a stand-alone document called the Code Requirements for Housing Accessibility (CRHA), which has been approved by HUD as a "safe harbor" for compliance with the Act.

IV. CROSS-COVERAGE

In some instances, projects may be covered by more than one federal accessibility law. In addition, those projects subject to federal accessibility requirements may also be subject to state and local accessibility laws and to building code accessibility requirements. For example, in a development with multifamily units covered by the FHA, rental offices and sales offices must be accessible according to "Requirement 2: Accessible and Usable Public and Common Use Areas." The rental and sales offices are also covered under Title III of the ADA, as they are considered a place of public accommodation where the general public, not just the building occupants and their visitors, is expected to visit. If the construction of the project is financed in whole or in part with federal funding, the accessibility requirements of Section 504 of the Rehabilitation Act may also apply.

V. REASONABLE ACCOMMODATIONS AND REASONABLE MODIFICATIONS

In addition to the design and construction requirements of the FHA as they apply to covered multifamily housing projects, the FHA also includes provisions for reasonable modifications of existing premises and reasonable accommodations in rules, policies, practices, or services.

If a resident requests a modification to an existing dwelling unit or to the public and common space to suit a particular disability—widening doorways to better accommodate a wheelchair, for example—the owner cannot refuse to make the modification if the resident agrees to pay the additional costs for the modifications and agrees to return the modification to its original condition if the modification may interfere with the next resident's use of the dwelling unit. If the modification does not interfere with the next resident's use of the dwelling unit, then it may be unreasonable for the owner to request that the resident return the modification to its original condition. For example, a resident may require that a bedroom door be widened to accommodate his or her wheelchair. The owner must grant the permission to widen the doorway if the resident agrees to pay for the added expense. However, it is unreasonable for the owner to request that the resident return the widened doorway to its original width when the resident vacates the unit because a widened doorway does not affect the next resident's use of the unit. If a resident requests that counters be lowered in the kitchen, for example, it is reasonable for the owner to request that the resident return the counters to their original height because lower-than-standard countertop heights may have an affect on the next resident's use of the kitchen.

It is against the law to refuse to make "reasonable accommodations" in rules, policies, practices, or services when it is necessary to enable people with disabilities to have equitable use to housing. For example, a policy may be in place that prohibits residents from having pets. The concept of reasonable accommodations makes it unlawful to refuse to make an exception to the "no pets" policy for a resident with blindness who needs the help of a seeing-eye dog.

In Part 2, we cover the Fair Housing Act's Accessibility Guidelines, and the technical requirements for satisfying the Act. The Guidelines are structured according to seven design and construction requirements:

Requirement 1. Accessible Building Entrance on an Accessible Route
Requirement 2. Accessible and Usable Public and Common Use Areas
Requirement 3. Usable Doors
Requirement 4. Accessible Route into and through the Covered Unit
Requirement 5. Light Switches, Electrical Outlets, Thermostats and Other Environmental Controls in Accessible Locations
Requirement 6. Reinforced Walls for Grab Bars
Requirement 7. Usable Kitchens and Bathrooms

Frequently Asked Questions

Q. **If my project involves an addition of a newly constructed laundry facility and three attached dwelling units to an existing building, must the laundry facility comply with the design and construction requirements of the FHA?**

A. No. In order to assess whether a common-use space (such as a laundry facility) must comply with the design and construction requirements of the FHA, it is important to first assess whether a project contains covered multifamily dwellings. If a project does not contain covered multifamily dwellings, then the public and common-use space is not required to comply with the accessibility requirements of the FHA?

A building contains covered dwelling units if there are at least four attached dwelling units built for first occupancy after March 13, 1991. According to the question, there are only three attached units being constructed. Even though they are being constructed as an addition to an existing building, they are considered newly constructed. Since the number of units is fewer than four, the project does not contain covered dwelling units. Because there are no covered dwelling units, the laundry facility is not required to comply with the accessibility requirements of the FHA. It is important to note that although a project may not be required to comply with the accessibility requirements of the FHA, it may be subject to other federal, state, or local accessibility laws in addition to accessibility requirements of applicable building codes.

Q. **An old chocolate manufacturing plant was completely gutted and rehabilitated into a multifamily residential complex. During the gut rehabilitation, everything but the structural skeleton of the original building was removed. Fifty new residential units were designed around the existing skeleton. Are the new units and the common-use spaces required to comply with the accessibility requirements of the FHA?**

A. No. Before determining the number of units and public spaces, if any, that must be accessible according to the design and construction requirements of the FHA, it is important to make sure that the multifamily housing project is covered by the FHA. At first glance, it seems that the new construction of 50 units built after March 13, 1991 must comply with the FHA. However, the building must have been built for "first occupancy" after March 13, 1991.

In order for a building to be built for "first occupancy," it must have never before been used for any other purpose. According to the question, the building was originally a chocolate manufacturing plant, used at one time for another purpose. As a result, the building does not qualify as a project covered by the design and construction requirements of the FHA, because it does not qualify as a building built for "first occupancy" after March 13, 1991.

Q. I am designing my multifamily project according to the International Building Code's (IBC) requirements for accessibility in Chapter 11. Chapter 11 contains the following definition for Dwelling Unit, Type B:

> A dwelling unit designed and construction for accessibility in accordance with ICC/ANSI A117.1–1998, intended to be consistent with the technical requirements of fair housing required by federal law.

> I understand that the IBC's Type B Dwelling Unit is intended to be consistent with dwelling units that are required to be accessible by the FHA. If I incorporate all of the IBC's Type B Dwelling Unit requirements into the dwelling units that I have designed and that are covered by the FHA, can I safely assume that I have incorporated all of the FHA's requirements for accessible dwelling units?

A. No. Like BOCA's National Building Code, ICBO's Uniform Building Code, and SBCCI's Standard Building Code, ICC's International Building Code 2000 includes provisions that do not meet the design and construction requirements of the FHA. However, the ICC responded to the need for a code document that incorporates the design and construction requirements of the FHA when it published the Code Requirements for Housing Accessibility (CRHA) in the spring of 2000. The CRHA is a stand-alone code document, available for adoption by states and local jurisdictions, that incorporates the design and construction requirements of the FHA in code language. In fact, HUD has approved the CRHA as an additional "safe harbor" for compliance with the design guidelines of the FHA (see Table 1-5 on page 6 for all approved "safe harbors").

VI. THE GUIDELINES

It is important to note that the Fair Housing Accessibility Guidelines issued by HUD are not mandatory and only provide minimal requirements to ensure that housing is accessible to people with disabilities. Architects, builders, developers, and others may vary from those requirements if access to housing is, at a minimum, equivalent to that required by the Act. In addition, the provisions of other laws or codes that require housing to be accessible to a greater extent than required by the FHA take precedence over the Act.

The purpose of the Guidelines is to serve as a safe harbor for compliance with the accessibility requirements of the Fair Housing Amendments Act of 1988. Architects, developers, builders, and others involved with the design and construction of covered multifamily buildings can depart from the requirements of the Guidelines, but must demonstrate that the accessibility requirements of the FHA have been met.

Definitions

Section 2 of the Guidelines provides definitions of terms used in the Guidelines. Some of the terms defined in the Guidelines have significantly different definitions from the same terms defined by building codes. As a result, it is important for developers, architects, builders, and others involved with the design and construction of multifamily housing to understand the definitions of terms provided in Section 2 as they apply to the Guidelines. Applying a building code's definition of a term defined in the Guidelines is inaccurate, and may incorrectly exempt some projects from FHA coverage.

Some of the more critical definitions of terms included in the Guidelines are as follows:

Accessible *"When used with respect to the public and common use areas of a building containing covered multifamily dwellings, means that the public or common-use areas of the building can be approached, entered, and used by individuals with physical handicaps. The phrase 'readily accessible to and usable by' is synonymous with 'accessible.' A public or common-use area that complies with the appropriate requirements of ANSI A117.1–1986, a comparable standard or these guidelines is 'accessible' within the meaning of this paragraph."*

Adaptable dwelling units *"When used with respect to covered multifamily dwellings, means dwelling units that include the features of adaptable design specified in 24 CFR 100.205 (c) (2)–(3)."*

Comment

The FHA includes requirements for both accessible and adaptable design features. Usually, "accessible design" includes those accessible features or elements that are designed and constructed in place and are intended to be permanent. "Adaptable design," on the other hand, is the design of a feature or element that is intended to be modified at a later time when needed. For example, one of the requirements for accessible routes is that they slope no more than 8.33 percent (1:12). Accessible routes are designed and constructed so that their slopes are not greater than 8.33 percent at the time of construction, and they are not intended to be modified in the future. Similarly, public and common-use doors, for example, must be designed from the onset to provide the proper maneuvering clearances and hardware on either side of the door so that they can be "approached, entered, and used by individuals with physical handicaps." The accessible hardware and maneuvering clearances cannot be modified in the future, and must remain as-is.

Adaptable designs or features are those that can be modified at a later time when the need arises. For example, Requirement 6 of the FHA requires that bathroom walls be reinforced for grab-bar installation; however, grab bars are not required to be installed. As long as the reinforcement is in place, the occupant has the option of installing grab bars when the need arises. Similarly, removable sink-base cabinets are adaptable features because they can be removed by the occupant if kneespace is needed.

An adaptable unit is one that includes the adaptable features specified in Requirement 3: "Usable Doors"; Requirement 4: "Accessible Route into and through the Covered Unit"; Requirement 5: "Light Switches, Electrical Outlets, Thermostats, and Other Environmental Controls in Accessible Locations"; Requirement 6: "Reinforced Walls for Grab Bars"; and Requirement 7: "Usable Kitchens and Bathrooms." Units that comply with the FHA are referred to as adaptable units.

> **Bathroom** *"Means a bathroom which includes a water closet (toilet), lavatory (sink), and bathtub or shower. It does not include single-fixture facilities or those with only a water closet and lavatory. It does include a compartmented bathroom. A compartmented bathroom is one in which the fixtures are distributed among interconnected rooms. A compartmented bathroom is considered a single unit and is subject to the Act's requirements for bathrooms."*

Comment

Building codes, for the most part, refer to "toilet rooms and bathing facilities," not "bathrooms." To be equivalent to the Guidelines' definition of "bathroom" a "toilet room and bathing facility" must contain a toilet, sink, and a bathtub or shower in the same room. If a unit contains a toilet and a bathtub in one room, and a sink only in an adjacent, interconnected room, for example, the FHA considers both interconnected rooms as one compartmented bathroom, and both rooms must comply with the accessibility requirements provided under Requirement 7: "Usable Kitchens and Bathrooms." Similarly, any bathroom design that is "compartmented" is considered by the FHA to be one bathroom and each compartmented room must comply with the applicable provision under Requirement 7.

According to the Guidelines, a facility that contains only a toilet and a sink is considered a powder room and, under certain conditions, is exempt from the Guidelines' requirements for usable bathrooms. In addition to compliance with Requirements 3 through 5 of the Guidelines, powder rooms are required to have reinforced walls for grab bars (Requirement 6) and provide the maneuvering and clear floors spaces required by Requirement 7: "Usable Kitchens and Bathrooms," *only when they are located on the primary entry level of a multistory unit in an elevator building and only when there are no other bathrooms located on that level.* However, no matter where they are located in covered units, they must always contain usable doors (Requirement 3), be on an accessible route (Requirement 4), and have controls in accessible locations (Requirement 5).

The Guidelines allow two bathroom design options: Type A and Type B. If the Type A option is taken, all bathrooms in the covered unit must be Type A. If the Type B option is taken, only one bathroom is required to be designed to the Type B requirements, and all other bathrooms must comply with Requirements 3, 4, 5, and 6 only.

Building *"Means a structure, facility, or portion thereof that contains or serves one or more dwelling units."*

Covered multifamily dwellings or covered multifamily dwellings subject to the Fair Housing Amendments *"Means buildings consisting of four or more dwelling units if such buildings have one or more elevators; and ground-floor dwelling units in other buildings consisting of four or more dwelling units. Dwelling units within a single structure separated by firewalls do not constitute separate buildings."*

Comment

The FHA considers a building that includes several dwelling units separated by firewalls to be one building. On the other hand, it is commonly understood by those who are familiar with building codes that dwelling units built within a single structure that are separated by firewalls are considered separate buildings. That said, Chapter 11: "Accessibility," of the model codes, eliminates the firewall criteria for the purposes of determining accessibility required by code. For example, if a firewall separates three units on one side from two units on the other side, the codes classify such a design as two distinct buildings: one building contains three units and the other contains two units. However, Chapter 11: "Accessibility," *of the model codes eliminates the firewall criteria.* As a result, for the purposes of counting the number of dwelling units that must be accessible in buildings and for the purposes of Chapter 11: "Accessibility" only, the preceding example contains more than four attached dwelling units (five units total) and is covered under the FHA.

The Guidelines provide that a structural connection by a walkway or stairs between dwelling units creates one building. For example, if an overhead walkway structurally connects one structure containing two dwelling units to another structure containing two dwelling units, the entire structure is considered by the FHA as one building with four units, and thus is a covered multifamily building. The codes might not consider such a configuration as one building.

Dwelling unit *As defined in the regulations that implement the Fair Housing Amendments Act: "A single unit of residence for a family of one or more persons. Examples of dwelling units include: a single-family home; an apartment unit within an apartment building; and in other types of dwellings in which sleeping accommodations are provided by toileting or cooking facilities are shared by occupants of more than one room or portion of the dwelling, rooms in which people sleep. Examples of the latter include dormitory rooms and sleeping accommodations in shelters intended for occupancy as a residence for homeless persons."*

Dwelling *As defined in the regulations that implement the Fair Housing Amendments Act: "Means any building, structure or portion thereof which is occupied as, or designed or intended for occupancy as, a residence by one or more families, and any vacant land which is offered for sale or lease for the construction or location theron of any such building, structure, or portion therof."*

Comment

Typically, building codes define a dwelling unit as a unit that includes "complete and independent" living facilities. Complete and independent living facilities include permanent provisions for living, sleeping, eating, cooking, and sanitation within the same unit. For example, a sleeping room in a dormitory is considered by the FHA to be a dwelling unit, even though cooking and sanitation facilities are not included in the room. The building codes, on the other hand, do not consider such a sleeping room to be a dwelling unit because it does not contain permanent provisions for cooking (a kitchen) or sanitation (a bathroom) within the room itself.

An understanding of the regulation's definition of "dwelling unit" is extremely important when determining whether a project is covered by the FHA. For example, if a unit contains four sleeping rooms, each occupied by unrelated people all of whom share one kitchen and bathroom facility (such as a dormitory suite for example) the FHA considers such a unit as having four dwelling units, and thus a covered multifamily dwelling. (A single-family home with four or more bedrooms occupied by related people, or occupied by unrelated persons that operates as a single household [such as a group home, for example], is exempt from FHA coverage.) However, the building codes do not consider such a building as having four distinct dwelling units because each room does not contain "complete and independent living facilities," that is, a kitchen and a bathroom within each sleeping room. As a result, the codes' definition of "dwelling unit" in this case will incorrectly exempt it from FHA coverage because the FHA covers "dwelling units," and the codes do not consider a dormitory sleeping room as a dwelling unit. Applying the commonly understood code definition of "dwelling unit" to the FHA may incorrectly exempt some buildings from coverage by the FHA.

Whether a residential care or assisted-living facility is covered by the FHA depends on whether the facility is used as a residence for more than a brief period of time. The Questions and Answers about the Guidelines (Q&As) state that, "The new construction requirements of the FHA would apply to continuing-care facilities if the facility includes at least one building with four or more dwelling units. Whether a facility is a 'dwelling' under the Act depends on whether the facility is to be used as a residence for more than a brief period of time. As a result, the operation of each continuing-care facility must be examined on a case-by-case basis to determine whether it contains dwellings."

Some types of transient housing facilities—including timeshares, residential hotels and motels, and homeless shelters—may be subject to the design and construction requirements of the FHA. It is important to understand when a transient facility may be covered by the FHA's accessibility requirements.

The codes' 30-days-or-less occupancy measure to assess whether a facility is "transient" is inaccurate when assessing FHA coverage as it applies to these facilities. Aside from length of stay, other factors to consider when assessing whether a facility is a covered multifamily dwelling are as follows:

- Whether the rental rate for the unit will be calculated on a daily, weekly, monthly, or annual basis;
- Whether the terms and length of occupancy will be established through a lease or other written agreement;
- What amenities will be included inside the unit, including kitchen facilities;
- How the purpose of the property is marketed to the public;
- Whether the resident possesses the right to return to the property; and
- Whether the resident has anywhere else in which to return.

These factors should be considered when determining FHA coverage as it applies to short-term occupancies.

Examples of other types of dwelling units that are covered under the FHA include, but are not limited to, condominiums, cooperatives, mobile homes, manufactured homes, and timeshares. FHA coverage has nothing to do with type of ownership, such as condominiums or timeshares. Regardless if a dwelling unit is privately owned, rented, leased, and so on, it must comply with the design and construction requirements of the FHA if it is newly constructed, built for first occupancy after March 13, 1991, and contains four or more attached dwelling units.

> **Ground floor** *"Means a floor of a building with a building entrance on an accessible route. A building may have one or more ground floors. Where the first floor containing dwelling units in a building is above grade, all units on that floor must be served by a building entrance on an accessible route. This floor will be considered to be a ground floor."*

Comment

To those familiar with building codes, any code reference to a ground floor is usually considered to be a floor of a building that can be accessed at grade. However, according to the Guidelines' definition, a ground floor is not necessarily a grade-level floor. Furthermore, a building can have more than one ground floor, although only one is required. If a building contains more than one floor designed to have an entrance on an accessible route, then each floor with an entrance on an accessible route is a ground floor and all dwelling units on those floors are covered. For example, if a building containing four or more dwelling units includes grade-level retail space and a second level of dwelling units located above the retail space, the first floor containing dwelling units (which is actually the second level of the building) is considered to be the ground floor and all units on that floor are covered. The retail space at grade is not covered by the FHA because it is not multifamily housing or common space for the residential units above grade and on the second level. However, other federal, state, and local accessibility regulations, such as the ADA, may apply to the retail space, in addition to other building code requirements for accessible commercial spaces.

A building may have more than one ground floor although only one is required. For example, if a building without elevators is built into the side of a hill and has two entrances served by an accessible route, one building entrance accessed at the bottom of the hill, and a second building entrance accessed at the top of the hill, the building has two ground floors at different elevations and all dwelling units on those floors are covered by the FHA. If the building just described is three stories high, and the top and bottom stories are ground floors, and thus covered by the FHA, the middle level does not have to comply with the accessibility requirements of the FHA if it does not contain any common-use space. In other words, if the middle level contains dwelling units only, it is exempt from FHA coverage because only the ground floors are covered in buildings not served by elevators. In addition, a route connecting the upper ground floor with the lower ground floor is not required.

> **Multistory dwelling unit** *"Means a dwelling unit with finished living space located on one floor and the floor or floors immediately above or below it."*

Comment

According to the regulations, multistory dwelling units in buildings without elevators are not covered by the FHA because the entire unit is not on a ground floor. Multistory units in elevator buildings are covered units; however, the level of the multistory unit served by the elevator must be the primary entry level, and only that level is covered. In addition, multistory units with internal elevators, such as a multistory townhouse with an internal elevator, are also covered units, and must comply with the Guidelines.

According to the common code definition, a multistory unit is one with "habitable or bathroom space" located on more than one story. However, according to the Guidelines, a multistory unit is one with finished living space located on more than one floor. Therefore, according to the Guidelines, a unit cannot be multistory if a bathroom is the only room located on a story, because a bathroom space is not finished living space. Similarly, a multistory unit cannot be defined as one where the entry foyer is the only room located on the entry floor, because a foyer is also not finished living space. Locating a bathroom only, or any other "nonhabitable" space such as storage, powder rooms, closets, halls, a foyer, or utility spaces, on one story and all of the living space on another story does not constitute a multistory unit under the FHA.

In addition, a single-story unit with a finished basement at the time of design and construction is considered a multistory unit and is not covered by the Guidelines if "habitable space" is located in the basement. Conversely, a single-story unit with an unfinished basement is a covered unit and not considered multistory, because the basement does not contain habitable space. It is important to apply the definition of "multistory dwelling unit" contained in the regulations or the Guidelines when determining FHA coverage as it applies to multistory units.

> **Loft** *"Means an intermediate level between the floor and ceiling of any story, located within a room or rooms of a dwelling."*

Comment

Lofts are intermediate levels within a room that share the same ceiling as the room they overlook. These intermediate levels must be open to the room they overlook and must not exceed 33.3 percent of the floor area of the room in which they are located. Lofts can be incorporated into covered units, and are not required to be linked with the rest of the dwelling unit by an accessible route if they contain secondary function areas only, such as a second bedroom, a TV room, or an office, for example. They cannot contain bathrooms or kitchens, for example, because all primary function areas in the dwelling unit must be on an accessible route. Primary function areas are permitted to be located in lofts if they are provided with an accessible route. Lofts are not permitted to interrupt the accessible route throughout the dwelling unit.

REQUIREMENT 1: ACCESSIBLE BUILDING ENTRANCE ON AN ACCESSIBLE ROUTE

Covered multifamily dwellings shall be designed and constructed to have at least one building entrance on an accessible route unless it is impractical to do so because of terrain or unusual characteristics of the site.

What This Requirement Calls For

Regardless of whether a project contains a single building or multiple buildings, each building must have an entrance on an accessible route unless it cannot be achieved because of extreme terrain (such as a site located on the side of a steep hill) or unusual characteristics of the site (such as a floodplain or a wetland). At least one entrance must be made accessible to any ground floor of a building, except in those cases where ground-floor dwelling units have separate exterior entrances, or where separate entrances serve separate clusters of dwelling units in a building. In these cases, analysis of the site will determine how many entrances must be made accessible. When entrances to dwelling units are accessed off a corridor from within a building with one common entrance, the common entrance typically used by occupants must be the accessible entrance served by an accessible route.

It is important to note that a service entrance, a door to a loading dock, or any other point of entry not typically used to enter the building cannot be considered a "building entrance" for the purposes of Requirement 1. If a building has a back-door used by some residents to enter the building lobby from a nearby street, for example, it is not this entrance that is required to be accessible because it is not typically used by most for entering the building. If the entrance used by most to enter the building is the one located off the main parking area in front of the building, for example, that entrance is required to be accessible, and to be served by an accessible route, because it is the typical building entrance. For buildings with more than one ground floor, each ground floor must be served by an accessible entrance on an accessible route to covered dwelling units.

Site Impracticality

The Guidelines recognize that in certain rare instances an accessible route is not practical to design because of extreme terrain or unusual characteristics of the site. The FHA itself does not include language that exempts projects from providing an accessible route due to extreme terrain or unusual site characteristics. The preamble to the FHA regulations notes that Congress understands that there may be instances when "certain natural terrain may pose unique building problems." Developers, architects, builders, and others involved with the design and construction of multifamily housing are provided with site impracticality tests to help them to determine whether providing an accessible route is practical. In a court of law, those who design and construct the building, including but not limited to the architect and the builder for example, have the burden of proving site impracticality.

Site Impracticality Due to Terrain

If covered multifamily dwelling units are located in buildings with elevators, they must always be served by at least one accessible entrance on an accessible route, regardless of terrain. Buildings with elevators are not exempt from the accessibility requirements of the FHA because the site work involved with the design and construction of most elevator buildings typically results in a relatively level entrance and a passenger drop-off area where accessible routes can easily be designed and constructed.

Accessible entrances on accessible routes to covered multifamily dwelling units may be impractical to provide due to terrain only if the units are located in buildings without elevators. An accessible entrance on an accessible route to these units may be impractical to provide as determined by the individual building test or the site analysis test.

Individual Building Test

If the slopes of the undisturbed site measured between the planned entrance and all vehicular or pedestrian arrival points within 50 ft. of the planned entrance, and the slopes of the planned finished grade measured between the entrance and all vehicular or pedestrian arrival points within 50 ft. of the planned entrance exceed 10 percent, it is impractical to provide an accessible entrance on an accessible route. The closest vehicular or pedestrian arrival point is used to measure slopes if there is no vehicular or pedestrian arrival point within 50 ft. of the planned entrance. It is important to note that the slopes of the undisturbed site "and" the slopes of the planned finished grade must exceed 10 percent. If one exceeds 10 percent and the other does not, site impracticality due to terrain as determined by the individual building test cannot be claimed. If site impracticality cannot be claimed as determined by the test, the accessible route must be no greater than 8.33 percent (1:12).

Slopes are measured at ground level from the point of the planned entrance on a straight line to each vehicular and pedestrian arrival point within 50 ft. of the planned entrance. If there are no vehicular or pedestrian arrival points within 50 ft. of the planned entrance, then the closest vehicular or pedestrian arrival points shall be used. The closest pedestrian arrival point is the intersection between the common sidewalk and the sidewalk to the entrance. The closest point from parking areas to the planned entrance is measured from the entry point to the parking area located nearest to the planned entrance.

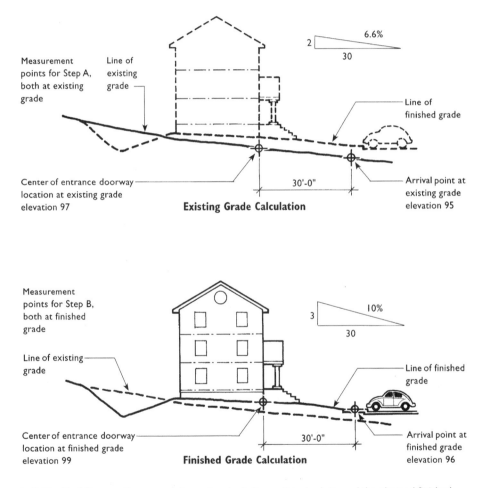

Individual building test. Tests are performed on both the undisturbed site and the planned finished grade. Here, both calculations do not exceed 10 percent; therefore, the developer must provide an accessible route to the entrance and all units on the ground floor served by the entrance are lowered.

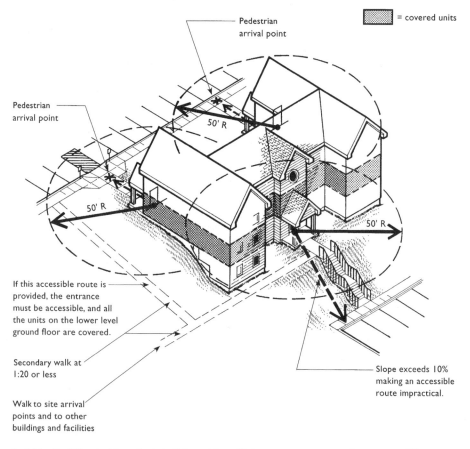

Pedestrian arrival point

= covered units

Pedestrian arrival point

50' R

50' R

50' R

If this accessible route is provided, the entrance must be accessible, and all the units on the lower level ground floor are covered.

Secondary walk at 1:20 or less

Walk to site arrival points and to other buildings and facilities

Slope exceeds 10% making an accessible route impractical.

Individual building test. In a single building with multiple common entrances, lower ground floor units may be covered.

Site Analysis Test

The site analysis test involves three steps, A through C. In step A, the percentage of the total buildable area of the undisturbed site with natural grades less than 10 percent slope is calculated. Floodplains, wetlands, or other restricted-use areas are not included in the buildable area. Step A is performed on a topographic survey with two-foot contour intervals and between each interval. A licensed engineer, landscape architect, architect, or surveyor must certify the slope analysis.

In step B, the minimum percentage of ground-floor units required to comply with the Guidelines is determined. That percentage must equal the percentage of the total buildable area of the undisturbed site, calculated in step A, that has an existing natural grade of less than 10 percent slope. For example, if the percentage of the total buildable area of the undisturbed site with natural grades of less than 10 percent slope equals 60 percent, then at least 60 percent of the total ground-floor units on the entire site must comply with the Guidelines.

In addition to the percentage of units required to be accessible, as determined by step A, step C requires that all ground-floor units in a building or ground-floor units served by a particular entrance be accessible if the unit entrances are on an accessible route. For example, in step B it was determined that at least 60 percent of all ground-floor units are required to comply with the Guidelines on a particular site. Suppose there are two buildings on the site, each containing 50 ground-floor dwelling units. One building contains a single

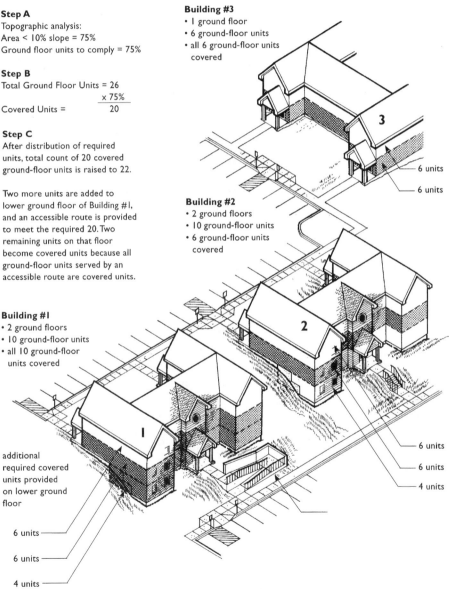

Step A
Topographic analysis:
Area < 10% slope = 75%
Ground floor units to comply = 75%

Step B
Total Ground Floor Units = 26
                    x 75%
Covered Units =   20

Step C
After distribution of required units, total count of 20 covered ground-floor units is raised to 22.

Two more units are added to lower ground floor of Building #1, and an accessible route is provided to meet the required 20. Two remaining units on that floor become covered units because all ground-floor units served by an accessible route are covered units.

Building #1
• 2 ground floors
• 10 ground-floor units
• all 10 ground-floor units covered

additional required covered units provided on lower ground floor

6 units
6 units
4 units

Building #3
• 1 ground floor
• 6 ground-floor units
• all 6 ground-floor units covered

6 units
6 units

Building #2
• 2 ground floors
• 10 ground-floor units
• 6 ground-floor units covered

6 units
6 units
4 units

Site analysis test. To meet the required number of covered units, an additional accessible entrance on an accessible route must be provided to another ground floor, thus making all the units on that floor covered.

common entrance to all 50 dwelling units on the ground floor, and the other building contains two clusters of dwelling units, each cluster with its own single, common entrance, and each cluster containing 25 dwelling units. The results of step B revealed that at least 60 percent of the total ground-floor units on the entire site, or 60 dwelling units (60 percent of 100 ground-floor units on the entire site), must be accessible according to the requirements of the Guidelines. An accessible entrance on an accessible route is provided to the ground floor of the building with the single, common entrance to all 50 ground-floor units. Ten additional ground-floor units must be accessible in order to comply with the results of step B. To capture the 10 ground-floor dwelling units needed to satisfy the results of step B, an accessible entrance on an accessible route is provided to one cluster containing 25 dwelling units in the other building. Since an accessible entrance on an accessible route is provided to the cluster containing 25 ground-floor dwelling units, all of the ground-floor units in that cluster, not just 10, must comply with the Guidelines. Why? Because step C requires that all ground-floor units in a building or all ground-floor units served by a particular entrance be accessible if the unit entrances are on an accessible route. Step C usually results in capturing additional ground-floor units that are required to comply with the Guidelines.

According to the 20 percent rule discussed in the next section, if step B determines that 16 percent of the total buildable area of a site has natural grades of less than 10 percent slope, then at least 20 percent, not 16 percent, of the total ground-floor units on the entire site must comply with the Guidelines. The 20 percent rule applies only to sites for which both the individual building test and the site analysis test can be used.

Site Impracticality Tests

Only the individual building test can be used to determine site impracticality due to terrain on a site with a single building with a common entrance to covered multifamily dwelling units. If a site, for example, contains one covered building that is not served by an elevator, 15 covered ground-floor dwelling units, and one common entrance used to access all units in the building, then the individual building test is the only test that can be used to determine whether an accessible entrance on an accessible route is practical to provide.

Remember, the 20 percent rule applies only to a site where both the individual building test and the site analysis test can be used. So, in the case where only the individual building test can be used, the 20 percent rule does not apply.

On sites other than those with only one building with one common entrance, either the individual building test or the site analysis test can be used to assess site impracticality due to terrain. If a site, for example, contains one building that is not served by an elevator, and has three separate entrances to three separate clusters of dwelling units, either test can be applied to determine the practicality of providing an accessible entrance on an accessible route to each of the three entrances, because there is more than one common entrance.

In this case, the site impracticality tests must be applied to each separate entrance to determine whether an accessible entrance on an accessible route to those entrances is practical. Similarly, if a site contains two covered buildings not served by elevators, each with only one common entrance, either test can be applied because the site contains more than one building.

The 20 Percent Rule

On all sites for which the individual building test or the site analysis test can be used to determine the practicality of providing an accessible entrance on an accessible route due to terrain, at least 20 percent of the total ground-floor units in buildings not served by elevators on the entire site must comply with the Guidelines.

The 20 percent rule does not apply to any building served by an elevator because buildings served by elevators are exempt from site impracticality. The rule also does not apply to sites for which only the individual building test can be used to determine whether an accessible entrance on an accessible route is practical. In other words, the 20 percent rule does not apply to one building having one common entrance or to a building served by an elevator. If the individual building test determines that it is impractical to provide an accessible entrance on an accessible route to a single covered building having only one common entrance, then none of the units are required to comply with the Guidelines. Conversely, if a site contains two covered buildings, each having five ground-floor units, then at least 20 percent (at least two units) of the total number of ground-floor units (10) on the entire site must comply with the Guidelines because either the individual building test or the site analysis test can be used to determine site impracticality. No matter what, a building served by an elevator cannot claim site impracticality.

Site Impracticality Due to Unusual Characteristics

Like site impracticality due to terrain, if covered multifamily dwelling units are located in buildings with elevators, they must always be served by at least one accessible entrance on an accessible route, regardless of unusual characteristics of the site. Sites with unusual characteristics are those located in a federally designated floodplain, coastal high-hazard area, and all other sites to which similar requirements of law or code apply, and those on which the lowest floor or the lowest structural member of the lowest floor must be raised to a level at or above the base flood elevation.

An accessible entrance on an accessible route may be impractical due to unusual characteristics of the site if the unusual characteristics result in a difference in finished-grade elevation exceeding 30 in. and 10 percent measured between an entrance and all vehicular or pedestrian arrival points within 50 ft. of the planned entrance; or if there are no vehicular or pedestrian arrival points within 50 ft. of the planned entrance, the unusual characteristics result in a difference in finished-grade elevation exceeding 30 in. and 10 percent measured

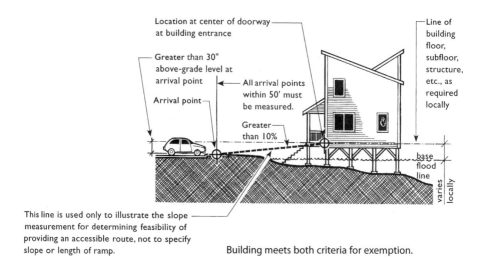

Location at center of doorway
at building entrance

Greater than 30"
above-grade level at
arrival point

All arrival points
within 50' must
be measured.

Arrival point

Greater
than 10%

Line of
building
floor,
subfloor,
structure,
etc., as
required
locally

base
flood
line

varies
locally

This line is used only to illustrate the slope
measurement for determining feasibility of
providing an accessible route, not to specify
slope or length of ramp.

Building meets both criteria for exemption.

between an entrance and the closest vehicular or pedestrian arrival point. A pedestrian or vehicular arrival point includes parking areas, public transportation stops, passenger loading zones, and public streets or sidewalks. It is important to note that the difference in finished grade between an entrance and vehicular or pedestrian arrival points must exceed 30 in. "and" 10 percent. Both conditions must be true.

Exceptions to Site Impracticality

Regardless of site impracticality due to terrain or unusual characteristics of the site, an accessible entrance on an accessible route must be provided to all buildings that have an elevator, even if that elevator connects a parking area with ground-floor dwelling units only, or when an elevated walkway or bridge with a slope no more than 10 percent connects a building entrance and a vehicular or pedestrian arrival point. The 10 percent slope criterion triggers the feasibility of providing an accessible route. For example, if the slope of the elevated walkway is no more than 10 percent, it is feasible to provide an accessible entrance on an accessible route. If the accessible route is feasible, as determined by the 10 percent criterion, then the slope of the elevated walkway must be reduced to no more than 8.33 percent (1:12), the maximum slope for accessible routes.

If an elevator is provided to create access to dwelling units on the ground floor only (from below-grade parking or from a lobby area, for example), the building is not considered an elevator building, and only the ground-floor units and at least one of each type of public and common use area must comply with the Guidelines. Similarly, if an elevator is used to access ground-floor units only, and other floors above or below the ground floor are accessed by other means (stairs for example) the building is not considered an elevator building because the elevator does not serve floors other than the ground floor.

An elevator building is one in which an elevator provides the means of accessing units in addition to those on the ground floor. For example, if a building contains an elevator that is used to access dwelling units on all of the floors containing dwelling units, the building is considered an elevator building, hence all units must comply with the Guidelines.

Buildings with elevators that provide access to floors in addition to the ground floor, but not all floors, are not permitted. For example, an elevator is not permitted to access ground-floor dwelling units on the first floor and penthouse dwelling units on the tenth floor, skipping all of the floors between the ground floor and the penthouse. If the elevator is provided to access dwelling units on floors other than those on a ground floor, it must provide access to all floors. However, if an elevator provides access to floors containing multistory dwelling units, it is only required to service the primary entry level of the multistory unit. In other words, the elevator is not required to service the second story of a multistory unit in an elevator building.

An entrance that complies with ANSI A117.1–1986, Section 4.14, and an accessible route that complies with ANSI A117.1–1986, Section 4.3, meets the requirements of the Guidelines. An entrance and an accessible route that complies with the comparable sections of the ANSI A117.1–1992, and 1998 editions, also meets the Guidelines.

Vehicular Route

If the slope of the finished grade between covered multifamily dwellings and a public or common-use facility (from a covered multifamily building entrance to a parking lot or tennis court, for example) exceeds 8.33 percent (1:12), or if other natural or manmade physical barriers or legal restrictions (all of which are outside the owner's control) do not allow provisions for an accessible pedestrian route, vehicular access is permitted. In these rare instances, if a vehicular route in place of an accessible pedestrian route is provided, there must be accessible parking spaces and necessary site provisions (such as access aisles and curb cuts) provided at each common facility. *It is important to note that a deliberate manipulation of the site to achieve slopes greater than 8.33 percent in order to avoid the requirements for accessible pedestrian routes is against the law.*

Any common-use areas such as parking lots, community rooms, and recreation areas must be on an accessible route from dwelling units according to Requirement 2 of the Guidelines: "Accessible Public and Common Use Areas." However, the FHA recognizes that some site grades prevent the design of an accessible pedestrian route. For example, on a steep site, an accessible route provided from site arrival points to the accessible building entrance may not be able to connect the covered dwelling units with the pool, because the pool may be located at the base of a steep cliff on a route with a slope much greater than 8.33 percent. Aside from a steep flight of stairs, the only way to access the pool area is by driving to it from the common parking area in front of the building. Because the slope of the finished grade in this case far exceeds 8.33 percent, an

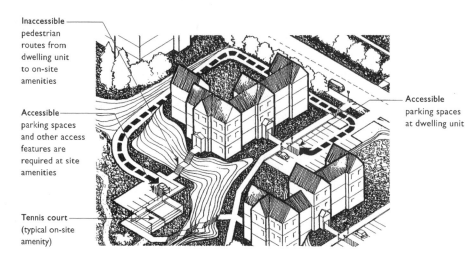

Inaccessible pedestrian routes from dwelling unit to on-site amenities

Accessible parking spaces and other access features are required at site amenities

Tennis court (typical on-site amenity)

Accessible parking spaces at dwelling unit

In some circumstances, site access by vehicle may be acceptable.

accessible vehicular route is allowed from the accessible parking area in front of the building to the pool area.

It is important to note that "sufficient" accessible parking must also be provided at the pool. In addition, an accessible route must be provided from the accessible parking spaces at the pool area to the pool itself. However, there is no requirement to provide an accessible route into the pool.

Accessible Routes

According to the Guideline's definition, an accessible route is a continuous and unobstructed path connecting accessible elements and spaces in a building or within a site that can be negotiated by a person with a severe disability using a wheelchair, and that is also safe for, and usable by, people with other disabilities. Interior accessible routes may include corridors, floors, ramps, elevators, and lifts. Exterior accessible routes may include parking access aisles, curb ramps, walks (5 percent or 1:20 maximum slope), ramps (8.33 percent or 1:12 maximum slope), and lifts. In certain circumstances, a vehicular route may be provided in place of an accessible pedestrian route.

The Act makes it illegal to require a person to negotiate steep walks, unnecessary changes in level, or stairs as the only means of access to newly constructed multifamily housing and associated sites and facilities. Requiring a person who may use a wheelchair to be carried up several steps in order to enter a building covered by the FHA, or any deliberate manipulation of site grades to exempt projects from coverage, is discriminatory housing practice and a violation of the Act.

During the early stages of planning a project subject to the design and construction requirements of the FHA, developers, architects, builders, and others involved with the design and construction of multifamily housing should attempt to visualize or diagram the routes whereby a building's occupants will arrive at the site, utilize the site, and enter buildings, dwelling units, and site facilities. Once a person enters the project site, the design and construction requirements of the FHA require that he or she be able to use the site and enter covered buildings by way of at least one continuous, unobstructed path. These accessible routes must be planned to allow "equitable use" of the entire site and associated buildings for people with disabilities, so that they can enjoy the same benefits of living there as are afforded to residents without disabilities.

Site-Arrival Points

A person arrives at the site before he or she can enter the buildings on it. There are several types of site-arrival points. Pedestrians can arrive from a public street or sidewalk that may connect a public transportation stop (an adjacent bus stop for example) with the building entrance. They may drive to the site, park their car in a front parking lot, and walk from the parking lot to the building entrance. Or, occupants or visitors may be driven to the site and dropped off at the building entrance by a relative or friend. According to the definition provided in the Guidelines, a vehicular or pedestrian arrival point includes public or resident parking areas, public transportation stops, passenger loading zones, and public streets or sidewalks.

Unless it is impractical to do so, the Guidelines indicate that an accessible route be provided from vehicular or pedestrian arrival points to accessible building entrances. An accessible entrance must be the one typically used by most to enter the building. Service-area doors or loading docks are not considered legitimate building entrances, hence are not required to be accessible, even if they are used by occupants to enter.

Accessible Route Locations

There are specific guidelines as to where accessible routes must be provided. For example, a site may include two buildings, each having dwelling units and its own common-use areas, that is, each building contains its own laundry room, community room, lobby area, and so on. The Guidelines indicate that accessible routes be provided from site-arrival points to each building's accessible entrances. In this case, the Guidelines do not indicate that an accessible route connect each building containing dwelling units because each building has its own common use areas. A person in one building is not required to use any of the facilities in the other building.

If a site contains three buildings—two containing only dwelling units and the third containing only common-use facilities, such as a laundry room—an accessible route is required to be provided from the site-arrival points to each building's accessible entrance. In addition, an accessible route must be provided from each building containing dwelling units to the building containing only common-use facilities because all residents must be able to get to the common-use areas provided in the separate building. However, because the two buildings that contain only dwelling units do not contain any common-use areas, an accessible route between them is not required.

If a site contains two buildings—both containing dwelling units but only one containing the common-use laundry room that people in both buildings are expected to use—then the Act requires that an accessible route be provided from site-arrival points to each building's accessible entrances, and also from one building to the next. An accessible route between each building will ensure that everyone can use the common-use area provided in only one of the buildings. If an accessible route is not planned between the two buildings, occupants who may use wheelchairs and live in the building without the laundry room are prevented from "equitable use" of the laundry room in the other building.

Elevator Buildings

An elevator building is one in which one or more elevators provides service to floors other than the ground floor. A building with an elevator installed as a means of providing an accessible route to the ground floor only is not considered an elevator building. For example, if an elevator provides the only accessible route to the dwelling units on the ground floor from below-grade parking, and does not go up to any other floor, the building is not considered an elevator building. If the same elevator serves floors other than the ground floor, it must provide service to every floor. In other words, the elevator cannot provide service to some floors and not others. All elevator buildings and buildings with an elevator provided as the only means of creating an accessible route to dwelling units on the ground floor are exempt from site impracticality. An accessible entrance served by an accessible route must always be provided to these buildings.

Structural Connections

Suppose a high-rise building served by an elevator is connected to a low-rise nonelevator wing that has dwelling units on two stories; the first story of dwelling units is accessed at grade and the second story is accessed by a flight of stairs. Because the FHA considers the two wings as one building (because they are structurally connected) and the building to be an elevator building (because there is at least one elevator that serves floors containing dwelling units other than the ground floor) all units in both wings are covered. As a result, all units must be accessible, and an accessible route must serve the accessible entrances of the dwelling units on the second level of the nonelevator wing. In order to accomplish this, installing a second elevator to serve the second-story units may be most practical. However, careful assessment of the project, and understanding of the technical requirements of the FHA during project planning, can prevent costly postconstruction remedies to meet the FHA's technical requirements.

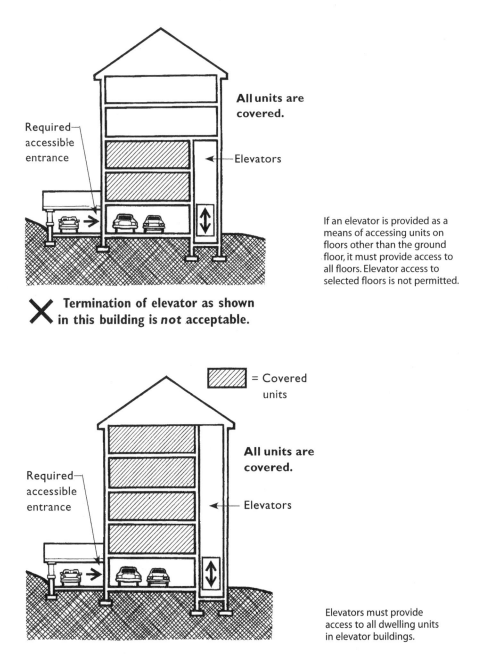

All units are covered.

Required accessible entrance

Elevators

If an elevator is provided as a means of accessing units on floors other than the ground floor, it must provide access to all floors. Elevator access to selected floors is not permitted.

✗ Termination of elevator as shown in this building is *not* acceptable.

▨ = Covered units

All units are covered.

Required accessible entrance

Elevators

Elevators must provide access to all dwelling units in elevator buildings.

If two buildings are connected to an elevator shaft by overhead walks or bridges, all dwelling units in both buildings are covered and must provide accessible entrances served by accessible routes to all dwelling units. However, if the only elevator on-site is freestanding, not connected to any building, and serves only to transport people from one level of the site to another, then the buildings are not considered elevator buildings. For example, a person may be required to

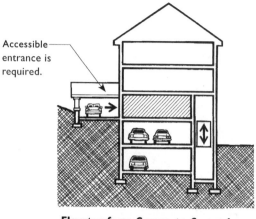

**Elevator from Garage to Covered
Ground-Floor Units**

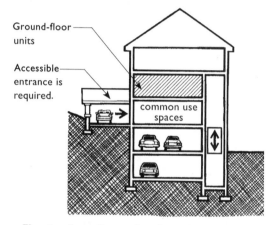

**Elevator from Garage-Levels to Ground-Floor
Units above Common-Use, Grade-Level Floor**

Even though the buildings at right contain elevators, they are provided as a means of creating access to units on the ground floor only, either from parking or from another common-use space space (such as a lobby). Since the elevator does not provide access to any other floor containing dwelling units, the building is not considered an elevator building, and only the units on the ground floor are covered by the Guidelines.

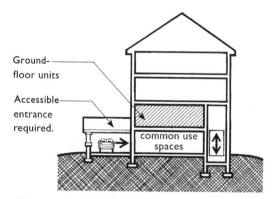

**Elevator from Grade-Level Common-Use Spaces
to Covered Ground-Floor Units Above**

park on one level of the site and use the exterior freestanding elevator to access dwelling unit entrances on another level of the site. The elevator provides the accessible route from parking to dwelling unit entrances on the other side of the building, but the buildings themselves are not served by elevators. Only the ground-floor units in these buildings are covered by the design and construction requirements of the FHA.

Buildings without Elevators

In buildings not served by elevators, only the ground-floor dwelling units are covered and must be served by an accessible entrance on an accessible route. In rare instances, extremes of terrain or unusual characteristics of the site will make it impractical to provide an accessible entrance on an accessible route to buildings without elevators. As a result, the number of covered dwelling units may be reduced (see the discussion of site impracticality on page 20). Buildings with an elevator provided only as a means of creating an accessible route to dwelling units on the ground floor only are not elevator buildings (see the discussion of elevator buildings on page 30).

When the First Level of Living in Buildings without Elevators is Above Grade

According to the Guidelines' definition, a ground floor is "a floor of a building with a building entrance on an accessible route. A building may have one or more ground floors. Where the first floor containing dwelling units in a building is above grade, all units on that floor must be served by a building entrance on

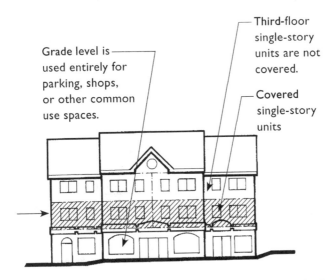

Grade level is used entirely for parking, shops, or other common use spaces.

Third-floor single-story units are not covered.

Covered single-story units

The first level of living is entirely above grade and considered by the Guidelines to be the ground floor. When the first level of living is entirely above retail shops or parking, for example, covered single-story units must be served by an accessible entrance on an accessible route.

an accessible route. This floor will be considered to be a ground floor." For example, the grade level of a building may contain only retail shops with all of the dwelling units above the retail shops, on the second level. The first level containing dwelling units is the level above the retail shops, and is considered by the FHA to be the ground floor, even though the dwelling units are not accessed at ground level. An accessible entrance served by an accessible route to the dwelling units located on the ground floor above the retail shops is required.

Installing an elevator to access the first level of dwelling units above the retail shops is one way to achieve an accessible route to that level. Installing an elevator only as a means of creating an accessible route to dwelling units on the ground floor does not create an elevator building, and only the ground-floor units are covered. If the elevator does provide service to other floors with dwelling units, in addition to the ground floor, then the building is an elevator building and all units are covered. Similarly, if the first level containing dwelling units is above a series of parking garages, then the level above the parking garages is the ground floor, and an accessible entrance served by an accessible route must be provided to each dwelling unit on that level.

When the First Level of Living in Buildings without Elevators Is At Grade

There may be circumstances when several retail shops, for example, are accessed at grade level and attached to one or more dwelling units, which are also accessed at grade level with other dwelling units accessed above grade, or a series of garages at grade level attached to one unit at grade level, with other units on a second level. Since the one unit accessed at grade is the first level containing dwelling units, and can be designed to have a building entrance on an accessible route, it establishes the ground floor of the building; hence, only that unit is covered. The other units above retail or garages are on the second level containing dwelling units in a building not served by elevators, and thus are not covered units.

One or more grade-level accessible units establishes a ground floor, and eliminates the need for accessible routes to units over garages or shops.

Frequently Asked Questions

Q. I am designing several buildings in which covered ground-floor dwelling units are accessed off a breezeway that is open to the front and back of the building. I performed the individual building test to find out whether I could claim site impracticality due to terrain because the site is extremely hilly. I took my measurements from the closest site-arrival points to the breezeway entrance at the front and back of the building. Since results of the site impracticality test showed that I can claim site impracticality, are all of the ground-floor dwelling units accessed off the breezeway exempt from FHA accessibility requirements?

A. No. The measurements should not have been taken from the site-arrival points to the breezeway entrance. Instead, in this case, measurements must be taken from site-arrival points to each dwelling unit entry door. As stated, the breezeway entrance is not the entrance to the building. The dwelling unit doors accessed off the open breezeway on the ground floor are the entrances to the "building." If the breezeway were closed, measurements would be taken from the door to the breezeway to the closest site-arrival points, since the door to the breezeway in this case is the entry to the building.

If a building has one common entrance or separate exterior entrances either to individual units or to clusters of dwelling units, measurements to assess site impracticality are taken from site arrival points to each building entrance.

Q. I am designing a project that incorporates a raised bridge with a 7 percent slope to provide access to ground-floor dwelling units from the parking lot in front of the building. Is it true that I cannot claim site impracticality even though I am designing my building on an extremely hilly site?

A. Yes. Site impracticality cannot be claimed if any one of the following conditions exists:

- Buildings are served by one or more elevators;
- Elevator access is provided to ground floor dwelling units only; or
- Raised walkways with slopes no more than 10 percent connect site-arrival points to a building entrance.

Q. I am constructing 20 attached single-story units each with its own private garage. The Q&As clarify the minimum width for garages and for the garage doors to ensure that people who may use wheelchairs can get out of the garage without obstruction from a parked vehicle. Must I follow the guidance provided in the Q&As as it applies to my garages?

A. No. The clarification contained in the Q&As does not pertain to private garages. There are no minimum measurements required for private garages or their doors. However, there are minimum width requirements for common-use garages and their doors. The Q&As Question 14(c) clarifies these measurements.

REQUIREMENT 2: ACCESSIBLE AND USABLE PUBLIC AND COMMON-USE AREAS

Covered multifamily dwellings with a building entrance on an accessible route shall be designed in such a manner that the public and common use areas are readily accessible to and usable by handicapped persons.

What This Requirement Calls For

Public and common-use areas are required to be accessible to people with disabilities so that they can enjoy and utilize site facilities in the same manner as people without disabilities. Only the public and common-use areas of housing developments containing covered dwelling units must comply with Requirement 2: "Accessible and Usable Public and Common-Use Areas." Common-use spaces that are a part of a housing development that does not contain multifamily units covered by the design and construction requirements of the FHA are not required, by the FHA, to be accessible. However, other federal accessibility laws, such as the ADA and Section 504 of the Rehabilitation Act of 1973, state and local mandates, and building code accessibility requirements might apply.

Under Requirement 2, the Guidelines include a chart outlining 15 elements or spaces in public and common-use areas that are required to be accessible. The elements or spaces required to be accessible, the ANSI A117.1–1986 technical criteria and comparable technical criteria contained in the ANSI A117.1–1992, and 1998 editions to which they must comply, and the Guidelines' explanatory text on the application of each are outlined in the following subsections.

Accessible Routes

Where required, accessible routes within the boundary of the site that comply with ANSI A117.1–1986, Section 4.3, or comparable sections in the ANSI A117.1–1992 and 1998 editions, meet the accessible route requirements of the FHA.

Where required, accessible routes within the boundary of the site. This includes:

- Accessible routes must be provided from public transportation stops, accessible parking spaces, accessible passenger loading zones, and public streets or sidewalks to accessible building entrances.
- Accessible routes must connect accessible buildings, facilities, elements, and spaces that are on the same site. On-grade walks or paths between separate buildings with covered multifamily dwellings, while not required, should be accessible unless the slope of the finished grade exceeds 8.33 percent at any point along the route. Handrails are not required on these accessible walks.
- Accessible routes must connect accessible building or facility entrances with accessible spaces and elements within the building or facility, including adaptable dwelling units.

- Where site or legal constraints prevent the installation of a route accessible to wheelchair users between covered multifamily dwellings and public or common-use facilities elsewhere on the site, an acceptable alternative is the provision of access via a vehicular route, as long as there is accessible parking on an accessible route to at least 2 percent of covered dwelling units, and necessary site provisions such as accessible parking and curb cuts are available at the public or common-use facility.

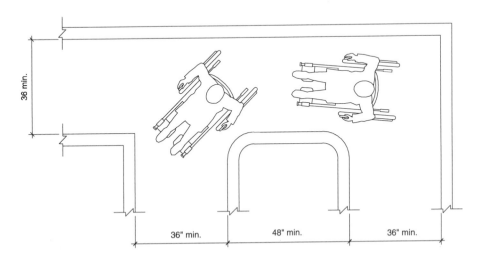

When a person in a wheelchair must make a turn around an obstruction that is no less than 48 in. wide, the minimum width of the accessible route around the obstruction must be at least 36 in.

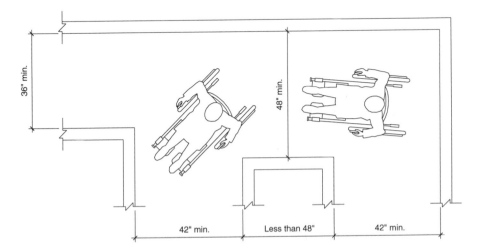

When a person in a wheelchair must make a turn around an obstruction that is less than 48 in. wide, the minimum width of the accessible route around the obstruction must increase to at least 42 and 48 in.

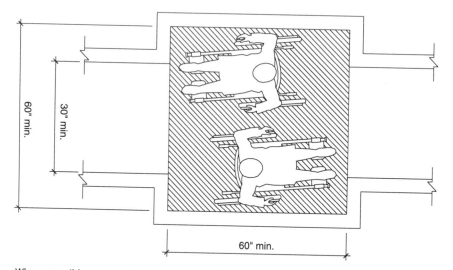

60" min.

30" min.

60" min.

When accessible routes are less than 60 in. wide, a 60 × 60-in. passing space must be provided at least every 200 ft. The passing space can also be a T-shaped turning space created by the intersection of two halls, walks, or corridors.

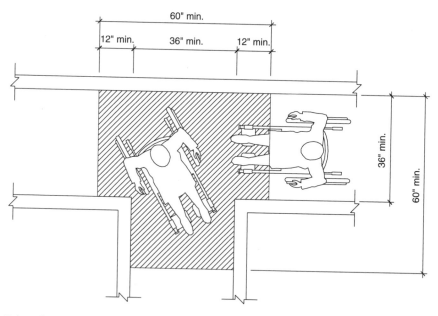

60" min.

12" min. | 36" min. | 12" min.

36" min.

60.0" min.

T-shaped turning space

Protruding Objects

Protruding objects that comply with ANSI A117.1–1986, Section 4.4, or comparable sections in the ANSI A117.1–1992 and 1998 editions, meet the Guidelines.

Where required: Protruding objects on accessible routes or in maneuvering space, including, but not limited to, halls, corridors, passageways, or aisles.

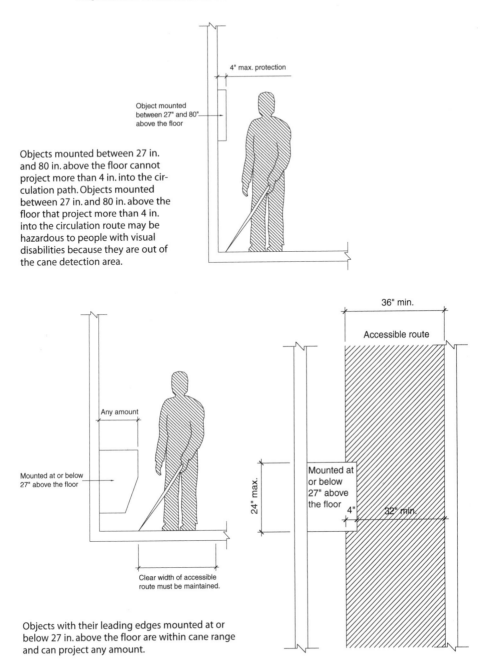

Objects mounted between 27 in. and 80 in. above the floor cannot project more than 4 in. into the circulation path. Objects mounted between 27 in. and 80 in. above the floor that project more than 4 in. into the circulation route may be hazardous to people with visual disabilities because they are out of the cane detection area.

Objects with their leading edges mounted at or below 27 in. above the floor are within cane range and can project any amount.

Ground and Floor Surface Treatments

Ground and floor surface treatments that comply with ANSI A117.1–1986, Section 4.5, or comparable sections in the ANSI A117.1–1992 and 1998 editions, meet the Guidelines.

Where required: On accessible routes, in rooms and spaces, including floors, walks, ramps, stairs, and curb ramps.

Parking and Passenger Loading Zones

Parking and passenger loading zones that comply with ANSI A117.1–1986, Section 4.6, or comparable sections in the ANSI A117.1-1992 and 1998 editions, meet the Guidelines.

Where required: If provided at the site, the following are required:

- Designated accessible parking at the dwelling units on request of residents with disabilities, on the same terms and with the full range of choices (e.g., surface parking or garage) that are provided for other residents of the project, with accessible parking on a route accessible to wheelchairs for at least 2 percent of the covered dwelling units;
- Accessible visitor parking, sufficient to provide access to grade-level entrances of covered multifamily dwellings; and
- Accessible parking at facilities (e.g., swimming pools) that serve accessible buildings.

Curb Ramps

Curb ramps that comply with ANSI A117.1–1986, Section 4.7, or comparable sections in the ANSI A117.1–1992 and 1998 editions, meet the Guidelines.

Where required: Where accessible routes cross curbs.

Ramps

Ramps that comply with ANSI A117.1–1986, Section 4.8, or comparable sections in the ANSI A117.1–1992 and 1998 editions, meet the Guidelines.

Where required: On accessible routes with slopes greater than 1:20.

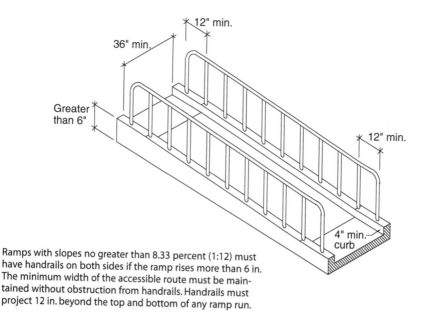

Ramps with slopes no greater than 8.33 percent (1:12) must have handrails on both sides if the ramp rises more than 6 in. The minimum width of the accessible route must be maintained without obstruction from handrails. Handrails must project 12 in. beyond the top and bottom of any ramp run.

Stairs

Stairs that comply with ANSI A117.1–1986, Section 4.9, or comparable sections in the ANSI A117.1–1992 and 1998 editions, meet the Guidelines.

Where required: Along accessible routes connecting levels not connected by an elevator.

Elevators

Elevators that comply with ANSI A117.1–1986, Section 4.10, or comparable sections in the ANSI A117.1–1992 and 1998 editions, meet the Guidelines.

Where required: For elevators that serve covered multifamily buildings, at least one must be accessible.

Platform Lift

Platform lifts that comply with ANSI A117.1–1986, Section 4.11, or comparable sections in the ANSI A117.1–1992 and 1998 editions, meet the Guidelines.

Where required: On platform lifts used in lieu of an elevator or ramp to provide accessibility. They may be used under certain conditions.

Drinking Fountains and Water Coolers

Drinking fountains and water coolers that comply with ANSI A117.1–1986, Section 4.15, or comparable sections in the ANSI A117.1–1992 and 1998 editions, meet the Guidelines.

Where required: Fifty percent of fountains and coolers on each floor, or at least one, if provided in the facility or at the site, must be accessible.

Toilet Rooms and Bathing Facilities

Toilet rooms and bathing facilities (including water closets, toilet rooms and stalls, urinals, lavatories and mirrors, bathtubs, shower stalls, and sinks) that comply with ANSI A117.1–1986, Section 4.22, or comparable sections in the ANSI A117.1–1992 and 1998 editions, meet the Guidelines.

Where required: In public-use and common-use facilities, at least one of each fixture provided per room must be accessible.

Seating, Tables, or Work Surfaces

Seating, tables, or work surfaces that comply with ANSI A117.1–1986, Section 4.30, or comparable sections in the ANSI A117.1–1992 and 1998 editions, meet the Guidelines.

Where required: If provided in accessible spaces, at least one of each type provided must be accessible.

Places of Assembly

Places of assembly that comply with ANSI A117.1–1986, Section 4.31, or comparable sections in the ANSI A117.1–1992 and 1998 editions, meet the Guidelines.

Where required: In the facility or at the site, places of assembly must be accessible.

Common-Use Spaces and Facilities

Common-use spaces and facilities (including swimming pools, playgrounds, entrances, rental offices, lobbies, elevators, mailbox areas, lounges, halls, corridors, and the like) that comply with ANSI A117.1–1986, Sections 4.1 through 4.30, or comparable sections in the ANSI A117.1–1992 and 1998 editions, meet the Guidelines.

Where required: If provided in the facility or at the site:

- Where multiple recreational facilities (e.g., tennis courts) are provided, sufficient accessible facilities of each type to assure equitable opportunity or use by persons with handicaps must be accessible; and
- Where practical, access to all or a portion of nature trails and jogging paths must be accessible.

Laundry Rooms

Laundry rooms that comply with ANSI A117.1–1986, Section 4.32.6, or comparable sections in the ANSI A117.1–1992 and 1998 editions, meet the Guidelines.

Where required: If provided in the facility or at the site:

- At least one of each type of appliance provided in each laundry area, except that laundry rooms serving covered multifamily dwellings would not be required to have front-loading washers. Where front-loading washers are not provided, management will be expected to provide assistive devices on request if necessary to permit a resident to use a top-loading washer.

Parking

Accessible Parking

Accessible parking spaces shall be located on the shortest route to an accessible building entrance. Parking areas that serve covered multifamily buildings are required to include accessible parking spaces for a minimum of 2 percent of the covered dwelling units. For example, on a site that includes an elevator building with 100 units, a minimum of two accessible parking spaces are required because all 100 units are covered (2 percent of 100 covered units = 2 accessible parking spaces). If a building is not served by an elevator and includes 50 units, 25 units on two floors, then the minimum number of accessible parking spaces that must be provided is equal to 2 percent of the covered units. Or, in this case, 2 percent of 25 ground-floor units, since only the ground-floor units in buildings not served by elevators are covered. Since 2 percent of 25 is less than one, a minimum of at least one accessible parking space must be provided.

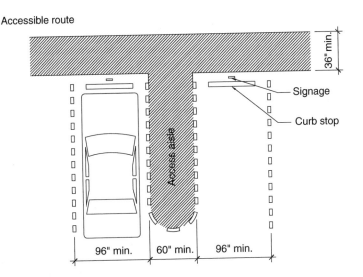

Two accessible parking spaces can share one access aisle. The access aisle is part of the accessible route.

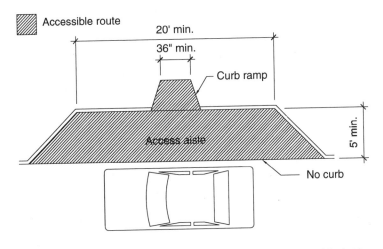

If provided, passenger drop-off areas must include an adjacent access aisle that is an integral part of the accessible route.

The Guidelines indicate that accessible parking be located on the same terms and with the full range of choices that are provided for other residents. As a result, when more than one type of parking is provided, at least one accessible space for each type of parking is required to be accessible even if that number exceeds 2 percent. For example, parking may include an outdoor parking lot directly in front of a building, as well as carport and garage parking located several hundred feet away from the front entrance. If two accessible parking spaces are required, then they must be located on the shortest route to the building entrance. Locating the two accessible spaces in the front parking lot meets the 2 percent requirement for accessible spaces and the requirement that they be located on the shortest route to the entrance. However, since carport and garage parking is also provided, in addition to the outdoor parking lot, the Guidelines indicate that at least one carport space and at least one garage space be made accessible, because people with disabilities must have the same parking choices afforded to other residents without disabilities. In this case, at least four accessible parking spaces must be provided, which is greater than 2 percent of the covered units.

Accessible Visitor Parking and Parking at Site Facilities

If parking includes designated visitor parking, then Requirement 2 provides that a "sufficient" number of visitor parking spaces must be accessible to provide access to grade-level entrances of covered multifamily dwellings. If separate parking is provided at site facilities, such as at a tennis court or other recreation area, in addition to the parking that serves a covered multifamily building, then accessible parking located on an accessible route to the site facility must also be provided at the facility. The accessible parking at the site facility must be provided in addition to the parking that serves covered multifamily buildings.

Accessible Common Garage Parking

The "Supplement to Notice of Fair Housing Accessibility Guidelines: Questions and Answers about the Guidelines (Q&As)" clarifies that where garage parking is the only type of common use parking provided at the site, and there are several individual parking garages grouped together either in a separate area of the building (such as at one end of the building) or in a detached building, for assignment or rental to residents, at least 2 percent of the garages must be at least 14 ft. 2 in. wide and have a vehicular door at least 10 ft. wide. This guideline does not apply to private garages. Although specific measurements for common garage doors are provided, architects and designers may design garages that provide equivalent or greater accessibility. The purpose of the clarification in the Q&As is to ensure that people with disabilities have enough maneuvering space to exit the automobile parked in the garage and to exit the garage through the garage door without interference from the parked automobile. Garage designs that have a smaller garage door and a separate exit door that has a clear width of at least 32 in. and is located on an accessible route to the covered unit are permitted because they provide equivalent accessibility.

Recreational Facilities

The Guidelines indicate that where multiple recreational facilities are provided —for example, swimming pools or tennis courts—a "sufficient" number of each type of facility must be accessible. For example, if a site contains one covered multifamily building that is served by one pool and one tennis court, both are required to be accessible since only one of each type exists. It is important to note that the Guidelines require that people with disabilities be provided access to the pool (but not into the pool itself) via an accessible route from covered dwelling units.

If a site contains two or more buildings, and each building is served by its own pool and tennis court, for example, then an accessible route from the covered dwelling units in each building to the recreational facilities that serve that particular building is required. The recreational facilities in this case are not required to be connected by an accessible route to covered dwelling units in the other buildings because the other buildings are served by separate recreational facilities of the same type. If multiple pools or tennis courts serve a covered multifamily building on a site, then a "sufficient" number of the facilities of the same type are required to be accessible. It is important to note that when assessing "facilities of the same type" care must be taken to ensure that the facilities are exactly the same. For example, a lap pool is not the same as a separate pool meant only for toddlers. Similarly, a clay tennis court is not the same as one made of concrete.

Stairs

Stairs and Accessible Routes

Since accessible routes cannot have a level change greater than ½ in. unless it can be negotiated by an elevator, ramp, or other means of access, stairs are not permitted on accessible routes. However, stairs are required to comply with the ANSI A117.1 stair provisions when they connect levels not connected by an elevator. For example, if a covered multifamily building includes a mailbox area located in a sunken or raised area of the lobby, and is connected to the main lobby level by a ramp and nearby stairs, the stairs must comply with the ANSI A117.1 provisions for stairs that connect levels not connected by an elevator. If the main lobby level and the raised or sunken mailbox area are connected by an elevator, the stairs do not need to comply with the ANSI A117.1 stair provisions. *It is important to check all applicable code requirements for stairs that may exceed the Guidelines' stair requirements.*

Stairs Connecting Floor Levels in Covered Multifamily Buildings

Since only ground-floor dwelling units are covered in a multifamily building not served by an elevator, stairs connecting the ground floor with other levels of the building are not required to be accessible. However, if, for example, the first floor containing dwelling units is located up several steps from a common lobby area that is connected to the ground floor by a ramp, the steps connecting these levels must be accessible, since the levels are not connected by an elevator. Fire stairs in elevator buildings, for example, or any other stair that connects floor levels already connected by an elevator, are exempt from the requirements for accessible stairs.

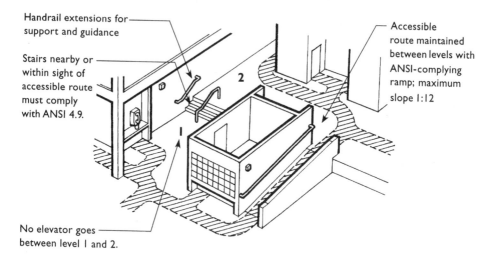

Handrail extensions for support and guidance

Stairs nearby or within sight of accessible route must comply with ANSI 4.9.

Accessible route maintained between levels with ANSI-complying ramp; maximum slope 1:12

No elevator goes between level 1 and 2.

Stairs at accessible routes between levels not connected by an elevator must meet ANSI requirements.

Laundry Rooms

Laundry rooms provided for the use of the residents must be accessible. For example, they must be located on an accessible route, must have accessible doors with proper maneuvering clearance; and, if folding tables, seating areas, sinks, soap dispensers, and other features are provided, at least one of each type must be accessible. In addition, if a bathroom is provided in a common laundry area, it must be accessible, and one of each type of fixture within the bathroom must also be accessible.

If one common laundry room is located in a covered multifamily building, with or without an elevator, an accessible route to it is required from each covered dwelling unit. If each floor of a covered multifamily building with an elevator contains a laundry room, then each laundry room on each floor must be accessible. If, however, more than one laundry room is provided in a building not served by an elevator, an accessible route is required from the covered units to at least one laundry room.

Within accessible laundry rooms, at least one of each type of appliance provided must be accessible and be located on an accessible route. For example, a 30 by 48-in. clear floor space is required to be located at accessible washers and dryers to facilitate a parallel approach to the appliance. The Guidelines do not require front-loading washers if the building management can provide assistive equipment to facilitate use of a top-loading washer upon request of a resident with a disability. Accessible washers and dryers must have any operable parts, such as control buttons, dials, coin slots, and so on, within the ANSI A117.1 reach range. Any operable parts must also comply with the ANSI A117.1 requirements for controls and operating mechanisms.

Frequently Asked Questions

Q. I am in the design development stage of a project that incorporates three buildings on a relatively flat site. One of the buildings is a community center for the residents of the new residential complex. It includes the laundry room, fitness center, and swimming pool, in addition to other common-use spaces. The two other buildings include dwelling units only. Is an accessible route required to connect each building containing dwelling units with the community center only since it contains all of the common-use space?

A. Yes. In this case, an accessible route is required to connect each building containing dwelling units to the community center because it contains the only common-use space. An accessible route is not required to connect the two buildings containing dwelling units only. However, if one of the buildings contained any common-use space that residents in the other building are expected to access, then an accessible route between the buildings would be required.

Q. The building I am designing includes two elevators. One of the elevators is accessible according to the ANSI A117.1 technical criteria for elevators. Are both elevators required to be accessible?

A. No. At least one accessible route must be provided from a building entrance to accessible dwelling units. Elevators are parts of accessible routes. Since at least one accessible route must connect building entrances with accessible dwelling units, at least one elevator must be accessible.

Q. Is it true that clear floor space positioned for a forward or side approach to the washing machine and dryer in my apartment is not required by the Act?

A. Yes. The Act does not require that clear floor space be provided at washers or dryers within dwelling units. However, clear floor space in front of at least one washer and dryer is required in common-use laundry rooms.

REQUIREMENT 3: USABLE DOORS

Covered multifamily dwellings with a building entrance on an accessible route shall be designed in such a manner that all the doors designed to allow passage into and within all premises are sufficiently wide to allow passage by persons in wheelchairs.

What This Requirement Calls For

Requirement 3 applies to doors that are parts of accessible routes in public and common-use areas, the exterior side of the primary entry door to covered dwelling units, and to all doors within dwelling units intended for user passage. Doors that are parts of accessible routes and only the exterior side of the primary entry door to covered units are parts of the public and common-use areas. If they comply with ANSI A117.1–1986, Section 4.13, or comparable sections in the ANSI A117.1–1992 and 1998 editions, they satisfy the FHA's accessibility requirements for public and common use doors.

Public and common-use doors must provide a 32-in. minimum clear opening width between the face of the door and the stop when the door is open 90 degrees; must include accessible hardware; are subject to maneuvering space requirements; and must comply with threshold and opening-force requirements. *Public and common-use doors and the primary entry door to covered dwelling units must provide a clear opening width not less than 32 in. This is an exact, not nominal, dimension.* Because public and common-use doors and the exterior side of primary entry doors to covered dwelling units are subject to more stringent requirements than doors within dwelling units, including hardware, threshold, opening force, and maneuvering clearance, they are referred to as "accessible doors."

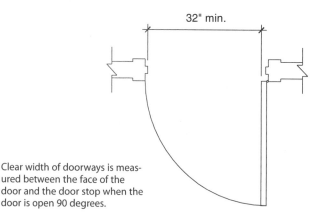

32" min.

Clear width of doorways is measured between the face of the door and the door stop when the door is open 90 degrees.

Doors within Dwelling Units

Doors within covered dwelling units and the interior side of the primary entry door to covered units are not part of public and common-use areas, and are exempt from the technical requirements for maneuvering clearance, accessible hardware, thresholds, and opening force. Because they are subject to less stringent requirements, they are referred to as "usable" doors, not "accessible" doors.

Every door within a dwelling units that is meant for user passage (such as walk-in closet doors, all bathroom and powder room doors, secondary doors that open onto decks, patios, or balconies) must provide a 32-in. nominal clear opening width, measured between the face of the door and the stop when the door is open 90 degrees. Since doors within dwelling units are required to provide a "nominal" clear width, tolerances between ¼ and ⅛ in. are acceptable. A 34-in.-wide door and a standard 6-ft.-wide sliding door, commonly used to access back patios, balconies, and decks, for example, provides the acceptable 32-in. wide nominal clear width.

Doors within dwelling units that are exempt from coverage are those not intended for user passage, such as a coat closet or linen closet door, and doors to small mechanical closets that house furnaces or hot water heaters. Even doors to locations that are inaccessible to people who use wheelchairs, such as a door to an unfinished basement or a door from the dwelling unit to the garage, are required to be usable because they are meant for user passage.

Double-Leaf Doors and Doors in Series

If double-leaf doors with two active leaves, such as French doors that open onto patios, are part of a covered dwelling unit, they must provide a nominal 32-in. clear width between the two door faces when they are both open 90 degrees. If only one leaf is active, the 32-in. nominal clear width must be provided between the face of the active leaf and the door stop when the active leaf is open 90 degrees. The same is true for double-leaf doors in public and common-use areas; however, the clear opening width is required to be at least 32 in. between the faces of the doors when they are open 90 degrees, or, if only one leaf is active, between the face of the active leaf and the door stop when the active leaf is open 90 degrees.

It is not uncommon for dwelling units with separate exterior entrances to include a vestibule area on the interior side of the primary entry door. Access to the interior of the dwelling unit from the vestibule area is provided through a second door that swings just beyond the swing of the primary entry door. The entry to the vestibule and the entry to the interior of the unit is through two doors in series. Doors in series may also be found in public and common-use areas, such as in lobby areas.

Maneuvering clearance required at doors that are parts of accessible routes: Maneuvering clearance is required only on the exterior side of a primary entry door to a dwelling unit because the exterior side of the primary entry door is part of common-use space. There are no maneuvering space requirements at the interior side of the primary entry door to dwelling units or on either side of doors within dwelling units or secondary egress doors that open onto patios, balconies, terraces, decks, patios, and so on.

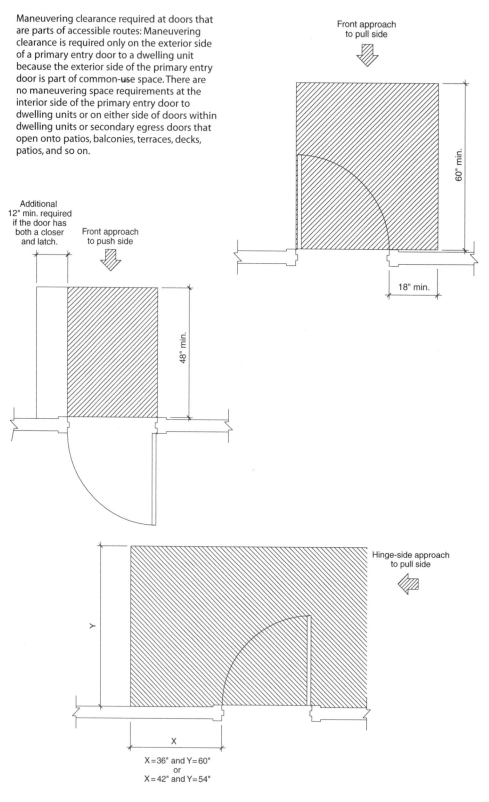

Front approach to pull side

60" min.

18" min.

Additional 12" min. required if the door has both a closer and latch.

Front approach to push side

48" min.

Hinge-side approach to pull side

Y

X

X = 36" and Y = 60"
or
X = 42" and Y = 54"

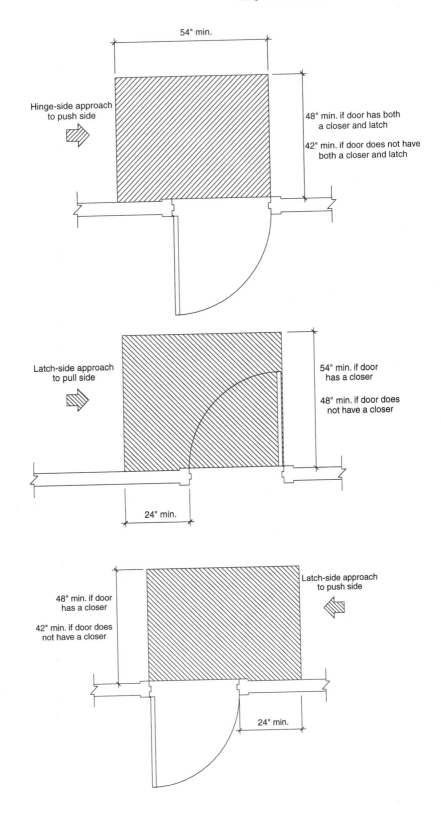

54" min.

Hinge-side approach
to push side

48" min. if door has both
a closer and latch

42" min. if door does not have
both a closer and latch

Latch-side approach
to pull side

54" min. if door
has a closer

48" min. if door does
not have a closer

24" min.

48" min. if door
has a closer

42" min. if door does
not have a closer

Latch-side approach
to push side

24" min.

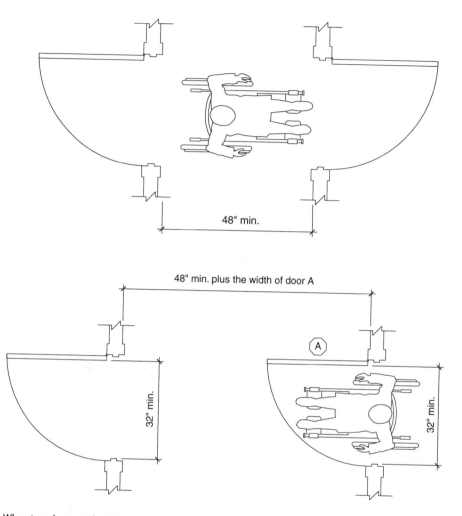

When two doors are in series, they cannot both swing into the space created between them. Only one door is permitted to swing into the space, or both doors must swing away from the space. If both doors swing away from the space, the space between the two doors must be no less than 48 in. If one door swings into the space, the space must be no less than 48 in. plus the width of the door swinging into the space.

When two doors are in series, a 48-in. space must be provided between them so people who use wheelchairs can easily access both doors. If the doors swing in the same direction, the 48-in. space must be provided between the leading edge of one door when it is open 90 degrees and the face of the second door when it is closed. In other words, the 48-in. space must be provided in addition to the space required and taken up by the open door. If the doors swing in opposite directions, the 48-in. space must be provided between the faces of both doors when they are closed. Two doors in series cannot both swing into the space between them.

Maximum Depth

Any opening in public and common-use areas and within dwelling units, such as an archway, greater than 24 in. in depth is not considered a doorway. If openings greater than 24 in. deep are on accessible routes, they must comply with the accessible route requirements, that is, they must be at least 36 in. wide. However, a passageway, archway, or doorway that measures 24 in. or less in depth is required to provide the 32-in. clear width. When the opening exceeds 24 in. in depth, the minimum 36-in. width requirement for accessible routes must be provided.

Frequently Asked Questions

Q. **Must there be maneuvering clearance that complies with ANSI A117.1 technical criteria on both sides of the entry door to my unit?**

A. No. Maneuvering clearance that complies with the ANSI A117.1 criteria must be provided on the exterior side only of the primary entry door to the unit. Maneuvering clearance is not required on the interior side of the primary entry door to the unit or on any side of doors within dwelling units.

Q. **Is it true that the clear opening width of a door that opens onto an exterior deck from a living room can be 32 in. nominal as opposed to 32 in. exactly?**

A. Yes. At secondary exit doors, or doors that open onto patios, terraces, decks, balconies, and so on, the required opening width at doors is 32 in. nominal. Tolerances between ⅛ and ¼ in. are permitted at these doors and at doors within dwelling units. The clear opening width provided at a door on the accessible route and at the primary entry door to the unit must be exactly 32 in. No tolerance is allowed at these doors.

Q. **Is it true that the 32-in.-wide by 26-in.-deep archway that connects my kitchen with my dining room must be widened to at least 36 in.?**

A. Yes. The clear width at doorways, or archways in this case, is permitted to be no less than 32-in. nominal for a maximum depth of 24 in. In other words, a doorway or archway that measures at least 32 in. in width must be widened to at least 36 in. if it is deeper than 24 in. If the doorway or archway is no more than 24 in. deep, it is permitted to measure at least 32 in. in width.

REQUIREMENT 4: ACCESSIBLE ROUTE INTO AND THROUGH THE COVERED DWELLING UNIT

All covered multifamily dwellings with a building entrance on an accessible route shall be designed and constructed in such a manner that all premises within covered multifamily dwelling units contain an accessible route into and through the covered dwelling units.

What This Requirement Calls For

An accessible route through a covered dwelling unit is required to be at least 36 in. wide and must connect all spaces within the unit. Routes are permitted to be wider, but not less than 36 in. Unlike the requirements for accessible routes in public and common-use areas, those within the dwelling unit are exempt from the technical requirements for headroom and protruding objects. *It is important to note that building codes or other federal, state, or local laws may require routes wider than 36 in.*

Design Features

Within covered units, "design features" such as lofts or raised or sunken areas are permitted. If a covered unit contains a design feature, such as a loft, split-level entry, or a raised or sunken area, all other spaces within the unit must be on an accessible route that is not interrupted by the design feature itself.

A covered unit cannot contain more than one design feature. A unit that contains a loft bedroom, for example, cannot also contain a raised or sunken area anywhere in the entire unit. Similarly, if a unit contains a sunken living room, it cannot contain a loft den area, or any other special design feature. A kitchen, bathroom, and any other primary function area must always be on an accessible route, and cannot be designed into any special design feature unless an accessible route is provided to these specific rooms.

Split-Level Entries

Although split-level entries are permitted, an alternate means of access to the remainder of the unit must be provided at the entry so that people in wheelchairs can access the unit. A unit can be raised or sunken above or below an entry foyer by several steps, for example, if a nearby accessible route (such as a ramp with a slope no greater than 8.33 percent) connecting the primary entry with the unit is provided.

Lofts

Lofts must be open to the room in which they are located, and must not exceed 33.3 percent of the floor area of the room in which they are located. Lofts are intermediate levels within the same story and thus do not create multistory units. Any primary function area, including kitchens, bathrooms, the only bedroom in the unit, the living room, the dining room, and so on, cannot be located in a loft area unless they can be accessed via an accessible route. Only secondary areas, such as a den, second bedroom, or a study, are permitted to be located in a loft area. Similarly, only portions of rooms, not entire rooms, can be located in a raised or sunken area.

Doors That Are Part of Special Design Features

Since Requirement 3 requires all doors within dwelling units to be usable, any door meant for user passage (such as a walk-in closet door located in a loft or a sunken or raised area) must provide a 32-in. nominal clear opening width even though these doors may not be on an accessible route. Doors to spaces that cannot otherwise be accessed are not permitted to be located in raised or sunken areas. However, they are permitted to be located in these areas if an alternate door to the same space is provided on an accessible route.

Multistory Units in Elevator Buildings

Multistory dwelling units in buildings without elevators are not covered units. However, multistory units in elevator buildings are covered units, and accessibility must be provided to the story served by the elevator. The story served by the elevator must be the primary entry level to the multistory unit, must comply with Requirements 3 through 7 of the FHA for all spaces located on the primary entry level only, and must contain a usable bathroom or powder room, according to the provisions of Requirement 7. The primary entry level can also include a special design feature with the same restrictions and requirements as discussed previously.

If the primary entry level contains only a powder room and not a full bathroom, it must comply with Requirements 3 through 7. If a powder room in addition to a bathroom is provided on the primary entry level, it must comply with Requirements 3, 4, and 5, and the bathroom must comply with Requirements 3 through 7. The second level of a multistory unit in an elevator building is exempt from the design and construction requirements of the FHA.

Level Changes and the Accessible Route through the Unit

The accessible route through the covered dwelling unit must be at least 36-in. wide. Ideally, accessible routes without level changes are best because they are easiest to negotiate for a person in a wheelchair and for those with other disabilities. However, minimal level changes are permitted on the accessible route. In covered units, unbeveled level changes up to ¼ in. are permitted. Changes in level between ¼ and ½ in. are also permitted; however, any level change within this range must be beveled. The slope of the bevel must not exceed 1:2. Changes in level greater than ½ in. must be ramped or must include alternate means of access. Although negotiating a ½-in. level change may be easy for some people who use wheelchairs or scooters, it presents a tripping hazard for others. Level changes are measured from the finished floor or ground surfaces. For example, measurements for level changes between the interior and exterior of the unit are taken from the top of the finished floor to the top of the exterior ground or floor level.

Level Changes between the Unit Interior and the Exterior Ground Surface at Secondary Exits

Threshold height at secondary exterior doors used to access the exterior from within the dwelling unit must not exceed ¾ in. According to the level-change requirement, the surfaces of exterior decks, patios, or balconies must be located no more than ½ in. from the interior floor surface of the covered unit if the exterior surfaces are constructed of pervious materials or materials that water can penetrate. For example, a wood deck must be installed no more than ½-in. below the top of the floor surface of the unit because wood is a pervious material—that is, water can penetrate through wood. The ½-in. allowable level change must be beveled, and is in addition to the permissible ¾-in. maximum threshold height for exterior doors. As a result, the maximum measurement from the top of the ¾-in. threshold to the top of the pervious exterior floor surface (which is permitted to be ½ in. below the floor surface of the unit) is 1¼ in. Thresholds at exterior doors and changes in level between the interior and exterior of the unit must be beveled with a slope no more than 1:2.

If exterior decks, patios, or balconies are constructed of impervious materials, or materials through which water cannot penetrate, then their surfaces must be located no more than 4 in. below the top of the floor surface of the dwelling unit. Again, this permissible level change is in addition to the allowable maximum ¾-in. threshold height at secondary exterior doors. For example, a concrete deck should be installed not more than 4 in. below the dwelling unit because interior finished floor concrete is an impervious material. As a result, the maximum measurement from the top of the ¾-in. threshold to the top of the impervious exterior floor surface is 4¾ in.

Other laws or codes may have different requirements for level changes and threshold heights. If other laws or codes require level changes or threshold heights that do not meet the Guidelines, alternate means of accessibility at these locations must be provided.

A vertical level change of no more than ¼ in. is permitted without edge treatment. Vertical-level changes greater than ½ in. are not permitted unless they can be negotiated by a ramp or elevator. Level changes between ¼ and ½ in. must be beveled. The slope of the bevel must be no more than 1:2.

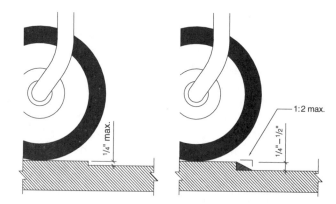

Threshold Heights and Level Changes

Threshold height at primary entry doors must not exceed ¾ in. The maximum level change allowed between the top of the interior floor surface of the dwelling unit and the exterior ground surface at the primary entry door is ½ in., regardless of whether the exterior floor or ground surface at the primary entry door is constructed of pervious or impervious materials. As a result, the maximum measurement from the top of the ¾-in. threshold to the top of the exterior floor surface (which is permitted to be ½ in. below the floor surface of the unit) is 1¼ in. The exterior ground surface at the primary entry door to the unit can be sloped no more than ⅛ in. per foot for drainage.

Other laws or codes may have different requirements for level changes and threshold heights. If other laws or codes require level changes or threshold heights that do not meet the Guidelines, alternate means of accessibility at these locations must be provided.

Frequently Asked Questions

Q. Is it true that my loft cannot be closed on all sides?

A. Yes. Lofts must be open to the room they overlook, and must not exceed 33.3 percent of the floor area of the room in which they are located. They also cannot contain any primary function areas (such as a bathroom or a kitchen) if they are not provided with an accessible route.

Q. The split-level entry foyer I am designing incorporates a short stairway that is adjacent to a ramp. Both the stairway and the ramp provide access from the entry foyer to the interior of the unit. Must I make the stairs accessible according to the ANSI A117.1 technical criteria for stairs?

A. No. The ANSI A117.1 technical criteria for stairs apply to stairs in public and common areas that connect levels not connected by an elevator. Stairs within dwelling units are not covered by the accessibility requirements of the FHA.

Q. Since I usually use my backdoor to enter my unit, does that mean that my concrete patio can be no more than ½ in. below the finished floor surface to my unit? In other words, must I apply the level change requirements for primary entry doors to my backdoor since it is the one I most often use to enter my unit?

A. No. The backdoor may be the one used to enter the unit, but it is not considered by the Guidelines to be the primary entry door. The exterior ground surface at the planned primary entry door cannot be more than ½ in. below the interior finished floor surface. It may also be sloped ⅛ in. per foot for drainage. Since the concrete patio is technically at a planned secondary exterior door, the nonpervious concrete patio is permitted to be no more than 4 in. below the interior floor surface of the unit.

REQUIREMENT 5: LIGHT SWITCHES, ELECTRICAL OUTLETS, THERMOSTATS, AND OTHER ENVIRONMENTAL CONTROLS IN ACCESSIBLE LOCATIONS

All covered multifamily dwellings with a building entrance on an accessible route shall be designed and constructed in such a manner that all premises within covered multifamily dwelling units contain light switches, electrical outlets, thermostats, and other environmental controls in accessible locations.

What This Requirement Calls For

Light switches, electrical outlets, thermostats, and other environmental controls must be located within accessible reach ranges between 15 and 48 in. above the finished floor. Environmental controls include those used to operate any heating, ventilation, or air conditioning equipment, including thermostats and switches that operate electric ceiling fans, air conditioners, and skylights. The Guidelines do not indicate that the controls comply with any force or type-of-motion criteria.

Requirement 5 does not apply to every control in a dwelling unit. It applies only to controls when no others that perform the same function are located within the same general area. For example, if the only outlet in the general area is located below a window sill that is located less than 15 in. above the floor, it is not permitted because it is out of the accessible reach range. However, an inaccessible outlet is permitted if another outlet within the accessible reach range is located in the same general area and performs the same function. Similarly, an inaccessible floor-mounted outlet is permitted only if another outlet that performs the same function is located nearby and within the accessible reach range.

Outlets are not permitted to be located over counters at the inside corners of kitchens if they are not at least 36 in. away from an adjacent wall. However, if a nearby outlet that performs the same function is located more than 36 in. away from the corner and is within the allowable obstructed reach range, then an inaccessible outlet close to an adjacent wall is permitted.

Controls Not Covered

Appliance outlets and controls are not covered by the Guidelines. Among these are controls used to operate circuit breakers and those that are part of the appliance itself including controls on ranges, range hoods, and washing machines. However, when switches used to operate range hood fans or range hood lights are mounted on a wall, not on the appliance itself, they must be with the accessible reach range. Outlets for refrigerators, microwaves, ovens, washing machines, dryers, and other appliances are not covered because they are not used regularly. Controls for garbage disposals and emergency interrupt switches to mechanical equipment are also not covered controls.

Reach Range for a Perpendicular or Forward Approach to Controls

The acceptable unobstructed forward reach range permitted to access light switches, electrical outlets, thermostats, and other environmental controls by a person in a wheelchair is between 15 and 48 in. above the floor. If the reach to these controls is over an obstruction (such as a wall shelf) that projects from the wall between 20 and 25 in., then the "high forward" maximum reach range is reduced from 48 in. to 44 in. Controls cannot be located so that a person must reach over an obstruction that projects from the wall more than 25 in. However, standard countertops are permitted a tolerance of ½ in. beyond the 25-in. projection limit for a maximum countertop projection of 25½ in. To make a forward approach to controls located over obstructions, a 30-in. wide kneespace must be provided below the obstruction. That clear kneespace must be as deep as the reach distance.

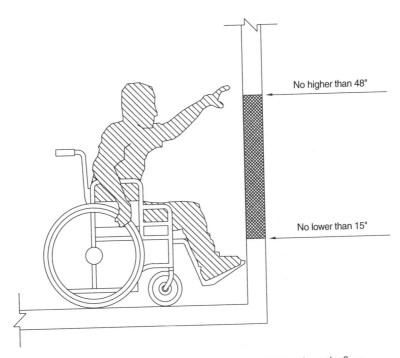

No higher than 48"

No lower than 15"

Accessible reach range for a seated user is between 15 and 48 in. above the floor.

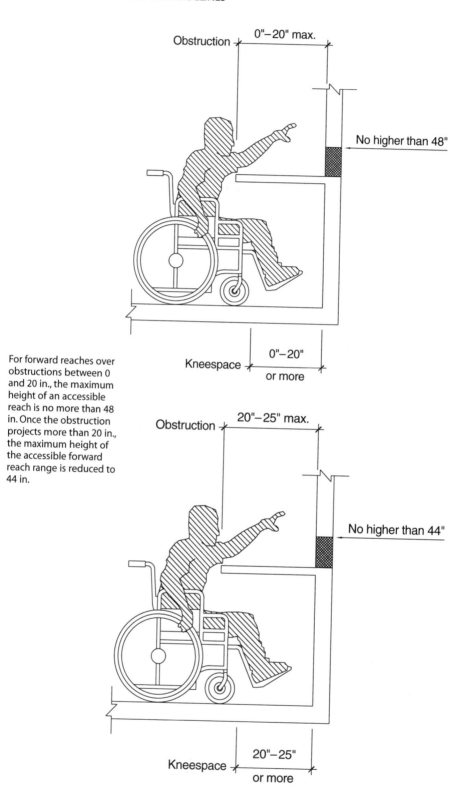

Obstruction   0"–20" max.

No higher than 48"

For forward reaches over obstructions between 0 and 20 in., the maximum height of an accessible reach is no more than 48 in. Once the obstruction projects more than 20 in., the maximum height of the accessible forward reach range is reduced to 44 in.

Kneespace   0"–20"
or more

Obstruction   20"–25" max.

No higher than 44"

Kneespace   20"–25"
or more

Reach Range for a Parallel or Side Approach to Controls

The Guidelines do not address an unobstructed side approach to controls. However, side approaches to controls located over obstructions are addressed. This type of approach is commonly found in kitchens where a person must reach over base cabinets to access controls. If access to the controls located over an obstruction requires a side, or parallel, approach, then the "high side" maximum reach is reduced from 48 to 46 in.

Base cabinets cannot obstruct a side reach by more than 24 in. HUD permits the same industry tolerance of ½ in. for countertops, as discussed previously for a maximum projection of 25½ in. Controls located so that a person must reach over obstructions greater than 25½ in. are not permitted.

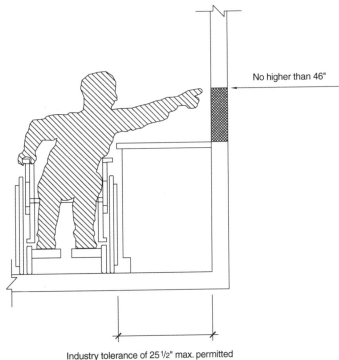

No higher than 46"

Industry tolerance of 25 1/2" max. permitted for countertops; other obstructions must not protrude more than 25"

The maximum height of an obstructed side reach is 46 in.

Frequently Asked Questions

Q. The ceiling light in my walk-in closet is turned on by pulling on a chain that's attached to the light itself, or by flicking the light switch just outside the closet door. Must I make both controls accessible?

A. No. Since the switch and the pull-chain perform the same function, and are located within the same general area, only one must be accessible. As long as the light switch is located between 15 and 48 in. above the floor, the pull-chain can be out of the accessible reach range. Moreover, a pull chain is not accessible because it must be grasped tightly and pulled. Switches are much easier to operate for most people, including those with manual dexterity problems.

Q. In order to operate the only light switch in my kitchen, I must reach over a wall-hung shelf that protrudes from the wall 26½ in. Must the maximum height of the switch be 44 in. above the floor in this case?

A. No. Obstructions cannot protrude more than 25 in. from the wall. The maximum high forward reach is 44 in. for a forward approach to controls located over obstructions that protrude between 20 and 25 in. The wall-hung shelf in this case must be removed or reduced to no more than 25 in. in depth; or the switch must be relocated, or another switch that performs the same function and is located within the same general area must be added within an accessible reach range.

Q. Is it true that the control for the light on my range hood is not covered by the Guidelines?

A. Yes. Controls that are parts of appliances are not covered. However, if the light on the hood is hard-wired to a switch on the wall, the switch must be located within accessible reach range.

REQUIREMENT 6: REINFORCED WALLS
FOR GRAB BARS

Covered multifamily dwellings with a building entrance on an accessible route shall be designed and constructed in such a manner that all premises within covered multifamily dwelling units contain reinforcements in bathroom walls to allow later installation of grab bars around the toilet, tub, shower stall, and shower seat, where such facilities are provided.

What This Requirement Calls For

Reinforced walls to allow for the later installation of grab bars is an example of an adaptable feature that allows the occupant of the dwelling unit to easily install grab bars when needed. All bathrooms must have walls reinforced for the later installation of grab bars at the toilet, bathtub, and shower stall at the time of construction and at specific locations outlined in the Guidelines.

In an elevator building, since only the story of a multistory unit served by the elevator must comply with the Guidelines, only those bathrooms on that story must provide reinforced walls for grab bars. Powder rooms must comply with Requirement 6 if they are the only bathing facility on the primary entry level of a multistory unit in an elevator building. Powder rooms in covered single-story units are exempt from Requirement 6 because there will always be a bathroom, in addition to the powder room, that must comply with Requirements 3 through 7.

Grab Bar Reinforcement at Toilets
Locating a toilet adjacent to a reinforced side wall allows for the easy installation of standard grab bars. The minimum reinforcement length at a wall adjacent to a toilet is 24 in., although longer reinforcement allows for the installation of a longer grab bar (which may be more convenient for some users). It is recommended that the leading edge of the reinforcement be at least 36 in. from the back wall. If a toilet is installed next to an adjacent short wall that does not allow the leading edge of the reinforcement to be located at least 36 in. away from the back wall, then at least 24 in. of reinforcement must still be provided, even if the leading edge of the reinforcement is exactly 24 in. from the back wall.

If a toilet is not installed adjacent to a side wall (a toilet may be placed between a sink and a bathtub, for example) reinforcement must be provided for the installation of other types of grab bars, including a wall-mounted foldaway, floor-mounted, or a wall-and-floor-mounted grab bar. The centerline of the alternative grab bar should be 15¾ in. from the centerline of the toilet, which is equivalent to the measure between the centerline of a standard wall-hung grab bar and the centerline of the toilet. When reinforcement for alternative grab bars is installed, care must be taken to ensure that the alternative grab bars, once installed, will not encroach on any clear floor space or block fixtures. For example, the installation of a floor-mounted grab bar at the toilet is not permitted to encroach on the clear floor space required at the toilet.

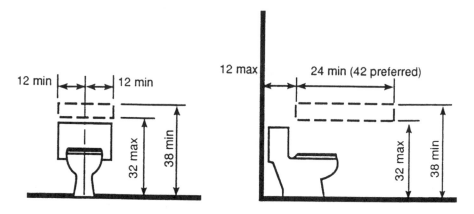

Wall reinforcement locations at the toilet, in inches.

Grab Bar Reinforcement at Bathtubs and Shower Stalls

The Guidelines identify specific areas on the walls that surround conventional bathtubs that must be reinforced to allow for the later installation of grab bars. However, there are also instances when nonconventional bathtubs or shower stalls are located away from walls, such as a sunken tub or a glass-walled shower stall. The Guidelines permit this type of bathroom design only if reinforcement provisions are made for the later installation of alternative grab bars. Whenever possible, the specific guidance on grab bar reinforcement locations provided in the Guidelines should be followed. For example, if a wall is present on the long side of a sunken tub, the specific guidance provided for reinforcement locations on the long wall at conventional bathtubs should be followed.

If a shower stall is the only bathing fixture in a covered single-story unit or on the primary entry level of a multistory unit in an elevator building, it must measure at least 36 in. by 36 in. and reinforcements at specific locations for the later installation of grab bars and a wall-hung bench seat must be provided. If shower stalls are not the only bathing fixture in a covered unit, they must be reinforced for the later installation of grab bars and are permitted to measure any size or configuration. Reinforcement is not required at these showers for the later installation of a wall-hung bench seat. It is important to note that glass showers must include reinforcement at any solid wall. Reinforcement installation is not required at glass walls or shower floors.

Frequently Asked Questions

Q. There is a special device I heard about that functions like a giant molly bolt that can be fastened anywhere on a wall and will allow grab bars to be installed onto it. If I purchase these devices and provide them to the residents of the covered units I am constructing, can I avoid reinforcing bathroom walls at fixtures for the later installation of grab bars?

A. No. Requirement 6 of the Guidelines indicates that covered dwelling unit bathrooms include the adaptable feature of reinforced walls for the later installation of grab bars. A resident may choose to use these special devices that function like giant molley bolts and allow the installation of grab bars, but they must be used in addition to the reinforced walls. In other words, no matter what, bathroom walls must always be reinforced for the later installation of grab bars at specific locations outlined in the Guidelines. However, installing grab bars using the giant molley bolts without reinforced walls at the time of construction may provide equivalent accessibility to reinforced walls without grab bars installed. It is the architect or the builder who must demonstrate that equivalent accessibility is achieved in all cases when they veer from the Guidelines or other approved "safe harbors."

Q. **I intend to install a floor-and-wall-mounted grab bar next to the toilet. If I do so, the part of the grab bar that is installed into the floor encroaches on the clear floor space required at the toilet. Is this arrangement okay?**

A. No. Grab bars cannot interfere with clear floor spaces needed at fixtures.

Q. **My bathtub is located away from any surrounding walls. Am I exempt from the grab bar reinforcement requirement?**

A. No. Reinforcements must be in place for the later installation of alternative grab bars such as a floor-mounted grab bar.

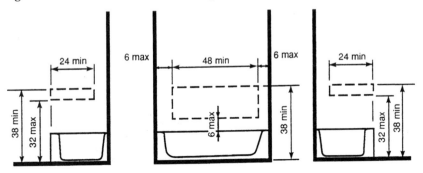

Wall reinforcement locations at the bathtub.

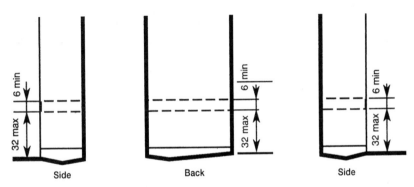

Side   Back   Side

Wall reinforcement locations at a stall shower.

REQUIREMENT 7: USABLE KITCHENS AND BATHROOMS

Covered multifamily dwellings with a building entrance on an accessible route shall be designed and constructed in such a manner that all premises within covered multifamily dwelling units contain usable kitchens and batrhooms such that an individual in a wheelchair can maneuver about the space.

What This Requirement Calls For

Kitchens and bathrooms within covered dwelling units must provide access for people with disabilities. Among all spaces within a dwelling unit, the kitchen and bathroom are perhaps two of the most important primary function areas. The Guidelines allow a minimal level of accessibility in the kitchen. Two design options are permitted for bathrooms: A and B. Option B typically provides a greater level of accessibility. As a result, when designing an Option B bathroom, only one bathroom is required to comply with the Option B requirements, and all other bathrooms are exempt from clear floor space requirements at fixtures (Requirement 7). However, in this case, all of the other bathrooms are required to comply with Requirements 3 through 6. If the Option A design in chosen, then all bathrooms in the unit must comply with the Option A requirements. That is, they must comply with Requirements 3 through 7.

Usable Kitchens

Clear Floor Space

The Guidelines indicate that a clear floor space that measures at least 30 in. by 48 in. be provided at the range or cooktop and the sink, to permit a person in a wheelchair to use the appliance by positioning the wheelchair parallel to the appliance. The clear floor space may be positioned for a perpendicular (forward) approach to the range or cooktop and the sink if kneespace is provided below the appliances. Compliance with ANSI A117.1 technical criteria for kneespace satisfies the Guidelines' requirement for kneespace. A clear floor space that measures at least 30 in. by 48 in. provided at the oven, dishwasher, refrigerator/freezer, or trash compactor is required for a person in a wheelchair to use the appliance by making a parallel (side) or perpendicular (front) approach to the appliance.

All clear floor spaces must be centered on the appliance (including the sink) they serve and must join the accessible route that connects the kitchen with the remainder of the dwelling unit. Clear floor spaces provided in the kitchen are permitted to overlap. When sinks incorporate more than one bowl, the clear floor space must be centered on the entire sink, not on the bowls.

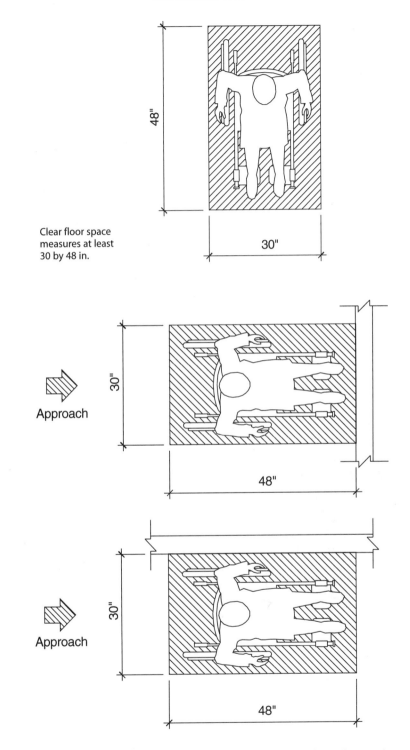

Clear floor space measures at least 30 by 48 in.

Approach

Approach

Clear floor space can be positioned for both a perpendicular or forward approach and a parallel or side approach.

U-Shaped Kitchens

For most kitchen arrangements, the minimum clearance allowed between the face of opposing base cabinets, countertops, appliances, or walls is 40 in. However, in U-shaped kitchens with a sink, range, or cooktop located at the base of the U, an unobstructed turning circle that measures at least 60 in. in diameter is required so that a person in a wheelchair can use the appliance located at the base of the U by pulling up parallel to the appliance. As a result, a U-shaped kitchen design that has a sink, range, or cooktop located at the base of the U must have a minimum measurement of at least 60 in. between opposing base cabinets, countertops, appliances, or walls. The clear floor space required at the sink, range, or cooktop located at the base of the U must be centered for a parallel approach on the appliance, that is, 48 in. must be centered on the appliance.

In a U-shaped kitchen, if removable base cabinets are provided below the sink, range, or cooktop located at the base of the U (allowing a person in a wheelchair to use the appliance by approaching it from a forward direction), the 60-in. diameter turning radius may be eliminated. However, the minimum measurement between opposing base cabinets, countertops, appliances, or walls in a U-shaped kitchen with a sink, range, or cooktop with kneespace or removable base cabinets below and located at the base of the U is 40 in.

Frequently Asked Questions

Q. **My U-shaped kitchen has two sinks. One is located at the base of the U and the other is located on an adjacent wall. The measurement between opposing base cabinets and appliances in the kitchen is 42 in. Do I have to provide the 60-in. turning circle?**

A. No. Since there are two sinks and the one on the adjacent wall is provided with the 30-in.-by-48-in. clear floor space positioned for a side approach to the sink, the 60-in. turning circle is not required. However, in a U-shaped kitchen with the only sink or cooktop in the kitchen located at the base of the U, the 60-in. turning circle must be provided so that a person can make a parallel approach to the appliance. In this case, if kneespace or removable base cabinets are provided below the sink or cooktop located at the base of the U, the 60-in. circle need not be provided.

Q. **Can I provide a front approach to the kitchen sink?**

A. Yes. Although the Guidelines allow a parallel approach to the kitchen sink, a front approach is permitted if removable base cabinets are, or open kneespace is, provided below the sink.

Q. **The controls on my cooktop are located so that a person must reach over burners to access them. Is this allowed?**

A. Yes. Although reaching over burners to access controls may be hazardous, the Guidelines do not cover controls on appliances.

Usable Bathrooms

There are two types of bathroom arrangements permitted in covered dwelling units: Type A and Type B. The Guidelines require either of the following:

- All bathrooms in the unit comply with the requirements for a Type A bathroom, or
- At least one bathroom must comply with the Type B requirements; all other bathrooms within the dwelling unit are exempt from clear floor space requirements at fixtures, but must have usable doors (Requirement 3), be on an accessible route (Requirement 4), have switches, outlets, and environmental controls in accessible locations (Requirement 5), and have reinforced walls for grab bars (Requirement 6).

Powder Rooms

If a powder room is provided in a covered unit, in addition to one or more bathrooms, it is exempt from clear floor space requirements at fixtures (Requirement 7) and from grab bar reinforcement requirements (Requirement 6), but it must comply with Requirements 3 through 5.

Only the bathrooms on the story served by the elevator in covered multistory dwelling units must comply with the requirements for usable bathrooms (Requirement 7). In many instances, a powder room is the only facility located on the covered story of a multistory unit, with full bathrooms located on an inaccessible, noncovered, story. The Guidelines permit this type of dwelling unit design; however, if the powder room is the only facility located on the covered story of a multistory dwelling unit, it must have usable doors (Requirement 3); be on an accessible route (Requirement 4); have switches, outlets, and environmental controls in accessible locations (Requirement 5); have reinforced walls for the later installation of grab bars (Requirement 6); and comply with the Type A or Type B bathroom provisions, including the requirements for maneuvering and clear floor space at fixtures (Requirement 7).

Type A Bathroom Requirements

All Type A bathrooms must provide "sufficient" maneuvering space so that a person in a wheelchair can enter the bathroom, close the door, use the fixtures, reopen the door, and exit. If "sufficient" maneuvering space is provided, doors are permitted to swing into the clear floor space at fixtures. The space below bathroom fixtures (the space below a toilet or sink) is permitted to be a part of the maneuvering space.

Clear floor space requirements at the toilet, sink, bathtub, and shower stall are specified in the Guidelines (Appendix A). Like the clear floor space provided at appliances in kitchens, clear floor space provided at fixtures in the bathroom can overlap. At sinks, the 30-by-48-in. clear floor space must be provided for a parallel approach if base cabinets below the sink are not removable. If the clear floor space cannot be located to allow for a parallel approach to the sink, a perpendicular or front approach is permitted if base cabinets below the sink are removable to provide kneespace. Clear floor space at the sink must be centered on the sink basin.

Type B Bathroom Requirements

In general, Type B bathrooms provide a higher degree of usability in the bathroom. If the Type B bathroom specification is used, only one of the bathrooms in the covered dwelling unit is required to be Type B; all other bathrooms must comply with Requirements 3 through 6. The only time powder rooms are required to comply with Requirement 6 and 7 is when they are the only toilet facility provided on the primary entry level of covered multistory units (see the preceding discussion of Powder Rooms).

In-Swinging and Out-Swinging Bathroom Doors

If the door swings into the bathroom, there must be a 30-by-48-in. clear floor space provided beyond the door swing. The space below any fixture can be used as part of the required clear floor space. If the door swings out of the bathroom, the 30-by-48-in. clear floor space must be provided for a person using a wheelchair to use the fixtures, reopen the door, and exit.

When Two Bathing Fixtures are Provided

In Type B bathrooms, if both a bathtub and a separate shower stall are provided, at least one must be made accessible according to the clear floor space requirements provided in the Guidelines at those fixtures. Similarly, if two sinks are provided, at least one must provide the minimum 30–by-48-in. clear floor space positioned for a parallel (side) approach and centered on the sink basin if base cabinets are not removable. Or, the clear floor space must be positioned for a perpendicular (front) approach and centered on the sink basin if base cabinets are removable.

Toilets

The Guidelines provide three choices for clear floor space at the toilet. Whichever clear floor space specification is chosen, toilets must be positioned in bathrooms so that a grab bar can be installed on at least one side if the occupant chooses to do so. If the grab-bar side of the toilet is adjacent to a wall or fixture, the centerline of the toilet must be at least 18 in. from the obstacle, an exact measure of 18 in. is best. The nongrab-bar side of the toilet must be located at least 15 in. from any obstacle.

Sinks

Vanities and sinks must be located with the centerline of the fixture at least 15 in. horizontally from any adjoining wall or fixture if base cabinets below the sink are removable. If base cabinets are not removable, a parallel (side) approach must be centered on the sink. In this case, the centerline of the fixture must be located at least 24 in. horizontally from any adjoining wall or fixture. If two or more sinks are provided, at least one must be accessible. The top of the sink rim must be no more than 34 in. above the finished floor. If a kneespace is provided below the sink, the bottom of the apron must be at least 27 in. above the floor and the kneespace provided must measure at least 17 in. deep and no more than 19 in. deep.

Bathtubs

Bathtubs and tub/showers in Type B bathrooms must provide a clear access aisle adjacent to them that measures at least 30 by 48 in. This access aisle must be measured from the foot of the tub, or the control wall, and can overlap any clear floor space provided below adjacent fixtures.

Shower Stalls

If a shower stall is the only bathing facility provided in the covered unit, it must be at least 36 by 36 in. and provide reinforcement for a wall-hung bench seat. The seat itself is not required. If the shower stall in the Type B bathroom is not the only bathing facility in the unit, it can be of any size. In addition, if it is provided within a Type B bathroom in addition to a separate bathtub, either the stall or the tub must be accessible. If the tub is accessible—that is, provides the clear access aisle next to adjacent fixtures—then the shower stall is exempt from any clear floor space requirements. If the shower stall is accessible—that is, provides the 30-by-48-in. clear floor space measure from the control wall—then the bathtub is exempt from the clear floor space requirements, meaning there is no access aisle requirement.

Frequently Asked Questions

Q. **The single-story covered units that I am constructing have one bathroom each. The bathroom includes both a bathtub and a separate stall shower. I have chosen the Type A bathroom option. Must the tub and separate shower be accessible?**

A. Yes. The Type A bathroom option requires that clear floor space be provided at all fixtures. The Type B option requires that, "where both tub and shower fixtures are provided in the bathroom, at least one is made accessible," meaning that only the Type B bathroom offers the option of making either the tub or the shower stall accessible when they are both provided in a bathroom.

Q. A covered multistory unit in an elevator building contains two full bathrooms, one on the primary entry level, the other accessed from the master bedroom on the second floor. Since the Type A bathroom option was chosen, must both bathrooms comply with the Type A specifications?

A. No. Only bathrooms located on the primary entry level, which must be the level of the multistory unit served by the elevator, are covered. As a result, the bathroom accessed off the master bedroom is not subject to the design and construction requirements of the FHA

Q. In my bathroom, the toilet is between a bathtub on one side and a wing wall on the other side. The wing wall is 26 in. deep. Is this permitted?

A. No. Wing walls in bathrooms cannot protrude more than 24 in. The 26-in. wing wall in this case must be reduced to 24 in. deep.

PART 2

Compliance Checklist

INTRODUCTION

This checklist is designed to serve as a guide for conformance with the design and construction requirements of the Fair Housing Amendments Act of 1988. The checklist is structured according to the seven requirements of the Fair Housing Amendments Act, and incorporates both scoping and technical criteria.

The checklist is geared toward building-industry professionals, including developers, architects, and builders. It can be used by architects during schematic design, design development, and construction document phases of a project, and by builders in the field as a guide to ensure that housing covered by the FHA is constructed as required. The checklist also serves as a useful learning tool for students, who can apply it to multifamily housing projects that, in the real world, may be required to meet the accessibility guidelines of the FHA.

The checklist includes helpful reminders and references to figures contained in Part 1 of this book, to help clarify the design and construction requirements of the FHA and to help communicate a complete understanding of each requirement. It is helpful to use the Guidelines (Appendix A) and the Supplement to Notice of Fair Housing Accessibility Guidelines: Questions and Answers about the Guidelines (Q&As, Appendix B) as companion documents for reference when completing the checklist.

The technical criteria contained in the checklist comes from the FHA's referenced technical standard—the A117.1 Standard for Accessible and Usable Buildings and Facilities. Although the 1986 edition of the A117.1 standard is specifically referenced by the regulations that implement the FHA, according to the Final Report of HUD's "Review of Model Building Codes," published in the *Federal Register* on March 23, 2000, compliance with the 1992 and 1998 editions of the standard is also a "safe harbor" for compliance with the technical requirements of the FHA.

For example, the 1986 edition of the A117.1 standard requires 108 in. of vertical clearance at passenger loading zones. The 1992 and 1998 editions of the standard require 114 in. of vertical clearance at passenger loading zones. Because the 1992 and 1998 editions require more vertical clearance, the technical criterion for vertical clearance is taken from the 1992 and 1998 editions. Although compliance with the 1986 edition of the A117.1 standard satisfies the technical requirements of the FHA (i.e., 108 in. of vertical clearance will satisfy the requirements of the FHA), the model building codes reference later editions of the A117.1 standard for compliance with building code requirements for accessibility. As a result, compliance with later editions of the A117.1 standard may satisfy both the technical accessibility requirements of the FHA and of the model building codes.

The checklist should be used only as a guide for conformance, not as a "certification" for compliance. It is the responsibility of the building-industry professional to make sure that covered projects are compliant with the accessibility requirements of the FHA by demonstrating that they are met. This checklist is not meant to serve as proof of compliance. It is meant to be used as a tool to identify potential areas of nonconformance, and to help ensure that the basic technical criteria are addressed. It should be used only after reading Part 1 and Appendices A and B. Once the checklist is completed, it should be cross-checked against the Guidelines, the Q&As, and the technical criteria contained in the A117.1 standard. *Remember: developers, architects, builders, and others involved in the design and construction of multifamily housing may veer from incorporating the technical criteria contained in the A117.1 standard and from the Guidelines if it can be demonstrated that the minimum technical requirements of the FHA are satisfied by other means.*

When using the checklist, it is important to survey each building and each covered unit separately. Beginning on page 79, checking "Yes" means that the project conforms with the specific scoping or technical criterion. "No" answers might indicate potential violations of the accessibility requirements of the FHA. Since the Guidelines, the ANSI A117.1 standard, and the *Design Manual* are "safe harbors" for compliance with the design and construction requirements of the FHA, it is important to reference those documents for clarification of the material contained in Part 1: The Act and The Guidelines, and Part 2: The Compliance Checklist. HUD's *Design Manual* may be obtained from HUD USER by calling 800-245-2691 or 800-483-2209 (TDD), or by faxing to 301-251-5767. The 1986, 1992, and 1998 editions of the ANSI A117.1 standard may be obtained from the International Code Council, Inc., by calling 703-931-4533.

CHECKLIST

Is the Project Covered?

1. Is the project newly constructed, containing at least four attached dwelling units, and built for first occupancy after March 13, 1991?

Note: If the project includes more than one building on the site that contains dwelling units, survey each building separately.

❏ Yes   ❏ No

If yes, the project may be covered by the accessibility requirements of the FHA. Proceed with the survey to find out which, if any, dwelling units are covered.

REMINDER:

- Structurally connected buildings are treated as one building for the purposes of determining whether the building contains at least four dwelling units. As a result, three attached units structurally connected by a raised walkway to another building containing two attached units, for example, are considered one building with five units.
- For the purposes of determining whether a building contains at least four attached dwelling units, and thus possibly covered by the FHA, firewalls do not create separate buildings. For example, one structure that contains four units, each separated by firewalls, is considered one building with four units. If this building is built for first occupancy after March 13, 1991, then it is covered by the FHA.
- The addition of at least four attached dwelling units to an existing building is considered new construction and is covered by the FHA.
- If a construction project involves the addition of a new common area to a building containing dwelling units that was built for first occupancy after March 13, 1991, then the new common area is covered by the FHA and must be connected by an accessible route to covered dwelling units.
- If a construction project involves the addition of a new common area to a building built for first occupancy before March 13, 1991, then the new common area is not covered by the FHA because there are no covered dwelling units.
- Review the definitions of the following terms provided in Section 2 of the Guidelines:
  Building
  Covered multifamily dwellings or covered multifamily dwellings subject to
    the Fair Housing Amendments
  Dwelling unit
  First occupancy

Which Units are Covered?

2. Are the units in the building single-story or multistory?

> **Note:** Survey each building separately.

> ❏ All single-story   ❏ All multistory
> ❏ Combination of single-story and multistory

- If the units are all single-story proceed to the next question.
- If the units are all multistory and the answer to the next question is no, the building is not covered.
- If the units are all multistory or a combination of single-story and multistory units, and the answer to the next question is yes, all units are covered and should be surveyed.
- If the units are a combination of single-story and multistory and the answer to the next question is no, only the single-story ground-floor units are covered. Proceed with the checklist and survey only those single-story ground-floor units.

REMINDER:

- Survey each building separately.
- Review the definitions of the following terms provided in Section 2 of the Guidelines:

  Ground floor

  Multistory dwelling unit

  Single-story dwelling unit

3. Is the building an elevator building?

> ❏ Yes   ❏ No

Note: An elevator building must have at least one elevator that provides access to all dwelling units in the building.

Exemptions due to site impracticality cannot be claimed if the following conditions exist:

- The answer to question 3 is yes;
- The answer to question 3 is no, because an elevator is provided only as a means of creating an accessible route to ground-floor dwelling units. If this condition exists, then all single-story ground-floor dwelling units are covered;
- The answer to question 3 is no, but an elevated walkway is planned or located between an entrance and a vehicular or pedestrian arrival point, and the walkway has a slope no more than 10 percent. If this condition exists, all single-story ground-floor dwelling units are covered; and
- The answer to question 3 is no, and an elevator is not provided only as a means of creating an accessible route to ground-floor dwelling units, and an elevated walk-

way is not planned or located between an entrance and a vehicular or pedestrian arrival point. If the building is located on a site without extreme terrain or unusual characteristics, then all single-story ground-floor units are covered.

Exemptions due to site impracticality may be claimed if:

- The answer to question 3 is no; an elevator is not provided only as a means of creating an accessible route to the ground floor containing dwelling units; an elevated walkway is not planned or located between an entrance and a site-arrival point; and the building is located on a site with extreme terrain or unusual characteristics.

REMINDER:

- Multistory units in elevator buildings are covered units. The story served by the elevator must be the primary entry level to the unit and must contain a usable bathroom or powder room that complies with Requirement 7. Only the primary entry level is covered and should be surveyed.

- Buildings with elevators that are provided as a means of creating an accessible route to ground-floor dwelling units only are not elevator buildings. An elevator building must contain at least one elevator that serves floors containing dwelling units in addition to the ground floor.

- A building can have more than one ground floor. If a non-elevator building has more than one ground floor, single-story units on all ground floors are covered. A building is not required to have more than one ground floor.

- Review the definitions of the following terms provided in Section 2 of the Guidelines:

    Ground floor

    Multistory dwelling unit

    Single-story dwelling unit

    Vehicular or pedestrian arrival points

Requirement 1: Accessible Building Entrance on an Accessible Route

Accessible entrances that comply with the following meets the Guidelines:

ANSI A117.1–1986, Section 4.14

ANSI A117.1–1992, Section 4.14

ANSI A117.1–1998, Section 401

Accessible routes that comply with the following meets the Guidelines:

ANSI A117.1–1986, Section 4.3

ANSI A117.1–1992, Section 4.3

ANSI A117.1–1998, Section 401

4. Is there at least one accessible building entrance on an accessible route from vehicular or pedestrian arrival points with a slope no greater than 8.33 percent (1:12)?

 ❏ Yes ❏ No

REMINDER:

- There must be at least one building entrance on an accessible route to buildings containing covered dwelling units from vehicular or pedestrian arrival points with a slope no greater than 8.33 percent (1:12).

- If a building has one common entrance through which all covered dwelling units are accessed, then that building entrance must be accessible and served by an accessible route. An accessible route to the accessible entrances of covered dwelling units is also required.

- If a building contains clusters of dwelling units with a common entrance to each cluster, or dwelling units with separate exterior entrances, the accessible route from vehicular or pedestrian arrival points must serve the accessible entrance to each cluster and each separate exterior entrance to each dwelling unit.

- Review the definitions of the following terms provided in Section 2 of the Guidelines:

  Accessible route

  Building entrance on an accessible route

  Entrance

  Slope

  Vehicular or pedestrian arrival points

  Vehicular route

5. Is there an elevated walkway between a building entrance and a vehicular or pedestrian arrival point with a slope no more than 10 percent?

❏ Yes   ❏ No

- If yes, the slope of the walkway must be reduced to no more than 8.33 percent (1:12), and all single-story ground-floor units are covered.

REMINDER:

- If the building is a nonelevator building, site impracticality cannot be claimed if the answer to question 5 is yes.

- Site impracticality can never be claimed if the building is served by an elevator that provides access to all floors, if a raised walkway with a slope no more than 10 percent connects the building entrance to any vehicular or pedestrian arrival point, or if an elevator is provided to create an accessible route to dwelling units on the ground floor only.

- Review the definitions of the following terms provided in Section 2 of the Guidelines:

  Building entrance on an accessible route

  Entrance

  Slope

  Vehicular or pedestrian arrival points

6. Is the slope of the finished grade between covered multifamily dwellings and a public or common-use facility 8.33 percent (1:12) or less?

❏ Yes ❏ No

REMINDER:

- Buildings containing only covered dwelling units do not have to be connected by an accessible route to other buildings containing only covered units. However, the route between buildings must be accessible if that route serves as a route to a common-use facility.
- Review the definitions of the following terms provided in Section 2 of the Guidelines:

  Common-use areas

  Covered multifamily dwellings or covered multifamily dwellings subject to the Fair Housing Amendments

  Public use areas

  Slope

Requirement 2: Accessible and Usable Public and Common-Use Areas

Accessible route(s): The requirements for accessible routes apply to accessible routes located within the boundary of the site.

Exterior accessible routes: At least one accessible route must be provided from public transportation stops, accessible parking spaces, accessible passenger loading zones, and public streets or sidewalks to accessible building entrances.

Interior accessible routes: At least one accessible route must be provided that connects accessible building or facility entrances with accessible spaces and elements/spaces within the building or facility.

Compliance with the following ANSI criteria meets the Guidelines:

ANSI A117.1–1986, Section 4.3

ANSI A117.1–1992, Section 4.3

ANSI A117.1–1998, Section 401

REMINDER:

- Review the definitions of the following terms provided in Section 2 of the Guidelines:

  Accessible route

  Building entrance on an accessible route

  Common-use areas

  Entrance

  Public use areas

  Vehicular and pedestrian arrival points

Use the following questions to survey both the exterior and interior accessible route(s).

7. Is the clear width of the accessible route 36 in. minimum, except at doors?

On the exterior: ❏ Yes ❏ No
On the interior: ❏ Yes ❏ No

8. Do accessible routes with turns around obstructions that are less than 48 in. wide have a clear space of 42 in. by 48 in. minimum (see the illustration on page 37)?

On the exterior: ❏ Yes ❏ No
On the interior: ❏ Yes ❏ No

9. Do accessible routes with a clear width less than 60 in. provide either a 60-in.- by- 60-in. passing space at intervals of not more than 200 ft. or a T-shaped turning space created by the intersection of two halls, walks, or corridors (see the illustrations on page 38)?

On the exterior: ❏ Yes ❏ No
On the interior: ❏ Yes ❏ No

10. Is the carpet or carpet tile used on a ground or floor surface securely attached with either a firm cushion, pad, or backing, or no cushion or pad?

On the exterior: ❏ Yes ❏ No
On the interior: ❏ Yes ❏ No

11. Does the carpet or carpet tile have a pile height of no more than $\frac{1}{2}$ in.?

On the exterior: ❏ Yes ❏ No
On the interior: ❏ Yes ❏ No

12. Are exposed edges of carpets fastened to floor surfaces with trim along the entire length of the exposed edge?

On the exterior: ❏ Yes ❏ No
On the interior: ❏ Yes ❏ No

13. Are any changes in floor level between $\frac{1}{4}$ in. and $\frac{1}{2}$ in. high beveled with the slope of the bevel not steeper than 1:2 (see the illustration on page 56)?

Note: Level changes no greater than $\frac{1}{4}$ in. are permitted to be vertical and without edge treatment.

On the exterior: ❏ Yes ❏ No
On the interior: ❏ Yes ❏ No

14. Are changes in level greater than $\frac{1}{2}$ in. negotiated by a curb ramp, ramp, or elevator?

On the exterior: ❏ Yes ❏ No
On the interior: ❏ Yes ❏ No

15. Do gratings on accessible routes and in accessible spaces have openings no greater than $\frac{1}{2}$ in. wide in one direction; and are gratings with elongated openings placed so that the long dimension is perpendicular to the dominant direction of travel?

> On the exterior: ❑ Yes ❑ No
> On the interior: ❑ Yes ❑ No

Protruding Objects: The requirements for protruding objects apply to objects located on or along accessible routes, including, but not limited to, halls, corridors, passageways, and aisles.

Compliance with the following ANSI criteria meets the Guidelines:

> ANSI A117.1–1986, Section 4.4
> ANSI A117.1–1992, Section 4.4
> ANSI A117.1–1998, Section 307

16. Do objects with leading edges located more than 27 in. and no more than 80 in. above the floor protrude from the wall no more than 4 in. (see the illustration on page 39)?

Note: Objects mounted at or below 27 in. above the floor may protrude any amount (see the illustration on page 39).

> On the exterior: ❑ Yes ❑ No
> On the interior: ❑ Yes ❑ No

17. Is the clear width of an accessible route (at least 36 in.) maintained throughout that route with no interference from protruding objects?

> On the exterior: ❑ Yes ❑ No
> On the interior: ❑ Yes ❑ No

Note: When objects are mounted more than 27 in. and no more than 80 in. above the floor, they may protrude from walls no more than 4 in. When objects are mounted at or below 27 in. above the floor, they may protrude any amount. However, they are permitted to reduce the accessible route to a minimum width of 32 in. for a length of no more than 24 in. (see the illustration on page 39).

18. Do free-standing objects mounted on posts or pylons overhang no more than 12 in. when located more than 27 in. and no more than 80 in. above the ground or floor?

> On the exterior: ❑ Yes ❑ No
> On the interior: ❑ Yes ❑ No

19. Where a sign or other obstruction is mounted between posts or pylons more than 12 in. apart, is the lowest edge of such sign or obstruction 27 in. maximum or 80 in. minimum above the adjacent ground or floor surface?

> On the exterior: ❑ Yes ❑ No
> On the interior: ❑ Yes ❑ No

20. Is there at least 80 in. minimum headroom clearance on accessible routes?

On the exterior: ❑ Yes ❑ No

On the interior: ❑ Yes ❑ No

21. Are guardrails or other barriers provided where vertical clearance of the area adjoining an accessible route is less than 80 in. high?

On the exterior: ❑ Yes ❑ No

On the interior: ❑ Yes ❑ No

Note: The leading edge of the guardrail or barrier must be located no more than 27 in. above the floor.

Ground and Floor Surface Treatments: The requirements for ground and floor surface treatments apply to accessible routes, rooms, and spaces, including floors, walks, ramps, stairs, and curb ramps.

Compliance with the following ANSI criteria meets the Guidelines:

ANSI A117.1–1986, Section 4.5

ANSI A117.1–1992, Section 4.5

ANSI A117.1–1998, Section 302

22. Are ground and floor surfaces of accessible routes and in accessible rooms and spaces stable, firm, and slip resistant?

On the exterior: ❑ Yes ❑ No

On the interior: ❑ Yes ❑ No

Parking and Passenger Loading Zones

Compliance with the following ANSI criteria meets the Guidelines:

ANSI A117.1–1986, Section 4.6

ANSI A117.1–1992, Section 4.6

ANSI A117.1–1998, Section 502, 503

23. Are accessible parking spaces located on accessible routes, and provided for at least 2 percent of covered dwelling units?

❑ Yes ❑ No

24. Is designated visitor parking provided?

❑ Yes ❑ No

•   If yes, is there a "sufficient" number (at least one) of accessible visitor parking spaces?

❑ Yes ❑ No

25. Is there a variety of resident parking available such as outdoor, garage, carport, or other?

❏ Yes   ❏ No

If yes, are there accessible parking spaces with the full range of choices afforded to others without disabilities provided, even if the total number of accessible parking on the site exceeds 2 percent of the covered dwelling units?

❏ Yes   ❏ No

> **Note:** Suppose the number of accessible parking spaces provided in an outdoor parking lot directly in front of a building equals 2 percent of covered units. Those accessible spaces are required to be provided on the shortest route to the building entrance. Several hundred feet away from the outdoor parking lot are carport and garage spaces that are available to the residents. Because outdoor, carport, and garage parking are different parking options available to the residents, at least one accessible carport and one garage space must be provided in addition to the accessible spaces already provided in the outdoor lot, even if that number exceeds 2 percent.

26. Is separate parking provided at any public and common-use facility on the site?

❏ Yes   ❏ No

If yes, is there a "sufficient" number (at least one) of accessible parking spaces available at the public and common-use facility, with necessary site provisions such as curb cuts and access aisles that are a part of the accessible route through the facility's accessible entrance?

❏ Yes   ❏ No

27. Are accessible parking spaces at least 96 in. wide (see the illustration on page 43)?

❏ Yes   ❏ No

28. Do accessible parking spaces have an adjacent access aisle at least 60 in. wide (see the illustration on page 43)?

> **Note:** Two spaces may share one access aisle. An access aisle is a part of the accessible route.

❏ Yes   ❏ No

29. Is an accessible circulation route maintained (at least 36 in. wide) without interference by vehicle overhangs? For example, the width of an accessible route that runs along the perimeter of a parking lot cannot be reduced by overhanging parked vehicles (see the illustration on page 43.

❏ Yes   ❏ No

30. Are accessible parking spaces identified by a sign that shows the international symbol of accessibility and that is not obscured by a vehicle parked in the space?

Note: Signs painted on the ground surface of accessible parking spaces are not permitted, because they will be hidden by parked vehicles. Signs mounted high enough on posts will not be obstructed by parked vehicles and can be clearly seen.

❏ Yes   ❏ No

31. Do passenger loading zones provide an access aisle at least 60 in. wide and at least 20 ft. long, adjacent and parallel to the vehicle pull-up space, and at the same level as the roadway (see the illustration on page 43)?

Note: An access aisle is a part of the accessible route.

❏ Yes   ❏ No

32. Is a vertical clearance of at least 114 in. provided at accessible passenger loading zones and along vehicle access routes to such areas from site entrances?

❏ Yes   ❏ No

Note: 114 in. satisfies ANSI 1992 and 1998. ANSI 1986 is satisfied with 108 in.

Curb Ramps: Curb ramps must be provided on accessible routes that cross curbs.

Compliance with the following ANSI criteria meets the Guidelines:

ANSI A117.1–1986, Section 4.7

ANSI A117.1–1992, Section 4.7

ANSI A117.1–1998, Section 406

33. Are curb ramps provided where accessible routes cross curbs?

❏ Yes   ❏ No

34. Are the slopes of curb ramps no steeper than 8.33 percent (1:12)?

❏ Yes   ❏ No

35. Are curb ramps located or protected to prevent their obstruction by parked vehicles?

❏ Yes   ❏ No

36. Are transitions from curb ramps to walks, gutters, or streets flush?

❏ Yes   ❏ No

37. Are curb ramps 36 in. wide, not including the flared sides?

❏ Yes   ❏ No

38. Do curb ramps that are located where pedestrians must walk across the ramp have flared sides with slopes no more than 1:10?

❏ Yes   ❏ No

39. Where the width of the walking surface at the top of the curb ramp and parallel to the run of the ramp is less than 48 in. wide, do the flared sides of curb ramps have slopes no steeper than 8.33 percent (1:12)?

❏ Yes   ❏ No

40. Are curb ramps with returned curbs located where pedestrians cannot walk across the ramps?

❏ Yes   ❏ No

41. Are built-up curb ramps located so that they do not protrude into vehicular traffic lanes or into parking space access aisles?

Note: The slopes of the flared sides of built-up curb ramps may be no steeper than 1:10. ANSI A117.1 1998 does not provide technical criteria for built-up curb ramps.

❏ Yes   ❏ No

42. Excluding any flared sides, are curb ramps at marked crossings wholly contained within the markings?

❏ Yes   ❏ No

43. Do diagonal or corner-type curb ramps with returned curbs or other well-defined edges have the edges parallel to the direction of pedestrian flow?

❏ Yes   ❏ No

44. Do bottoms of diagonal curb ramps (the part of curb ramps that meets the street) have 48 in.-wide minimum clear space?

❏ Yes   ❏ No

45. Is the 48 in.-wide minimum clear space provided within the markings at marked crossings?

❏ Yes   ❏ No

46. At marked crossings, do diagonal curb ramps with flared sides have a segment of straight curb at least 24 in. long located on each side of the curb ramp and within the marked crossing?

❏ Yes   ❏ No

47. Do raised islands in crossings have a cut-through level with the street or curb ramps at both sides, and a level area at least 48 in. long by at least 36 in. wide, in the part of the island intersected by the crossing?

❏ Yes   ❏ No

Ramps: Accessible routes with slopes greater than 1:20 must comply with the ramp requirements of the Guidelines.

Compliance with the following ANSI criteria meets the Guidelines:

ANSI A117.1–1986, Section 4.8

ANSI A117.1–1992, Section 4.8

ANSI A117.1–1998, Section 405

48. Do all ramp runs rise 30 in. or less, with a slope not greater than 8.33 percent (1:12)?

On the exterior: ❏ Yes ❏ No

On the interior: ❏ Yes ❏ No

49. Is the clear width of ramps at least 36 in. (see the illustration on page 40)?

On the exterior: ❏ Yes ❏ No

On the interior: ❏ Yes ❏ No

50. Do ramps have level landings at the bottom and top of each run?

On the exterior: ❏ Yes ❏ No

On the interior: ❏ Yes ❏ No

51. Is the landing width at least as wide as the widest ramp run leading to it?

Note: The clear width at ramps must be at least 36 in.

On the exterior: ❏ Yes ❏ No

On the interior: ❏ Yes ❏ No

52. Is the landing length 60 in. minimum clear? (Ramp width must be at least 36 in.)

On the exterior: ❏ Yes ❏ No

On the interior: ❏ Yes ❏ No

53. For ramps that change direction at landings, is the landing at least 60 in. by 60 in. wide?

On the exterior: ❏ Yes ❏ No

On the interior: ❏ Yes ❏ No

54. Do ramps with a rise greater than 6 in. or a run longer than 72 in. have handrails (see the illustration on page 40)?

Note: Handrails are not required on ramps that rise less than 6 in.

On the exterior: ❏ Yes ❏ No

On the interior: ❏ Yes ❏ No

55. Are handrails provided on both sides of ramps on accessible routes with a rise greater than 6 in. or a run longer than 72 in. (see the illustration on page 40)?

On the exterior: ❏ Yes ❏ No

On the interior: ❏ Yes ❏ No

56. Are handrails continuous within the full length of each ramp run?

On the exterior: ❑ Yes ❑ No
On the interior: ❑ Yes ❑ No

57. Are inside handrails on switchback or dogleg ramps continuous between runs?

On the exterior: ❑ Yes ❑ No
On the interior: ❑ Yes ❑ No

58. Are the top of gripping surfaces of handrails mounted between 34 in. and 38 in. maximum, vertically above ramp surfaces, and at a consistent height above ramp surfaces?

On the exterior: ❑ Yes ❑ No
On the interior: ❑ Yes ❑ No

59. Is the clear space between handrail and wall at least 1$\frac{1}{2}$ in.?

On the exterior: ❑ Yes ❑ No
On the interior: ❑ Yes ❑ No

60. Are gripping surfaces of handrails continuous, without interruption by newel posts, other construction elements, or obstructions?

On the exterior: ❑ Yes ❑ No
On the interior: ❑ Yes ❑ No

61. Do handrails have a circular cross-section with an outside diameter of between 1$\frac{1}{4}$ in. and 2 in. or are they of a shape that provides an equivalent gripping surface?

On the exterior: ❑ Yes ❑ No
On the interior: ❑ Yes ❑ No

62. Are handrails and any wall or other surfaces adjacent to them free of any sharp or abrasive elements?

On the exterior: ❑ Yes ❑ No
On the interior: ❑ Yes ❑ No

63. Are handrails securely fastened to their fittings?

On the exterior: ❑ Yes ❑ No
On the interior: ❑ Yes ❑ No

64. At ramps (except for continuous handrails at the inside turn of ramps), do handrails extend horizontally 12 in. minimum beyond the top and bottom of ramp runs (see the illustration on page 40)?

On the exterior: ❑ Yes ❑ No
On the interior: ❑ Yes ❑ No

65. Do such extensions return to a wall, guard or the walking surface, or are they continuous to the handrail of an adjacent ramp run?

On the exterior: ❏ Yes   ❏ No
On the interior: ❏ Yes   ❏ No

66. Are the cross-slopes of ramp surfaces level?

On the exterior: ❏ Yes   ❏ No
On the interior: ❏ Yes   ❏ No

67. Do ramps and landings have curbs, walls, or railings that prevent people from traveling off the ramp or landing (see the illustration on page 40)?

On the exterior: ❏ Yes   ❏ No
On the interior: ❏ Yes   ❏ No

68. If curbs or barriers are provided, are they at least 4 in. high (see the illustration on page 40)?

On the exterior: ❏ Yes   ❏ No
On the interior: ❏ Yes   ❏ No

69. If curbs or barriers are not provided, do the ramps or landings protrude at least 12 in. beyond the inside surface of railings?

On the exterior: ❏ Yes   ❏ No
On the interior: ❏ Yes   ❏ No

70. Do outdoor ramps and approaches to them appear to be designed so that water will not accumulate on walking surfaces?

❏ Yes   ❏ No

Stairs: This section applies to stairs along accessible routes connecting levels not connected by an elevator.

Compliance with the following ANSI criteria meets the Guidelines:

ANSI A117.1–1986, Section 4.9
ANSI A117.1–1992, Section 4.9
ANSI A117.1–1998, Section 504

71. Is there a ramp or other means of access located within sight from stairs that connect levels not connected by an elevator?

On the exterior: ❏ Yes   ❏ No
On the interior: ❏ Yes   ❏ No

72. If a ramp or other means of access is not located within sight from stairs that connect levels not connected by an elevator, is there directional signage to a ramp or other means of access?

On the exterior: ❑ Yes ❑ No
On the interior: ❑ Yes ❑ No

73. Are all stair risers between 4 in. and 7 in. high?

On the exterior: ❑ Yes ❑ No
On the interior: ❑ Yes ❑ No

74. Are all stair treads at least 11 in. deep, measured from riser to riser?

On the exterior: ❑ Yes ❑ No
On the interior: ❑ Yes ❑ No

75. Do all stairs have closed risers?

On the exterior: ❑ Yes ❑ No
On the interior: ❑ Yes ❑ No

76. Do all nosings protrude no more than $1\frac{1}{2}$ in.?

On the exterior: ❑ Yes ❑ No
On the interior: ❑ Yes ❑ No

77. Do outdoor stairs and approaches to them appear to be designed so that water will not accumulate on walking surfaces?

❑ Yes ❑ No

78. Are handrails provided on both sides of stairs that are required to be accessible?

On the exterior: ❑ Yes ❑ No
On the interior: ❑ Yes ❑ No

Note: See the section about stairs on page 45.

79. Are handrails continuous within the full length of each stair flight?

On the exterior: ❑ Yes ❑ No
On the interior: ❑ Yes ❑ No

80. Are inside handrails on switchback or dogleg stairs continuous between flights?

On the exterior: ❑ Yes ❑ No
On the interior: ❑ Yes ❑ No

81. Are the tops of gripping surfaces of handrails mounted between 34 in. and 38 in. maximum, vertically above stair nosings, and at a consistent height above stair nosings?

On the exterior: ❑ Yes ❑ No
On the interior: ❑ Yes ❑ No

82. Is the clear space between handrail and wall at least $1\frac{1}{2}$ in.?

On the exterior: ❏ Yes   ❏ No
On the interior: ❏ Yes   ❏ No

83. Are gripping surfaces of handrails continuous, without interruption by newel posts, other construction elements, or obstructions?

On the exterior: ❏ Yes   ❏ No
On the interior: ❏ Yes   ❏ No

84. Do handrails have a circular cross section with an outside diameter of between $1\frac{1}{4}$ in. and 2 in., or a shape that provides an equivalent gripping surface?

On the exterior: ❏ Yes   ❏ No
On the interior: ❏ Yes   ❏ No

85. Are handrails and any wall or other surfaces adjacent to them free of any sharp or abrasive elements?

On the exterior: ❏ Yes   ❏ No
On the interior: ❏ Yes   ❏ No

86. Are handrails securely fastened to their fittings?

On the exterior: ❏ Yes   ❏ No
On the interior: ❏ Yes   ❏ No

87. At the top of stair flights, except for continuous handrails at the inside turn of stairs, do at least one of the following conditions apply: Handrails extend horizontally above the landing for 12 in. minimum, beginning directly above the first riser nosing, and return to a wall or guard; or handrails are continuous to the handrail of an adjacent stair flight?

On the exterior: ❏ Yes   ❏ No
On the interior: ❏ Yes   ❏ No

88. At the bottom of stair flights, except for continuous handrails at the inside turn of stairs, do at least one of the following conditions apply: Handrails extend 12 in. minimum horizontally, beginning directly above the last riser nosing, and return to a wall, guard, or the walking surface; or handrails are continuous to the handrail of an adjacent stair flight?

On the exterior: ❏ Yes   ❏ No
On the interior: ❏ Yes   ❏ No

Elevators and Lifts: At least one elevator must be accessible.

Compliance with the following ANSI criteria meets the Guidelines:

ANSI A117.1–1986, Section 4.10
ANSI A117.1–1992, Section 4.10
ANSI A117.1–1998, Section 407

Note: Although exterior elevators are rare, some sites include exterior free-standing elevators that provide exterior access to different site levels. For example, an exterior free-standing elevator may provide access from a lower parking level to an upper level that provides access to dwelling unit entrances; or an exterior elevator may be connected to a building by open elevated walkways. At least one of these types of elevators must be accessible if they are a part of the accessible route. If there are no exterior elevators, do not check the "On the exterior" selection in the following questions.

89. Does at least one accessible elevator provide access to all floors of the building?

On the exterior: ❏ Yes ❏ No

On the interior: ❏ Yes ❏ No

90. If not all elevators are accessible, are those that are clearly identified with the international symbol of accessibility?

On the exterior: ❏ Yes ❏ No

On the interior: ❏ Yes ❏ No

91. Are elevator cars automatically brought to floor landings within a tolerance of $1/2$ in.?

On the exterior: ❏ Yes ❏ No

On the interior: ❏ Yes ❏ No

92. Are raised-character and Braille floor designations provided on both jambs of elevator entrances, and centered at 60 in. above the floor?

On the exterior: ❏ Yes ❏ No

On the interior: ❏ Yes ❏ No

93. Are the raised-characters on the elevator jambs at least $5/8$ in. high and no more than 2 in. high, and in uppercase?

On the exterior: ❏ Yes ❏ No

On the interior: ❏ Yes ❏ No

94. Are the raised characters on the elevator jambs accompanied by Braille?

On the exterior: ❏ Yes ❏ No

On the interior: ❏ Yes ❏ No

95. Do elevator doors remain fully open in response to a car call for three seconds minimum?

On the exterior: ❏ Yes ❏ No

On the interior: ❏ Yes ❏ No

96. Do the inside dimensions of elevator cars provide space for people who use wheelchairs to enter the car, maneuver within reach of controls, and exit the car?

Note: Compliance with the ANSI guidance for the inside dimensions of elevator cars meets the Guidelines.)

On the exterior:	❑ Yes	❑ No
On the interior:	❑ Yes	❑ No

97. Is the clearance between the car platform sill and the edge of any hoistway landing no more than $1\frac{1}{4}$ in.?

On the exterior:	❑ Yes	❑ No
On the interior:	❑ Yes	❑ No

98. Are floor surfaces in elevator cars stable, firm, and slip-resistant?

On the exterior:	❑ Yes	❑ No
On the interior:	❑ Yes	❑ No

99. Are carpets or carpet tiles used on elevator floors securely attached with either a firm cushion, pad, or backing, or no cushion or pad?

On the exterior:	❑ Yes	❑ No
On the interior:	❑ Yes	❑ No

100. Is the pile height on carpet or carpet tiles laid in elevators no more than $\frac{1}{2}$-in.?

On the exterior:	❑ Yes	❑ No
On the interior:	❑ Yes	❑ No

101. Are the exposed edges of carpets used on elevator floors trimmed along the entire length of the exposed edges and fastened to floor surfaces?

On the exterior:	❑ Yes	❑ No
On the interior:	❑ Yes	❑ No

102. Is the highest operable part of a two-way emergency communication device in the elevator located no more than 54 in. above the floor for a parallel approach or no more than 48 in. above the floor for a front approach?

On the exterior:	❑ Yes	❑ No
On the interior:	❑ Yes	❑ No

103. Is the two-way emergency communication device, identified by raised symbols and lettering, located adjacent to the device?

On the exterior:	❑ Yes	❑ No
On the interior:	❑ Yes	❑ No

104. If instructions for the car emergency-signaling device are provided, are they presented in both tactile and visual form?

On the exterior: ❏ Yes ❏ No
On the interior: ❏ Yes ❏ No

105. Are the tops of the elevator hall call buttons located vertically between 35 in. and 54 in. above the floor?

On the exterior: ❏ Yes ❏ No
On the interior: ❏ Yes ❏ No

106. Is the button that designates the up direction located above the button that designates the down direction?

On the exterior: ❏ Yes ❏ No
On the interior: ❏ Yes ❏ No

107. Are both visible and audible signals provided at each elevator entrance, to indicate which car is answering a call?

On the exterior: ❏ Yes ❏ No
On the interior: ❏ Yes ❏ No

If yes, are the signals either in-car signals visible from the floor area adjacent to the hall call buttons or signals located outside the car, such as on a wall located adjacent to the elevator car?

On the exterior: ❏ Yes ❏ No
On the interior: ❏ Yes ❏ No

108. Are the hall signal fixtures centered at least 72. in. above the floor?

Note: These are the signals that light up and indicate which direction the elevator is traveling.

On the exterior: ❏ Yes ❏ No
On the interior: ❏ Yes ❏ No

109. Does the audible signal sound once for up and twice for down, or do verbal annunciators state either "up" or "down"?

On the exterior: ❏ Yes ❏ No
On the interior: ❏ Yes ❏ No

110. Do elevator doors have a reopening device that stops and reopens a car door and hoistway door if the door becomes obstructed?

On the exterior: ❏ Yes ❏ No
On the interior: ❏ Yes ❏ No

111. Are the buttons located on the elevator control panel at least $3/4$ in. in their smallest dimension?

On the exterior: ❏ Yes   ❏ No
On the interior: ❏ Yes   ❏ No

112. Is there contrast between characters/symbols and the background of the control panel?

On the exterior: ❏ Yes   ❏ No
On the interior: ❏ Yes   ❏ No

113. Are characters and symbols on the control panel raised and in uppercase, at least $5/8$ in. high and no more than 2 in. high?

On the exterior: ❏ Yes   ❏ No
On the interior: ❏ Yes   ❏ No

114. Are the raised characters and symbols on the control panel accompanied by Braille?

On the exterior: ❏ Yes   ❏ No
On the interior: ❏ Yes   ❏ No

115. Are raised characters or symbols with Braille designations located to the left of their respective control buttons?

On the exterior: ❏ Yes   ❏ No
On the interior: ❏ Yes   ❏ No

116. Is the in-car call button for the main entry floor designated by a star?

On the exterior: ❏ Yes   ❏ No
On the interior: ❏ Yes   ❏ No

117. Do the floor buttons in the elevators have visible indicators to show that a call has been registered?

On the exterior: ❏ Yes   ❏ No
On the interior: ❏ Yes   ❏ No

118. Do the visible indicators in the elevator cease when the call is answered?

On the exterior: ❏ Yes   ❏ No
On the interior: ❏ Yes   ❏ No

119. Are the controls inside the elevator located on a front wall if cars have center opening doors, and at the side wall or at the front wall next to the door if cars have side opening doors?

On the exterior: ❏ Yes   ❏ No
On the interior: ❏ Yes   ❏ No

120. If the building has a platform lift, does it comply with the relevant requirements listed previously, and provide the minimum 30 in. by 48 in. clear floor space?

On the exterior: ❏ Yes ❏ No

On the interior: ❏ Yes ❏ No

Drinking Fountains and Water Coolers: If provided in the building or at the site, at least one accessible drinking fountain (per floor) must be provided.

Compliance with the following ANSI criteria meets the Guidelines:

ANSI A117.1–1986, Section 4.15

ANSI A117.1–1992, Section 4.15

ANSI A117.1–1998, Section 602

121. Is the lowest leading edge of a water cooler or drinking fountain mounted no more than 27 in. above the floor (see the illustration on page 39)?

❏ Yes ❏ No

If no, and the water cooler or drinking fountain is mounted at or higher than 27 in. above the floor, it cannot protrude more than 4 in.

122. Is the 36-in. minimum width of the accessible route maintained without interference by the fountain, or is the 36-in. minimum width reduced by the fountain or cooler by no more than 4 in. for a maximum distance of 24 in.?

❏ Yes ❏ No

If no, the drinking fountain is not compliant with the Guidelines.

123. Does the fountain or water cooler protrude from the wall no more than 4 in.?

❏ Yes ❏ No

124. Is the water cooler or fountain spout outlet located at least 36 in. above the floor?

❏ Yes ❏ No

125. Are the spouts of drinking fountains and water coolers located at the front of the unit directing the water flow parallel or nearly parallel to the front of the unit?

❏ Yes ❏ No

126. Do wall-mounted and post-mounted cantilevered drinking fountains and water coolers have a clear knee space between the bottom of the apron and the floor or ground at least 27 in. high, 30 in. wide, and 17 in. to 19 in. deep?

❏ Yes ❏ No

127. Do wall-mounted and post-mounted cantilevered drinking fountains and water coolers have a clear floor space centered on the fixture that measures at least 30 in. by 48 in. to allow for a forward approach?

❏ Yes ❏ No

128. Do free-standing or built-in drinking fountains and water coolers have a clear floor space centered on the fixture, and that measures at least 30 in. by 48 in. to allow for a parallel approach?

❏ Yes   ❏ No

129. Can the operable parts located at or near the front edge of the fountain or water cooler be operated with one hand, without the need to grasp tightly, pinch, or twist the wrist?

❏ Yes   ❏ No

Toilet Rooms and Bathing Facilities

Where provided in public and common-use areas, at least one of each fixture must be accessible, including water closets, toilet rooms and stalls, urinals, lavatories, mirrors, bathtubs, shower stalls, and sinks.

Compliance with the following ANSI criteria meets the Guidelines:

ANSI A117.1–1986, Section 4.22

ANSI A117.1–1992, Section 4.16

ANSI A117.1–1998, Section 603 through 608

130. Is an unobstructed 60-in. diameter turning space provided in toilet rooms and bathing facilities?

❏ Yes   ❏ No

131. Is maneuvering space provided on both sides of the doors to toilet rooms and bathing facilities?

Note: See questions 180 through 188 for proper maneuvering clearances required at doors depending on the approach to them.

❏ Yes   ❏ No

If controls, dispensers, receptacles, or other equipment are provided, at least one of each must be on an accessible route, and the answers to questions 132 though 134 must be yes.

132. Is a clear floor that measures at least 30 in. by 48 in. provided to allow a forward or a parallel approach to controls, dispensers, receptacles, or other equipment by a person using a wheelchair?

❏ Yes   ❏ No

133. Is the highest operable part of all controls, dispensers, receptacles, and other operable equipment placed between 15 in. and 48 in. above the floor?

❏ Yes   ❏ No

134. Are controls operable with one hand, precluding the need to grasp tightly, pinch, or twist the wrist?

❏ Yes   ❏ No

135. Are medicine cabinets located with a usable shelf no higher than 44 in. above the floor?

❏ Yes   ❏ No

Water Closets Not in Stalls

136. Does the clear floor space provided at water closets comply with one of the following diagrams?

❏ Yes   ❏ No

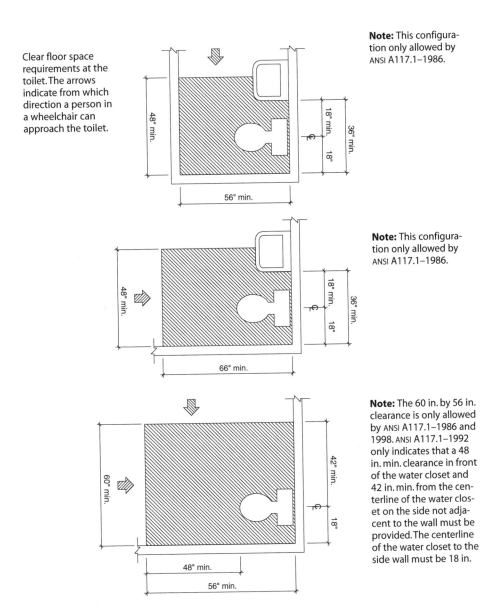

Clear floor space requirements at the toilet. The arrows indicate from which direction a person in a wheelchair can approach the toilet.

Note: This configuration only allowed by ANSI A117.1–1986.

Note: This configuration only allowed by ANSI A117.1–1986.

Note: The 60 in. by 56 in. clearance is only allowed by ANSI A117.1–1986 and 1998. ANSI A117.1–1992 only indicates that a 48 in. min. clearance in front of the water closet and 42 in. min. from the centerline of the water closet on the side not adjacent to the wall must be provided. The centerline of the water closet to the side wall must be 18 in.

137. Is the height of water closets between 17 in. to 19 in. above the floor?

Note: heights are measured to the top of the seat.

❏ Yes ❏ No

138. Do grab bars at water closets comply with the locations in the following diagrams and is their centerline located between 33 in. and 36 in. above the floor?

❏ Yes ❏ No

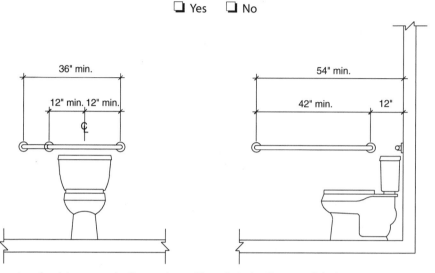

Location of grab bars around toilets not located in stalls. In the diagram at left, the 36-in. measure is required when wall space permits. In the diagram at right, the 12-in. measure is required to be an exact measure by ANSI A117.1–1986, and a maximum measure by ANSI A117.1–1992 and 1998.

139. Are controls for flush valves hand-operated or automatic, and located no more than 44 in. above the floor?

❏ Yes ❏ No

140. Are toilet paper dispensers installed within reach, with the centerline of the dispenser at least 19 in. above the floor?

Note: ANSI A117.1–1992 and 1998 requires that the dispenser be located 15 in. min. to 48 in. max. above the floor.

❏ Yes ❏ No

Toilet Stalls

141. For water closets located in stalls, is the answer to questions 136 and 137 yes?

❏ Yes ❏ No

142. Does the size and arrangement of toilet stalls comply with either of the diagrams in the following figure?

❏ Yes ❏ No

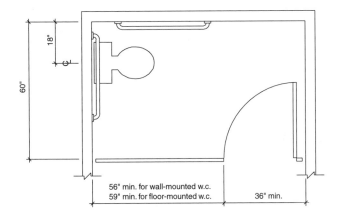

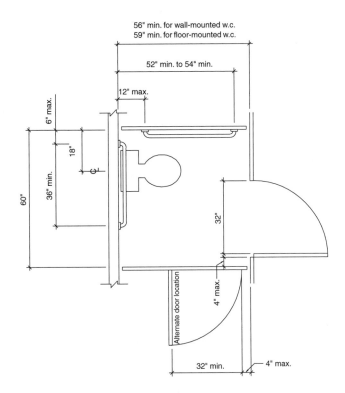

Accessible toilet stalls and grab bar locations for stall toilets. The 1992 and 1998 editions of ANSI A117.1 allow the leading edge of the side grab bar to be 54 in. away from the back wall. The 1986 edition of the A117.1 standard allows the leading edge to be 52 in. min. away from the back wall.

143. Do toilet stalls with a minimum depth of 56 in. or 66 in. have a wall-mounted water closet?

Note: If the depth of the 56 in.-deep and the 66 in.-deep stalls is increased 3 in., then a floor-mounted water closet may be used.

❏ Yes   ❏ No

144. For stalls less than 60 in. deep, does the front partition and at least one side partition have a toe clearance of at least 9 in. above the floor?

Note: Toe clearance is not required for stalls 60 in. or greater in depth.

❏ Yes   ❏ No

145. Is maneuvering space provided at stall doors?

Note: See questions 180 through 188 for proper maneuvering clearances required at doors, depending on the approach to them. If the only approach to the stall door is to the latch side of the door, the clearance between the exterior door surface and any obstruction may be reduced to a minimum of 42 in. (i.e., 42 in. minimum clearance required perpendicular to the door).

❏ Yes   ❏ No

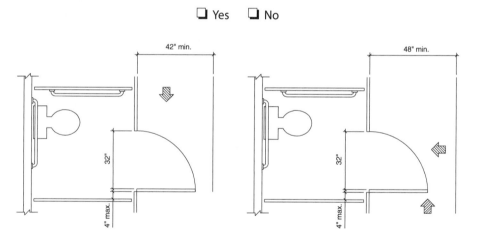

Maneuvering clearance requirements at stall doors.

146. Are grab bars that comply with the locations in the diagrams shown in the figures on page 101 provided in stalls?

Note: Grab bars must not interrupt the required clear floor space.

❏ Yes   ❏ No

Urinals

147. Are urinals stall-type or wall hung, with an elongated rim at a maximum of 17 in. above the floor?

❏ Yes   ❏ No

148. Is a clear floor space measuring at least 30 in. by 48 in. provided in front of urinals to allow a forward approach?

Note: Privacy shields allowing less than 30 in. clear width may not extend beyond the front edge of the urinal rim.

❏ Yes ❏ No

149. Are flush controls hand-operated or automatic, and mounted no more than 44 in. above the floor?

❏ Yes ❏ No

Lavatories and Mirrors

150. Are lavatories mounted with a clearance of at least 29 in. from the floor to the bottom of the apron?

❏ Yes ❏ No

151. Are lavatories mounted with their rims no more than 34 in. above the floor?

❏ Yes ❏ No

152. Is a clear floor space measuring at least 30 in. by 48 in. provided in front of a lavatory to allow a forward approach?

Note: The clear floor space must extend a maximum of 19 in. underneath the lavatory.

❏ Yes ❏ No

153. Are pipes under lavatories insulated or protected?

❏ Yes ❏ No

154. Are lavatory controls operable with one hand, precluding the need to grasp tightly, pinch, or twist the wrist?

❏ Yes ❏ No

155. Are mirrors mounted with the bottom edge of the reflecting surface no higher than 38 in. from the floor?

Note: ANSI A117.1–1986 requires that the bottom edge of the reflecting surface be mounted no higher than 40 in. above the floor.

❏ Yes ❏ No

Bathtubs

156. Is the clear floor space provided at bathtubs compliant with the following diagrams?

❏ Yes ❏ No

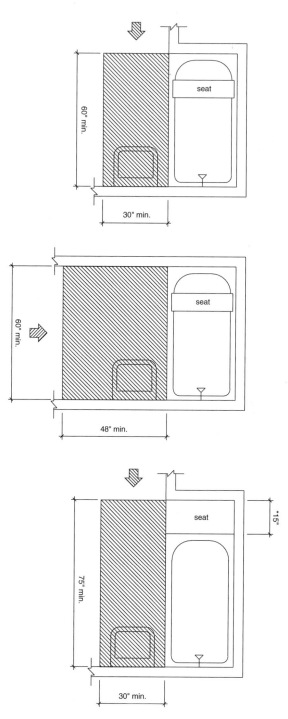

Clear floor space at bathtubs: Built-in seats must measure at least 15 in. in width. The 1998 edition of the ANSI A117.1 standard requires an additional 12-in. offset beyond the seat. The 1992 edition of the ANSI A117.1 standard requires that the clear floor space adjacent to tubs with built-in seats be at least 93 by 30 in.

157. Is an in-tub seat or a seat at the head end of the tub provided?

❏ Yes ❏ No

158. Are grab bars installed that comply with the following diagrams?

❏ Yes ❏ No

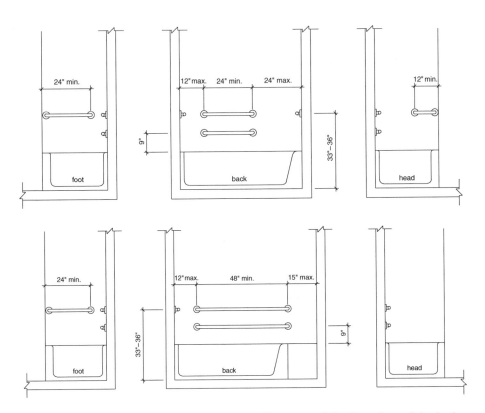

159. Are faucets and other bathtub controls offset toward the front face of the bath-tub?

Note: The front face of the bathtub is the exposed long end, as opposed to the back face of the bathtub which is the long side of the tub located at the back wall.

❏ Yes ❏ No

160. Is a shower spray unit provided that has a hose at least 60 in. long and that can be used as a fixed shower head or as a hand-held shower?

❏ Yes ❏ No

Shower Stalls

161. Does the size and clear floor space at shower stalls comply with the either one of the following diagrams?

❏ Yes ❏ No

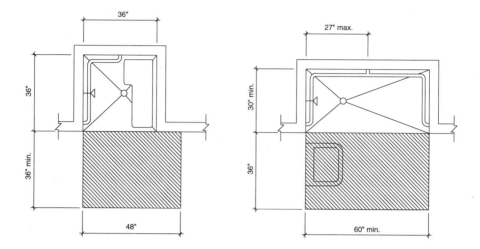

The 1998 edition of the A117.1 standard allows a 30- by 60-in. clear floor space adjacent to the roll-in shower. The 1986 and 1992 editions of the A117.1 standard shows a 36- by 60-in. adjacent clear floor space.

162. Is a seat provided in shower stalls that measure 36 in. by 36 in.?

❏ Yes   ❏ No

163. Is the seat mounted 17 in. to 19 in. above the floor, and does it extend the full depth of the stall?

❏ Yes   ❏ No

164. Is the seat on the wall opposite the controls?

❏ Yes   ❏ No

165. Are grab bars that comply with the locations shown in the following diagrams provided at stalls?

❏ Yes   ❏ No

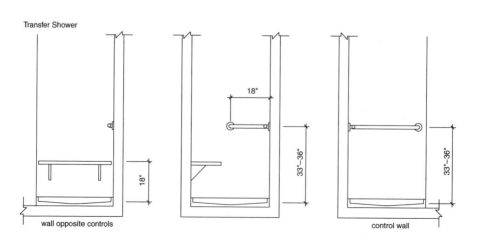

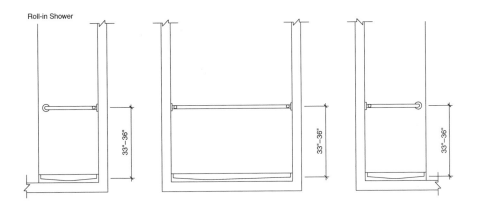

Roll-in Shower

166. Are all controls, faucets, and the shower unit in transfer showers mounted on the side wall opposite the seat? In roll-in showers, are the controls located on the back wall?

❏ Yes　❏ No

167. Is a shower spray unit provided with a hose at least 60 in. long, and that can be used as a fixed shower head or as a hand-held shower?

❏ Yes　❏ No

168. If provided, are curbs in shower stalls that are 36 in. by 36 in. no higher than 4 in.

Note: Stalls measuring 30 in. by 60 in. do not have curbs. Curbs are not addressed in ANSI 1992 or 1998.

❏ Yes　❏ No

Seating, Tables, or Work Surfaces: If provided in accessible spaces, at least of one of each type must be accessible.

Compliance with the following ANSI criteria meets the Guidelines:

ANSI A117.1–1986, Section 4.30

ANSI A117.1–1992, Section 4.31

ANSI A117.1–1998, Section 902

169. Do accessible seating spaces provided at tables and work surfaces for people in wheelchairs have a 30 in. by 48 in. minimum clear floor space that does not overlap kneespace by more than 19 in.?

❏ Yes　❏ No

170. If benches are provided, are they 20 in. to 24 in. wide, by 42 in. to 48 in. long, and are they fixed to a wall along the longer dimension, and mounted 17 in. to 19 in. above the floor?

❏ Yes　❏ No

171. Is a 30 in. by 48 in. clear floor space provided at accessible benches?

❏ Yes ❏ No

172. If benches are installed in wet locations, is the surface of the bench slip-resistant?

❏ Yes ❏ No

173. Does the accessible seating have kneespace at least 27 in. high, 30 in. wide, and 19 in. deep?

❏ Yes ❏ No

174. Are the tops of accessible portions of tables and work surfaces located 28 in. to 34 in. above the floor?

❏ Yes ❏ No

Places of Assembly: If provided, at least one of each type must be accessible.

Compliance with the following ANSI criteria meets the Guidelines:

ANSI A117.1–1986, Section 4.31

ANSI A117.1–1992, Section 4.32

ANSI A117.1–1998, Section 802

175. Are there spaces large enough for two wheelchairs to fit side by side, located at a variety of viewing positions within the assembly space?

❏ Yes ❏ No

Laundry Rooms: If provided, at least one of each type of appliance in each laundry area must be accessible; however, laundry rooms are not required to have front-loading washers.

Compliance with the following ANSI criteria meets the Guidelines:

ANSI A117.1–1986, Section 4.32.6

ANSI A117.1–1992, Section 4.33.5

ANSI A117.1–1998, Section 611

REMINDER:

- In addition to at least one accessible washer and dryer, folding tables, seating, benches, laundry sinks, soap dispensers, and so on must also be accessible.
- If front-loading washers are not available, assistive devices must be available from the management upon request by a resident, to help people with disabilities use a top-loading machine.

176. Is there clear floor space that measures at least 30 in. by 48 in. centered on at least one washer and one dryer, to allow for a forward or parallel approach?

❏ Yes ❏ No

Of the next two questions, either question 177 or question 178 must be marked yes for compliance.

177. Are operable parts of at least one washer and one dryer within the obstructed or unobstructed forward reach range if the approach to the appliance is from the front (see the illustrations on pages 59 and 60)?

Note: The coin slots of coin-operated laundry equipment must be within the accessible reach range.

❑ Yes ❑ No

178. Are operable parts of at least one washer and one dryer within the obstructed side reach range if the approach to the appliance is from the side (see the illustration on page 61)?

Note: The coin slots of coin-operated laundry equipment must be within the accessible reach range.

❑ Yes ❑ No

Requirement 3: Usable doors

Compliance with the following ANSI criteria meets the Guidelines:

ANSI A117.1–1986, Section 4.13

ANSI A117.1–1992, Section 4.13

ANSI A117.1–1998, Section 404

Use the following questions to survey both sides of doors in public and common-use areas, not including the exterior side of unit entry doors.

179. Do doorways have a clear opening of at least 32 in. when the door is open 90 degrees, measured between the face of the door and the stop (see the illustration on page 48)?

❑ Yes ❑ No

180. Front approach to the pull side of swinging door: Is there maneuvering space that extends 18 in. minimum beyond the latch side of the door and 60 in. minimum perpendicular to the doorway (see the illustration on page 50)?

❑ Yes ❑ No

181. Front approach to the push side of swinging door: For doors with *both* a closer and a latch, is there maneuvering space that extends 12 in. minimum beyond the latch side of the door, and 48 in. minimum perpendicular to the doorway? Or, for doors that do not have both a closer and latch, is there maneuvering space at least as wide as the door opening that extends 48 in. minimum perpendicular to the doorway (see the illustration on page 50)?

❑ Yes ❑ No

182. Hinge-side approach to pull side of swinging doors: If 60 in. minimum is provided perpendicular to the doorway, is there maneuvering space that extends 36 in. minimum beyond the latch side of the door, or if 54 in. minimum is provided perpendicular to the doorway, is there maneuvering space that extends 42 in. minimum beyond the latch side of the door (see the illustration on page 50)?

183. Hinge-side approach to push side of swinging doors: For doors with *both* a closer and a latch, is there maneuvering space of 54 in. minimum, parallel to the doorway and 48 in. minimum perpendicular to the doorway? Or, for doors that do not have both a closer and latch, is there maneuvering space at least 54 in. parallel to the doorway and 42 in. minimum perpendicular to the doorway (see the illustration on page 51)?

❏ Yes   ❏ No

184. Latch-side approach to pull side of swinging doors: For doors with a closer, is there maneuvering space that extends 24 in. minimum beyond the latch side of the door and 54 in. minimum perpendicular to the doorway? Or, for doors without a closer, is there maneuvering space that extends 24 in. minimum beyond the latch side of the door and 48 in. minimum perpendicular to the doorway (see the illustration on page 51)?

❏ Yes   ❏ No

185. Latch-side approach to push side of swinging door: For doors with a closer, is there maneuvering space that extends 24 in. minimum parallel to the doorway beyond the latch side of the door and 48 in. minimum perpendicular to the doorway? Or, for doors that do not have a closer, is there maneuvering space that extends 24 in. minimum parallel to the doorway beyond the latch side of the door and 42 in. minimum perpendicular to the doorway (see the illustration on page 51)?

186. Front approach to sliding and folding doors: Is there maneuvering space that is the same width as the door opening that extends 48 in. minimum perpendicular to the doorway?

❏ Yes   ❏ No

187. Slide-side approach to sliding and folding doors: Is there maneuvering space of 54 in. minimum, parallel to the doorway, and 42 in. minimum, perpendicular to the doorway?

❏ Yes   ❏ No

188. Latch-side approach to sliding and folding doors: Is there maneuvering space that extends 24 in. minimum beyond the latch side of the door that extends 42 in. minimum perpendicular to the doorway?

189. Is the floor or ground surface within the required maneuvering spaces of all doors on accessible routes and in public and common-use areas clear and virtually flat?

❑ Yes ❑ No

190. Is the space between two hinged or pivoted doors in a series 48 in. minimum plus the width of any door swinging into the space (see the illustration on page 52)?

❑ Yes ❑ No

191. Do hinged or pivoted doors in a series swing either in the same direction or away from the space between doors (see the illustrations on page 52)?

❑ Yes ❑ No

192. Are thresholds at doorways $1/2$ in. high maximum? (Exterior sliding door thresholds can be $3/4$ in. high maximum.)

❑ Yes ❑ No

193. Do handles, pulls, latches, locks, and other operable parts of accessible doors have a shape that is easy to grasp with one hand, precluding the need to grasp or pinch tightly, or twist the wrist to operate?

❑ Yes ❑ No

194. Is door hardware mounted between 15 in. and 48 in. above the floor?

Note: The ANSI A117.1–1998 criterion for the mounting height of hardware is between 34 in. and 48 in. above the floor.

❑ Yes ❑ No

195. When sliding doors are in the fully open position, is operating hardware exposed and usable from both sides?

❑ Yes ❑ No

196. Is the pushing or pulling force required to open interior hinged doors 5.0 lbs. maximum?

❑ Yes ❑ No

197. Is the pushing or pulling force required to open interior sliding or folding doors 5.0 lbs. maximum?

❑ Yes ❑ No

198. Is the pushing or pulling force required to open exterior hinged doors 8.5 lbs. maximum?

Note: Pushing or pulling force criteria for exterior hinged doors are provided in ANSI A117.1–1986 only.

❑ Yes ❑ No

199. Is the time it takes for power-operated doors to fully open three seconds or more?

Note: No criteria are provided in ANSI A117.1–1998.

❑ Yes   ❑ No

200. Is the force required to stop power-operated door movement 15 lb. maximum?

Note: No criteria provided in ANSI A117.1–1998.

❑ Yes   ❑ No

201. Does the bottom 12 in. of all doors (except automatic doors, power doors, and sliding doors) have a smooth uninterrupted surface, to allow the door to be opened by a wheelchair footrest without creating a trap or hazardous condition?

Note: This criterion is not provided in ANSI A117.1–1986.

❑ Yes   ❑ No

202. When narrow stile-and-rail doors are used, is there a 12-in. high minimum, smooth panel, extending the full width of the doors, installed on the push side of the doors, that will allow the doors to be opened by a wheelchair footrest without creating a trap or hazardous condition?

Note: This criterion is not provided in ANSI A117.1–1986.

❑ Yes   ❑ No

Use the following questions to survey the exterior side of the primary entry door to covered dwelling units.

203. Are changes in level between the exterior and interior floor or ground surfaces (excluding threshold) at the primary entry door no more than $1/2$ in.?

Note: Level changes between the exterior and interior floor or ground surfaces at the primary entry door can be no more than $1/2$ in., regardless of the finish material of the exterior floor or ground surface. Changes in level between $1/4$ in. and $1/2$ in. must be beveled with a slope no greater than 1:2. Changes in level less than $1/4$ in. are permitted to be vertical.

❑ Yes   ❑ No

204. Are thresholds no more than $1/2$ in. high at the primary entry door?

Note: Sliding doors are permitted as primary entry doors if all of the other units incorporate the same door as a primary entry door. If so, thresholds are permitted to be no more than $3/4$ in.

❑ Yes   ❑ No

205. Do doorways have a clear opening of 32 in. minimum, with the door open 90 degrees, measured between the face of the door and the stop when the door is open 90 degrees (see the illustration on page 48)?

❑ Yes   ❑ No

206. Front approach to the pull side of swinging door: Is there maneuvering space that extends 18 in. minimum beyond the latch side of the door, and 60 in. minimum perpendicular to the doorway (see the illustration on page 50)?

❏ Yes   ❏ No

207. Front approach to the push side of swinging door: For doors with both a closer and a latch, is there maneuvering space that extends 12 in. minimum beyond the latch side of the door and 48 in. minimum perpendicular to the doorway. Or, for doors that do not have both a closer and latch, is there maneuvering space at least as wide as the door opening that extends 48 in. minimum perpendicular to the doorway (see the illustration on page 50)?

❏ Yes   ❏ No

208. Hinge-side approach to pull side of swinging doors: If 60 in. minimum is provided perpendicular to the doorway, is there maneuvering space that extends 36 in. minimum beyond the latch side of the door; or, if 54 in. minimum is provided perpendicular to the doorway, is there maneuvering space that extends 42 in. minimum beyond the latch side of the door (see the illustration on page 50)?

❏ Yes   ❏ No

209. Hinge-side approach to push side of swinging doors: For doors with *both* a closer and a latch, is there maneuvering space of 54 in. minimum, parallel to the doorway and 48 in. minimum perpendicular to the doorway? Or, for doors that do not have both a closer and latch, is there maneuvering space at least 54 in. parallel to the doorway and 42 in. minimum perpendicular to the doorway (see the illustration on page 51)?

❏ Yes   ❏ No

210. Latch-side approach to pull side of swinging doors: For doors with a closer, is there maneuvering space that extends 24 in. minimum beyond the latch side of the door and 54 in. minimum perpendicular to the doorway? Or, for doors without a closer, is there maneuvering space that extends 24 in. minimum beyond the latch side of the door and 48 in. minimum perpendicular to the doorway (see the illustration on page 51)?

❏ Yes   ❏ No

211. Latch-side approach to push side of swinging door: For doors with a closer, is there maneuvering space that extends 24 in. minimum parallel to the doorway beyond the latch side of the door and 48 in. minimum perpendicular to the doorway? Or, for doors that do not have a closer, is there maneuvering space that extends 24 in. minimum parallel to the doorway beyond the latch side of the door and 42 in. minimum perpendicular to the doorway (see the illustration on page 51)?

❏ Yes   ❏ No

212. Front approach to sliding and folding doors: Is there maneuvering space that is the same width as the door opening that extends 48 in. minimum perpendicular to the doorway?

 Yes ☐ No

213. Slide-side approach to sliding and folding doors: Is there maneuvering space of 54 in. minimum, parallel to the doorway, and 42 in. minimum, perpendicular to the doorway?

☐ Yes ☐ No

214. Latch-side approach to sliding and folding doors: Is there maneuvering space that extends 24 in. minimum beyond the latch side of the door that extends 42 in. minimum perpendicular to the doorway?

☐ Yes ☐ No

215. Does the floor or ground surface within the required maneuvering spaces of all primary entry doors have a slope that is virtually flat?

Note: The ground surface outside the primary entry door is permitted to be sloped $1/8$ in. for drainage.

☐ Yes ☐ No

216. Is the space between two hinged or pivoted doors in a series 48 in. minimum plus the width of any door swinging into the space (see the illustrations on page 52)?

☐ Yes ☐ No

217. Do hinged or pivoted doors in a series swing either in the same direction or away from the space between doors (see the illustrations on page 52)?

☐ Yes ☐ No

218. Are thresholds at doorways $1/2$ in. high maximum?

Note: For doors with direct access to the exterior, thresholds can be no more than $3/4$ in. high.

☐ Yes ☐ No

219. Do handles, pulls, latches, locks, and other operable parts of accessible doors have a shape that is easy to grasp with one hand, precluding the need to grasp or pinch tightly, or twist the wrist to operate?

☐ Yes ☐ No

220. Is door hardware mounted within a high forward reach of 48 in. maximum and a low forward reach of 15 in. minimum above the floor?

Note: The ANSI A117.1–1998 criterion for the mounting height of hardware is between 34 in. and 48 in. above the floor.

☐ Yes ☐ No

221. Is the pushing or pulling force required to open interior hinged doors 5.0 lbs. maximum?

❏ Yes   ❏ No

222. Is the pushing or pulling force required to open interior sliding or folding doors 5.0 lbs. maximum?

❏ Yes   ❏ No

223. Is the pushing or pulling force required to open exterior hinged doors 8.5 lbs. maximum?

Note: Pushing or pulling force criterion for exterior hinged doors is provided in ANSI A117.1–1986 only.

❏ Yes   ❏ No

Use the following questions to survey all doors within dwelling units that are meant for user passage.

224. Do all doors intended for user passage within covered dwelling units have a nominal clear opening of at least 32 in. when the door is open 90 degrees measured between the face of the door and the stop?

Note: Survey doors, including, but not limited to, walk-in closet doors, doors from the unit to an attached garage, doors to unfinished basements, secondary exit doors, and any other doors meant for user passage within the unit, including doors located in lofts or raised or sunken areas. Doors that are not intended for user passage and doors to small mechanical rooms with furnaces or hot water heaters are excluded from Requirement 3. Clear-width tolerances of $1/4$ in. and $3/8$ in. are acceptable.

❏ Yes   ❏ No

225. Do all interior doors intended for user passage have no or low thresholds?

Note: Thresholds greater than $1/2$ in. are not permitted. Thresholds between $1/4$ in. and $1/2$ in. must be beveled with a slope no greater than 1:2.

❏ Yes   ❏ No

Surfaces of Balconies, Terraces, Patios, and Decks

226. Are thresholds at secondary doors no more than $1/2$ in. high?

Note: Thresholds for sliding doors are permitted to be no more than $3/4$ in high.

❏ Yes   ❏ No

227. If an exterior deck, patio, or balcony surface is constructed of impervious materials (such as concrete, brick, or flagstone) is it no more than 4 in. below the interior floor level of the dwelling unit?

❏ Yes   ❏ No

228. If an exterior deck, patio, or balcony surface is constructed of nonimpervious materials (such as sand, wood, or gravel) is it no more than $\frac{1}{2}$ in. below the floor level of the interior floor level of the dwelling unit?

❏ Yes   ❏ No

Requirement 4: Accessible Route into and through the Dwelling Unit

Review the definitions of the following terms provided in Section 2 of the Guidelines:

Accessible route

Loft

Story

229. Does the accessible route within the unit have a minimum clear width of 36 in.?

❏ Yes   ❏ No

230. Are changes in level between $\frac{1}{4}$ in. and $\frac{1}{2}$ in. along the accessible route through the dwelling unit beveled , with a slope of the bevel no greater than 1:2?

Note: Level changes less than $\frac{1}{4}$ in. do not need to be beveled.

❏ Yes   ❏ No

231. Except for design features, such as a loft or an area on a different level within a room (e.g., sunken are of a living room), are the changes in level no more than $\frac{1}{2}$ in?

❏ Yes   ❏ No

232. If changes in level are greater than $\frac{1}{2}$ in., is a ramp or other means of access provided?

❏ Yes   ❏ No

233. Where a single-story dwelling unit has a special design feature, such as a loft or a sunken or raised area, are all portions of the single-story unit, except the loft or the sunken or raised area, on an accessible route?

❏ Yes   ❏ No

234. Where a single-story unit contains a special design feature, such as a loft or a sunken or raised area, is there only one special design feature in the unit?

Note: Covered units cannot contain more than one special design feature, because more than one feature will reduce the usability of a significant portion of the dwelling unit for a person in a wheelchair.

❏ Yes   ❏ No

235. For covered units with a special design feature, is the accessible route through the remainder of the dwelling maintained without obstruction by the feature?

❑ Yes ❑ No

236. For covered units with a special design feature, are all bathrooms, powder rooms, and kitchens on an accessible route?

Note: Bathrooms, powder rooms, kitchens, or the only bedroom in the unit are primary function areas, and may not be a part of a special design feature unless they are served by an accessible route.

❑ Yes ❑ No

Requirement 5: Light Switches, Electrical Outlets, and Environmental Controls in Accessible Locations

REMINDER:

- Obstructions should not extend more than 25 in. from the wall beneath a control.
- A tolerance of $\frac{1}{2}$ in. is permitted to allow for the installation of some standard countertops that may protrude $25\frac{1}{2}$ in. from a wall.
- Controls or outlets that are out of accessible reach range are acceptable, provided that comparable controls or outlets that perform the same functions are provided within the same area, and are accessible.

237. Is the horizontal centerline of operable parts of light switches in the unit located between 15 in. and 48 in. above the floor?

❑ Yes ❑ No

238. Is the horizontal centerline of operable parts of electrical outlets in the unit located between 15 in. and 48 in. above the floor? (All electrical receptacles must be within the reach range specified.)

❑ Yes ❑ No

239. Is the horizontal centerline of operable parts of thermostats in the unit located between 15 in. and 48 in. above the floor?

❑ Yes ❑ No

240. Is the horizontal centerline of operable parts of other environmental controls in the unit located between 15 in. and 48 in. above the floor (including switches that operate ceiling fans or skylights, for example)?

❑ Yes ❑ No

241. For operable parts of light switches located over an obstruction between 20 and 25 in., is the maximum height of the operable parts located no higher than 44 in. above the floor for a forward approach, or 46 in. above the floor for a side approach (see the illustration on pages 60 and 61)?

242. For operable parts of electrical outlets located over an obstruction between 20 and 25 in., is the maximum height of the operable parts located no higher than 44 in. above the floor for a forward approach, or 46 in. above the floor for a side approach (see the illustration on pages 60 and 61)?

243. For operable parts of thermostats located over an obstruction between 20 and 25 in., is the maximum height of the operable parts located no higher than 44 in. above the floor for a forward approach, or 46 in. above the floor for a side approach (see the illustrations on pages 60 and 61)?

244. For operable parts of other environmental controls (e.g., switches that operate ceiling fans or skylights) located over an obstruction between 20 and 25 in., is the maximum height of the operable parts located no higher than 44 in. above the floor for a forward approach, or 46 in. above the floor for a side approach (see the illustrations on pages 60 and 61)?

245. If inaccessible controls (e.g., controls mounted at the inside corners of walls or floor-mounted outlets) are installed, are there accessible controls nearby that perform the same function, and are located between 48 in. and 15 in. above the floor?

Requirement 6: Reinforced Walls for Grab Bars

REMINDER:

- Where fixtures (e.g., toilet, bathtub, or shower stall) are not placed adjacent to a wall, provisions must be made for the installation of floor-mounted, foldaway, or similar alternative grab bars.
- Where the powder room (a room with a toilet and sink) is the only toilet facility located on an accessible level of a covered multistory dwelling unit, it must comply with Requirements 3 through 7.

Use the following questions to survey bathrooms and powder rooms within a covered units.

246. Are bathroom walls reinforced with plywood or solid blocking in locations indicated in Requirement 6 of the Guidelines (Appendix A) to allow later installation of grab bars around the toilet?

 Yes ❏ No

247. Are bathroom walls reinforced with plywood or solid blocking in locations indicated in Requirement 6 of the Guidelines (Appendix A) to allow later installation of grab bars around the tub?

❏ Yes ❏ No

248. Are bathroom walls reinforced with plywood or solid blocking in locations indicated in Requirement 6 of the Guidelines (Appendix A) to allow later installation of grab bars around the shower stall?

❏ Yes ❏ No

249. Are bathroom walls reinforced with plywood or solid blocking to allow later installation of grab bars around the shower seat if the shower is the only bathing facility in the unit or on the accessible level of a covered multistory unit?

 Yes ❏ No

250. If the toilet, bathtub, or shower stall is located away from walls, is reinforcement provided to allow for the installation of alternative grab bars at these fixtures?

❏ Yes ❏ No

Requirement 7: Usable Kitchens and Bathrooms
Usable Bathrooms

REMINDER:

- All bathrooms in covered units must have a 32-in. clear width at doorways (Requirement 3); be on an accessible route (Requirement 4); have switches, outlets, and controls in accessible locations (Requirement 5); have reinforcing for grab bars around toilets, tubs, and showers (Requirement 6); and meet either Type A or Type B specifications of Requirement 7.
- Powder rooms must have a 32-in. clear width at doorways (Requirement 3); be on an accessible route (Requirement 4); and have switches, outlets, and controls in accessible locations (Requirement 5). When the powder room is the only toilet facility on the entry level of a multistory unit in an elevator building, it must comply with Requirements 3 through 7.
- Required clear floor space at fixtures may overlap.
- Review the definitions of "bathroom" provided in Section 2 of the Guidelines.

Type A: *All* bathrooms in the dwelling unit must comply with questions 251 through 260.

Type B: If all bathrooms in the dwelling unit do not comply with questions 251 through 260 (Type A), then at least one bathroom in the dwelling unit must comply with questions 261 through 274, and all other bathrooms in the unit must have usable entry doors (Requirement 3); be on an accessible route (Requirement 4); have switches and outlets in accessible locations (Requirement 5); and have reinforced walls for grab bars (Requirement 6).

Type A Specifications

Type A bathrooms must have reinforced walls for the later installation of grab bars.

REMINDER:

- Doors may swing into the clear floor space provided at any fixture if the maneuvering space is provided. Maneuvering spaces may include any kneespace or toespace available below bathroom fixtures.

251. Where the door swings into the bathroom, is there a clear space (30 in. by 48 in.) within the room to position a wheelchair or other mobility aids clear of the path of the door as it is closing, and to permit use of fixtures?

Note: Clear space can include any kneespace and toespace available below bathroom fixtures.

 ❑ Yes   ❑ No

252. Where the door swings out, is a clear space provided within the bathroom for a person using a wheelchair or other mobility aid to position the wheelchair such that the person can use the fixtures and be able to reopen the door and exit?

❑ Yes   ❑ No

253. Is the clear floor space specified in Requirement 7 of the Guidelines provided at the toilet (in the Guidelines, see Figure 7(a), page 167, Appendix A)?

❑ Yes   ❑ No

254. Is the clear floor space specified in Requirement 7 of the Guidelines provided at the lavatory, and centered on the sink basin (in the Guidelines, see Figure 7(c), page 167, Appendix A)?

Note: If removable base cabinets are not provided below a sink, then the clear floor space must be centered on the sink basin for a parallel approach.

❑ Yes   ❑ No

255. If kneespace is provided below the vanity, is the bottom of the apron at least 27 in. above the floor?

 ❑ Yes   ❑ No

256. If kneespace is provided below the vanity, is it between 17 in. and 19 in. deep?

❏ Yes ❏ No

257. Is the clear floor space specified in Requirement 7 of the Guidelines provided at the tub (in the Guidelines, see Figure 7(b), page 167, Appendix A)?

❏ Yes ❏ No

258. Is clear floor space specified in Requirement 7 of the Guidelines provided at the shower stall (in the Guidelines, see Figure 7(d), page 168, Appendix A)?

❏ Yes ❏ No

259. If the shower stall is the only bathing facility provided in the covered dwelling unit, does it measure at least 36 in. by 36 in., and provide a 30-in.-by-48-in. clear floor space positioned at the stall as specified in Requirement 7 of the Guidelines (in the Guidelines, see Figure 7(d), page 168, Appendix A)?

❏ Yes ❏ No

260. Is the top of the lavatory rim a maximum height of 34 in. above the finished floor?

❏ Yes ❏ No

Type B Specifications

Type B bathrooms must have reinforced walls for the later installation of grab bars.

261. Where the door swings into the bathroom, is there a clear space (30 in. by 48 in.) within the room to position a wheelchair or other mobility aids clear of the path of the door as it is closed and to permit use of fixtures?

Note: This clear space can include any kneespace and toespace available below bathroom fixtures.

❏ Yes ❏ No

262. Where the door swings out, is a clear space provided within the bathroom for a person using a wheelchair or other mobility aid to position the wheelchair such that the person can use the fixtures and is able to reopen the door and exit?

❏ Yes ❏ No

263. When both tub and shower fixtures are provided in the bathroom, is at least one made accessible according to the clear floor space requirements provided in Requirement 7 of the Guidelines (in the Guidelines, see Figures 7(d) and 8, pages 168 and 169, Appendix A)?

❏ Yes ❏ No

264. When two or more lavatories in a bathroom are provided, is one made accessible according to the clear floor space requirements in Requirement 7 of the Guidelines (in the Guidelines, see Figure 7(c), page 167, Appendix A)?

❑ Yes   ❑ No

265. In locations where toilets are adjacent to walls or bathtubs, is the centerline of the fixture 18 in. from the wall or bathtub?

❑ Yes   ❑ No

266. Is the other (nongrab bar) side of the toilet fixture a minimum of 15 in. from the finished surface of adjoining walls or vanities or from the edge of a lavatory?

❑ Yes   ❑ No

267. If the lavatory is designed with removable base cabinets, is the required clear floor space for a front approach centered on the sink basin?

❑ Yes   ❑ No

268. If the vanity and lavatory are designed for a parallel approach, is the clear floor space centered on the sink basin, as specified in Requirement 7 of the Guidelines (in the Guidelines, see Figure 7(c), page 167, Appendix A)?

❑ Yes   ❑ No

269. Is the top of the lavatory rim a maximum height of 34 in. above the finished floor.?

❑ Yes   ❑ No

270. If kneespace is provided below the vanity, is the bottom of the apron at least 27 in. above the floor?

❑ Yes   ❑ No

271. If kneespace is provided below the vanity, is it between 17 in. and 19 in. deep?

❑ Yes   ❑ No

272. Are the bathtubs and tub/showers located in the bathroom so that there is a clear access aisle that is at least 30 in. wide and extends for a length of 48 in., measured from the foot (control end) of the bathtub, as specified in Requirement 7 of the Guidelines (in the Guidelines, see Figure 8, page 169, Appendix A)?

❑ Yes   ❑ No

273. Is the clear floor space specified in Requirement 7 of the Guidelines provided (in the Guidelines, see Figure 7(d), page 168, Appendix A) if the shower stall is the only bathing facility provided in a covered single-story unit; or on the accessible level of a covered multistory unit; or if both a bathtub and a shower stall are provided in the bathroom, and the shower stall is the accessible fixture?

Note: If a bathtub and a shower stall are provided in a Type B bathroom, only one must be accessible.

❑ Yes   ❑ No

274. If the shower stall is the only bathing facility provided in the covered dwelling unit, or on the accessible level of a covered multistory unit, does it measures at least 36 in. by 36 in, and does it have reinforcing to allow for installation of an optional wall-hung bench seat?

❑ Yes   ❑ No

Usable Kitchens

275. A 30-in.-by-48-in. clear floor space must be provided at sinks, ranges and cooktops to allow for a parallel approach. The clear floor space must be centered on the bowl or appliance. Do the following comply with the requirements for clear floor space:

the range or cooktop?	❑ Yes	❑ No
the sink?	❑ Yes	❑ No

276. A 30-in.-by-48-in. clear floor space must be provided at ovens, dishwashers, refrigerators, freezers, and trash compactors. The space may be oriented in either parallel or a perpendicular position and must be centered on the appliance. Do the following comply with the requirements for clear floor space:

Note: The Guidelines do not address clear floor space requirements at microwave ovens.

the oven?	❑ Yes	❑ No
the dishwasher?	❑ Yes	❑ No
the refrigerator/freezer?	❑ Yes	❑ No
the trash compactor?	❑ Yes	❑ No

277. If the kitchen is not U-shaped, is the clearance between counters and all opposing base cabinets, countertops, appliances, or walls at least 40 in?

❑ Yes   ❑ No

278. If the kitchen is U-shaped and has the sink, range, or cooktop located at the base of the U, is a 60-in. diameter turning circle provided to allow parallel approach to the sink, range, or cooktop? If the answer to this question is no, the answer to the next question must be yes.

❑ Yes   ❑ No

279. If the kitchen is U-shaped and has the sink, range, or cooktop located at the base of the U, are base cabinets designed to be removable at that location to allow kneespace for a forward approach to the sink, range, or cooktop?

❑ Yes   ❑ No

APPENDIX A

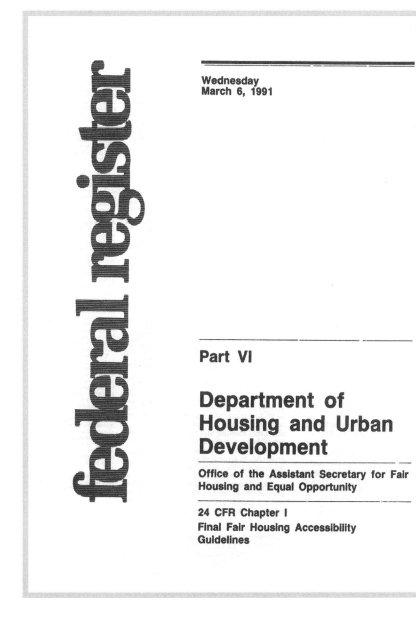

Wednesday
March 6, 1991

Part VI

Department of Housing and Urban Development

Office of the Assistant Secretary for Fair Housing and Equal Opportunity

24 CFR Chapter I
Final Fair Housing Accessibility Guidelines

9472 Federal Register / Vol. 56, No. 44 / Wednesday, March 6, 1991 / Rules and Regulations

DEPARTMENT OF HOUSING AND URBAN DEVELOPMENT

Office of the Assistant Secretary for Fair Housing and Equal Opportunity

24 CFR Ch. I

[Docket No. N-91-2011; FR 2665-N-06]

Final Fair Housing Accessibility Guidelines

AGENCY: Office of the Assistant Secretary for Fair Housing and Equal Opportunity, HUD.

ACTION: Notice of Final Fair Housing Accessibility Guidelines.

SUMMARY: This document presents guidelines adopted by the Department of Housing and Urban Development to provide builders and developers with technical guidance on how to comply with the specific accessibility requirements of the Fair Housing Amendments Act of 1988. Issuance of this document follows consideration of public comment received on proposed accessibility guidelines published in the Federal Register on June 15, 1990. The guidelines presented in this document are intended to provide technical guidance only, and are not mandatory. The guidelines will be codified in the 1991 edition of the Code of Federal Regulations as Appendix II to the Fair Housing regulations (24 CFR Ch. I, Subch. A, App. II). The preamble to the guidelines will be codified in the 1991 edition of the Code of Federal Regulations as Appendix III to the Fair Housing regulations (24 CFR Ch. I, Subch. A, App. III).

EFFECTIVE DATE: March 6, 1991.

FOR FURTHER INFORMATION CONTACT: Merle Morrow, Office of HUD Program Compliance, room 5204, Department of Housing and Urban Development, 451 Seventh Street, SW., Washington, DC. 20410-0500, telephone (202) 708-2618 (voice) or (202) 708-0015 (TDD). (These are not toll-free numbers.)

SUPPLEMENTARY INFORMATION:

I. Adoption of Final Guidelines

The Department of Housing and Urban Development (Department) is adopting as its Fair Housing Accessibility Guidelines, the design and construction guidelines set forth in this notice (Guidelines). Issuance of this document follows consideration of public comments received in response to an advance notice of intention to develop and publish Fair Housing Accessibility Guidelines, published in the Federal Register on August 2, 1989 (54 FR 31856), and in response to proposed accessibility guidelines published in the Federal Register on June 15, 1990 (55 FR 24730).

The Department is adopting as final Guidelines, the guidelines designated as Option One in the proposed guidelines published on June 15, 1990, with modifications to certain of the Option One design specifications. In developing the final Guidelines, the Department was cognizant of the need to provide technical guidance that appropriately implements the specific accessibility requirements of the Fair Housing Amendments Act of 1988, while avoiding design specifications that would impose an unreasonable burden on builders and significantly increase the cost of new multifamily construction. The Department believes that the final Guidelines adopted by this notice (1) are consistent with the level of accessibility envisioned by Congress; (2) simplify compliance with the Fair Housing Amendments Act by providing guidance concerning what constitutes acceptable compliance with the Act; and (3) maintain the affordability of new multifamily construction by specifying reasonable design and construction methods.

The Option One design specifications substantially revised in the final Guidelines include the following:

(1) Site impracticality. The final Guidelines provide that covered multifamily dwellings with elevators shall be designed and constructed to provide at least one accessible entrance on an accessible route regardless of terrain or unusual characteristics of the site. Every dwelling unit on a floor served by an elevator must be on an accessible route, and must be made accessible in accordance with the Act's requirements for covered dwelling units.

For covered multifamily dwellings without elevators, the final Guidelines provide two alternative tests for determining site impracticality due to terrain. The first test is an individual building test which involves a two-step process: measurement of the slope of the undisturbed site between the planned entrance and all vehicular or pedestrian arrival points; and measurement of the slope of the planned finished grade between the entrance and all vehicular or pedestrian arrival points. The second test is a site analysis test which involves an analysis of the existing natural terrain (before grading) by topographic survey with 2 foot contour intervals, with slope determination made between each successive contour interval.

A site with a single building (without an elevator), having a common entrance for all units, may be analyzed only under the first test—the individual building test. All other sites, including a site with a single building having multiple entrances serving either individual dwelling units or clusters of dwelling units, may be analyzed either under the first test or the second test. For sites for which either test is applicable (that is, all sites other than a site with a single nonelevator building having a common entrance for all units), the final Guidelines provide that regardless of which test is utilized by a builder or developer, at least 20% of the total ground floor units in nonelevator buildings, on any site, must comply with the Act's accessibility requirements.

(2) An accessible route into and through covered dwelling units. The final Guidelines distinguish between (i) single-story dwelling units, and (ii) multistory dwelling units in elevator buildings, and provide guidance on designing an accessible entrance into and through each of these two types of dwelling units.

(a) Single-story dwelling units. For single-story dwelling units, the final Guidelines specify the same design specification as presented in the proposed Option One guidelines, except that design features within the single-story dwelling units, such as a loft or a sunken living room, are exempt from the access specifications, subject to certain requirements. Lofts are exempt provided that all other space within the units is on an accessible route. Sunken or raised functional areas, such as a sunken living room, are also exempt from access specifications, provided that such areas do not interrupt the accessible route through the remainder of the unit. However, split-level entries or areas will need ramps or other means of providing an accessible route.

(b) Multistory dwelling units in buildings with elevators. For multistory dwelling units in buildings with elevators, the final Guidelines specify that only the story served by the building elevator must comply with the accessible features for dwelling units required by the Fair Housing Act. The other stories of the multistory dwelling units are exempt from access specifications, provided that the story of the unit that is served by the building elevator (1) is the primary entry to the unit; (2) complies with Requirements 2 through 7 with respect to the rooms located on the entry/accessible level; and (3) contains a bathroom or powder room which complies with Requirement 7.

(c) Thresholds at patio, deck or balcony doors. The final Guidelines provide that exterior deck, patio, or balcony surfaces should be not more

Federal Register / Vol. 56, No. 44 / Wednesday, March 6, 1991 / Rules and Regulations 9473

than ½ inch below the floor level of the interior of the dwelling unit, unless they are constructed of impervious materials such as concrete, brick or flagstone, in which case the surface should be no more than 4 inches below the floor level of the interior dwelling units, unless the local building code requires a lower drop. This provision and the following provision were included in order to minimize the possibility of interior water damage when exterior surfaces are constructed of impervious materials.

(d) Outside surface at entry door. The final Guidelines also provide that at the primary entry door to dwelling units with direct exterior access, outside landing surfaces constructed of impervious materials such as concrete, brick, or flagstone should be no more than ½ inch below the interior of the dwelling unit. The Guidelines further provide that the finished surface of this area, located immediately outside the entry door, may be sloped for drainage, but the sloping may be no more than ⅛ inch per foot.

(3) Usable bathrooms. The final Guidelines provide two alternative sets of specifications for making bathrooms accessible in accordance with the Act's requirements. The Act requires that an accessible or "usable" bathroom is one which provides sufficient space for an individual in a wheelchair to maneuver about. The two sets of specifications provide different approaches as to how compliance with this maneuvering space requirement may be achieved. The final Guidelines for usable bathrooms also provide that the usable bathroom specifications (either set of specifications) are applicable to powder rooms (i.e., a room with only a toilet and a sink) when the powder room is the only toilet facility on the accessible level of a covered multistory dwelling unit.

The details about, and the reasons for these modifications, and additional minor technical modifications made to certain design specifications of the Option One guidelines, are discussed more fully in the section-by-section analysis which appear later in this preamble.

Principal features of the Option One guidelines that were not changed in the final Guidelines include the following:

(1) Accessible entrance and an accessible route. The Option One guidelines for these two requirements remain unchanged in the final Guidelines.

(2) Accessible and usable public and common use areas. The Option One guidelines for public and common use areas remain unchanged in the final Guidelines.

(3) Door within individual dwelling units. The final Guidelines recommend that doors intended for user passage within individual dwelling units have a clear opening of at least 32 inches nominal width when the door is open 90 degrees.

(4) Doors to public and common use areas. The final Guidelines continued to provide that on accessible routes in public and common use areas, and for primary entry doors to covered units doors that comply with ANSI 4.13 meet the Act's requirement for "usable" doors.

(4) Thresholds at exterior doors. Subject to the exceptions for thresholds and changes in level at exterior areas constructed of impervious materials, the final Guidelines continue to specify that thresholds at exterior doors, including sliding door tracks, be no higher than ¾ inch.

(5) Reinforced walls for grab bars. The final Guidelines for bathroom wall reinforcement remains essentially unchanged from the Option One guidelines. The only change made to these guidelines has been to subject powder rooms to the reinforced wall requirement when the powder room is the only toilet facility on the accessible floor of a covered multistory dwelling unit.

The text of the final Guidelines follows the Preamble, which includes a discussion of the public comments received on the proposed guidelines, and the section-by-section analysis referenced above.

The design specification presented in the Fair Housing Accessibility Guidelines provide technical guidance to builders and developers in complying with the specific accessibility requirements of the Fair Housing Amendments Act of 1988. The Guidelines are intended to provide a safe harbor for compliance with the accessibility requirements of the Fair Housing Amendments Act, as implemented by 24 CFR 100.205 of the Department's Fair Housing regulations. The Guidelines are not mandatory. Additionally, the Guidelines do not prescribe specific requirements which must be met, and which, if not met, would constitute unlawful discrimination under the Fair Housing Amendments Act. Builders and developers may choose to depart from the Guidelines, and seek alternate ways to demonstrate that they have met the requirements of the Fair Housing Act.

II. Statutory and Regulatory Background

Title VIII of the Civil Rights Act of 1968 makes it unlawful to discriminate in any aspect relating to the sale, rental or financing of dwellings, or in the provision of brokerage services or facilities in connection with the sale or rental of a dwelling, because of race, color, religion, sex or national origin. The Fair Housing Amendments Act of 1988 (Pub. L. 100–430, approved September 13, 1988) (Fair Housing Act or the Act) expanded coverage of title VIII (42 U.S.C. 3601–3620) to prohibit discriminatory housing practices based on handicap and familial status. As amended, section 804(f)(3)(C) of the Act provides that unlawful discrimination includes a failure to design and construct covered multifamily dwellings for first occupancy after March 13, 1991 (30 months after the date of enactment in accordance with certain accessibility requirements. The Act defines "covered multifamily dwellings" as "(a) buildings consisting of 4 or more units if such buildings have one or more elevators; and (b) ground floor units in other buildings consisting of 4 or more units" (42 U.S.C. 3604).

The Act makes it unlawful to fail to design and construct covered multifamily dwellings so that:

(1) Public use and common use portions of the dwellings are readily accessible to and usable by persons with handicaps;

(2) All doors within such dwellings which are designed to allow passage into and within the premises are sufficiently wide to allow passage by persons in wheelchairs; and

(3) All premises within such dwellings contain the following features of adaptive design:

(a) An accessible route into and through the dwelling;

(b) Light switches, electrical outlets, thermostats, and other environmental controls in accessible locations.

(c) Reinforcements in bathroom walls to allow later installation of grab bars; and

(d) Usable kitchens and bathrooms such that an individual in a wheelchair can maneuver about the space.

The Act provides that compliance with (1) the appropriate requirements of the American National Standard for Buildings and Facilities—Providing Accessibility and Usability for Physically Handicapped People (commonly cited as "ANSI A117.1"), or (2) with the laws of a State or unit of general local government, that has incorporated into such laws the accessibility requirements of the Act, shall be deemed to satisfy the accessibility requirements of the Act. (See section 804(f)(4) and (5)(A).) The Act also provides that the Secretary of the Department of Housing and Urban

9474   **Federal Register** / Vol. 56, No. 44 / Wednesday, March 6, 1991 / Rules and Regulations

Development shall provide technical assistance to States and units of local government and other persons to implement the accessibility requirements of the Act. (See section 804(f)(5)(C).)

Congress believed that the accessibility provisions of the Act would (1) facilitate the ability of persons with handicaps to enjoy full use of their homes without imposing unreasonable requirements on homebuilders, landlords and non-handicapped tenants; (2) be essential for equal access and to avoid future *de facto* exclusion of persons with handicaps; and (3) be easy to incorporate in housing design and construction. Congress predicted that compliance with these minimal accessibility design and construction standards would eliminate many of the barriers which discriminate against persons with disabilities in their attempts to obtain equal housing opportunities. (See H.R. Rep. No. 711, 100th Cong. 2d Sess. 27–28 (1988) ("House Report").)

The Fair Housing Act became effective on March 12, 1989. The Department implemented the Act by a final rule published January 23, 1989 (54 FR 3232), and which became effective on March 12, 1989. Section 100.205 of that rule incorporates the Act's design and construction requirements, including the requirement that multifamily dwellings for first occupancy after March 13, 1991 be designed and constructed in accordance with the Act's accessibility requirements. The final rule clarified which multifamily dwellings are subject to the Act's requirements. Section 100.205 provides, in paragraph (a), that covered multifamily dwellings shall be deemed to be designed and constructed for first occupancy on or before March 13, 1991, if they are occupied by that date, or if the last building permit or renewal thereof for the covered multifamily dwellings is issued by a State, County or local government on or before January 13, 1990. The Department selected the date of January 13, 1990 because it is fourteen months before March 13, 1991. Based on data contained in the Marshall Valuation Service, the Department found that fourteen months represented a reasonable median construction time for multifamily housing projects of all sizes. The Department chose the issuance of a building permit as the appropriate point in the building process because such permits are issued in writing by governmental authorities. The issuance of a building permit has the advantage of being a clear and objective standard. In addition, any project that actually

achieves first occupancy before March 13, 1991 will be judged to have met this standard even if the last building permit or renewal thereof was issued after January 13, 1990 (55 FR 3251).

Section 110.205 of the final rule also incorporates the Act's provisions that compliance with the appropriate requirements of ANSI A117.1, or with State or local laws that have incorporated the Act's accessibility requirements, suffices to satisfy the accessibility requirements of the Act as codified in § 100.205. In the preamble to the final rule, the Department stated that it would provide more specific guidance on the Act's accessibility requirements in a notice of proposed guidelines that would provide a reasonable period for public comment on the guidelines.

III. Proposed Accessibility Guidelines

On August 2, 1989, the Department published in the **Federal Register** an advance notice of intention to develop and publish Fair Housing Accessibility Guidelines (54 FR 31856). The purpose of this document was to solicit early comment from the public concerning the content of the Accessibility Guidelines, and to outline the Department's procedures for their development. To the extent practicable, the Department considered all public comments submitted in response to the August 2, 1989 advance notice in its preparation of the proposed accessibility guidelines.

On June 15, 1990, the Department published proposed Fair Housing Accessibility guidelines (55 FR 24370). The proposed guidelines presented, and requested public comment on, three options for accessible design:

(1) Option one (Option One) provided guidelines developed by the Department with the assistance of the Southern Building Code Congress International (SBCCI), and incorporated suggestions received in response to the August 2, 1989 advance notice;

(2) Option two (Option Two) offered guidelines developed by the National Association of Home Builders (NAHB) and the National Coordinating Council on Spinal Cord Injuries (NCCSCI); and

(3) Option three (Option Three) offered "adaptable accommodations" guidelines, an approach that provides for identification of certain features in dwelling units that could be made accessible to people with handicaps on a case-by-case basis.

In the June 15, 1990 notice of proposed guidelines, the Department recognized that projects then being designed, in advance of publication of the final Guidelines may not become available for occupancy until after March 13, 1991. The Department advised that efforts to

comply with the proposed guidelines, Option One, in the design of projects which would be completed before issuance of the final Guidelines, would be considered as evidence of compliance with the Act in connection with the Department's investigation of any complaints. Following publication of the June 15, 1990 notice, the Department received a number of inquiries concerning whether certain design and construction activities in connection with projects likely to be completed before issuance of final Guidelines would be considered by the Department to be in compliance with the Act.

In order to resolve these questions, the Department, on August 1, 1990, published in the **Federal Register** a supplementary notice to the proposed guidelines (55 FR 31191). In the supplementary notice, the Department advised that it only would consider efforts to comply with the proposed guidelines, Option One, as evidence of compliance with the Act. The Department stated that evidence of compliance with the Option One guidelines, under the circumstances described in the supplementary notice, would be a basis for determination that there is no reasonable cause to believe that a discriminatory housing practice under section 804(f)(3) has occurred, or is about to occur in connection with the investigation of complaints filed with the Department relating to covered multifamily dwellings. The circumstances described in the August 1, 1990 supplementary notice that the Department found would be in compliance with the Act, were limited to:

(1) Any covered multifamily dwellings which are designed in accordance with the Option One guidelines, and for which construction is completed before publication of the final Fair Housing Accessibility Guidelines; and

(2) Any covered multifamily dwellings which have been designed in accordance with the Option One guidelines, but for which construction is not completed by the date of publication of the final Guidelines provided:

(a) Construction begins before the final Guidelines are published; or

(b) A building permit is issued less than 60 days after the final Guidelines are published.

On September 7, 1990, the Department published for public comment a Preliminary Regulatory Impact Analysis on the Department's assessment of the economic impact of the Guidelines, as implemented by each of the three design options then under consideration (55 FR 37072–37129).

Federal Register / Vol. 56, No. 44 / Wednesday, March 6, 1991 / Rules and Regulations   9475

IV. Public Comments and Commenters

The proposed guidelines provided a 90-day period for the submission of comments by the public, ending September 13, 1990. The Department received 562 timely comments. In addition, a substantial number of comments were received by the Department after the September 13, 1990 deadline. Although those comments were not timely filed, they were reviewed to assure that any major issues raised had been adequately addressed in comments that were received by the deadline. Each of the timely comments was read, and a list of all significant issues raised by those comments was compiled. All these issues were considered in the development of the final Guidelines.

Of the 562 comments received, approximately 200 were from disability advocacy organizations, or units of State or local government concerned with disability issues. Sixty-eight (68) additional commenters identified themselves as members of the disability community; 61 commenters identified themselves as individuals who work with members of the disability community (e.g., vocational or physical therapists or counselors), or who have family members with disabilities; and 96 commenters were members of the building industry, including architects, developers, designers, design consultants, manufacturers of home building products, and rental managers. Approximately 292 commenters supported Option One without any recommendation for change An additional 155 commenters supported Option One, but recommended changes to certain Option One design standards. Twenty-six (26) commenters supported Option Two, and 10 commenters supported Option Three. The remaining commenters submitted questions, comments and recommendations for changes on certain design features of one or more of the three options, but expressed no preference for any particular option, or, alternatively, recommended final guidelines that combine features from two or all three of the options.

The Commenters

The commenters included several national, State and local organizations and agencies, private firms, and individuals that have been involved in the development of State and local accessibility codes. These commenters offered valuable information, including copies of State and local accessibility codes, on accessibility design standards. These commenters included: the

Southern Building Code Congress International (SBCCI); the U.S. Architectural and Transportation Barriers Compliances Board (ATBCB); the Building Officials & Code Administrators International, Inc. (BOCA); the State of Washington Building Code Council; the Seattle Department of Construction and Land Use; the Barrier-free Subcode Committee of the New Jersey Uniform Construction Code Advisory Board; the Department of Community Planning, Housing and Department of Arlington County, Virginia; the City of Atlanta Department of Community Development, Bureau of Buildings; and members of the Department of Architecture, the State of University of New York at Buffalo. In addition to the foregoing organizations, a number of the commenters from the building industry submitted detailed comments on the proposed guidelines.

The commenters also included a number of disability organizations, several of which prepared detailed comments on the proposed guidelines. The comments of two disability organizations also were submitted as concurring comments by many individuals and other disability advocacy organizations. These two organizations are the Disability Rights Education & Defense Fund, and the Consortium for Citizens with Disabilities (CCD). The CCD represents the following organizations: the Association for Education and Rehabilitation of the Blind and Visually Impaired, Association for Retarded Citizens of the United States, International Association of Psychological Rehabilitation Facilities, National Alliance for the Mentally Ill, National Association of Protection and Advocacy Systems, National Association of Developmental Disabilities Councils, National Association of State Mental Health Program Directors, National Council of Community Mental Health Centers, National Head Injury Foundation, National Mental Health Association, United Cerebral Palsy Associations, Inc. Both the Disability Rights Education and Defense Fund and the CCD were strongly supportive of Option One.

A coalition of 20 organizations (Coalition), representing both the building industry and the disability community, also submitted detailed comments on the proposed guidelines. The members of the Coalition include: American Institute of Architects, American Paralysis Association, American Resort and Residential Development Association, American Society of Landscape Architects,

Apartment and Office Building Association, Association of Home Appliance Manufacturers, Bridge Housing Corporation, Marriott Corporation, Mortgage Bankers Association, National Apartment Association, National Assisted Housing Management Association, National Association of Home Builders (NAHB), National Association of Realtors, National Association of Senior Living Industries, National Conference of States on Building Codes and Standards, National Coordinating Council on Spinal Cord Injury (NCCSCI), National Leased Housing Association, National Multi Housing Council, National Organization on Disability, and the Paralyzed Veterans of America.

The commenters also included U.S. Representatives Don Edwards, Barney Frank and Hamilton Fish, Jr., who advised that they were the primary sponsors of the Fair Housing Act, and who expressed their support of Option One.

Comments on the Three Options

In addition to specific issues and questions raised about the design standards recommended by the proposed guidelines, a number of commenters simply submitted comments on their overall opinion of one or more of the options. Following is a summary of the opinions typically expressed on each of the options.

Option One. The Option One guidelines drew a strong reaction from commenters. Supporters stated that the Option One guidelines provided a faithful and clearly stated interpretation of the Act's intent. Opponents of Option One stated that its design standards would increase housing costs significantly—for everyone. Several commenters who supported some features of Option One were concerned that adoption of Option One in its entirety would escalate housing costs. Another frequent criticism was that Option One's design guidelines were too complex and cumbersome.

Option Two. Supporters of Option Two state that this option presented a reasonable compromise between Option One and Option Three. Supporters stated that the Option Two guidelines provided more design flexibility than the Option One guidelines, and that this flexibility would allow builders to deliver the required accessibility features at a lower cost. Opponents of Option Two stated that this option allowed builders to circumvent the Act's intent with respect to several essential accessibility features.

Option Three. Supporters of Option Three stated that Option Three presented the best method of achieving the accessibility objectives of the Act, at the lowest possible cost. Supporters stated that Option Three would contain housing costs, because design adaptation only would be made to those units which actually would be occupied by a disabled resident, and the adaptation would be tailored to the specific accessibility needs of the individual tenant. Opponents of Option Three stated that this option, with its "add-on" approach to accessibility, was contrary to the Act's intent, which, the commenter claimed, mandates accessible features at the time of construction.

Comments on the Costs of Implementation

In addition to the comments on the specific features of the three design options, one of the issues most widely commented upon was the cost of compliance with the Act's accessibility requirements, as implemented by the Guidelines. Several commenters disputed the Department's estimate of the cost of compliance, as presented in the Initial Regulatory Flexibility Analysis, published with the proposed guidelines on June 15, 1990 (55 FR 24384–24385), and in the Preliminary Regulatory Impact Analysis published on September 7, 1990 (55 FR 37072–37129). The Department's response to these comments is discussed in the Final Regulatory Impact Analysis, which is available for public inspection during regular business hours in the Office of the Rules Docket Clerk, room 10276, Department of Housing and Urban Development, 451 Seventh Street, SW., Washington, DC 20410–0500.

V. Discussion of Principal Public Comment Issues, and Section-by-Section Analysis of the Final Guidelines.

The following presents a discussion of the principal issues raised by the commenters, and the Department's response to each issue. This discussion includes a section-by-section analysis of the final Guidelines that addresses many of the specific concerns raised by the commenter, and highlights the differences between the proposed Option One guidelines and the final Guidelines. Comments related to issues outside the purview of the Guidelines, but related to the Act (e.g., enforcement procedures, statutory effective date), are discussed in the final section of the preamble under the preamble heading "Discussion of Comments on Related Fair Housing Issues".

1. Discussion of General Comments on the Guidelines

ANSI Standard

Comment. Many commenters expressed their support for the ANSI Standard as the basis for the Act's Guidelines, because ANSI is a familiar and accepted accessibility standard.

Response. In developing the proposed and final Guidelines, the Department was cognizant of the need for uniformity, and of the widespread application of the ANSI Standard. The original ANSI A117.1, adopted in 1961, formed the technical basis for the first accessibility standards adopted by the Federal Government, and most State governments. The 1980 edition of that standard was based on research funded by the Department, and became the basis for the Uniform Federal Accessibility Standards (UFAS), published in the Federal Register on August 4, 1984 (47 FR 33862). The 1980 edition also was generally accepted by the private sector, and was recommended for use in State and local building codes by the Council of American Building Officials. Additionally, Congress, in the Fair Housing Act, specifically referenced the ANSI Standard, thereby encouraging utilization of the ANSI Standard as guidance for compliance with the Act's accessibility requirements. Accordingly, in using the ANSI Standard as a reference point for the Fair Housing Act Accessibility Guidelines, the Department is issuing Guidelines based on existing and familiar design standards, and is promoting uniformity between Federal accessibility standards, and those commonly used in the private sector. However, the ANSI Standard and the final Guidelines have differing purposes and goals, and they are by no means identical. The purpose of the Guidelines is to describe minimum standards of compliance with the specific accessibility requirements of the Act.

Comment. Two commenters suggested that the Department adopt the ANSI Standard as the guidelines for the Fair Housing Act's accessibility requirements, and not issue new guidelines.

Response. The Department has incorporated in the Guidelines those technical provisions of the ANSI Standard that are consistent with the Act's accessibility requirements. However, with respect to certain of the Act's requirements, the applicable ANSI provisions impose more stringent design standards than required by the Act. (In the preamble to the proposed rule (55 FR 3251), and again in the preamble to the

proposed guidelines (55 FR 24370), the Department advised that a dwelling unit that complies fully with the ANSI Standard goes beyond what is required by the Fair Housing Act.) The Department has developed Guidelines for those requirements of the Act where departures from ANSI were appropriate.

Comment. A few commenters questioned whether the Department would revise the Guidelines to correspond to ANSI's periodic update of its standard.

Response. The ANSI Standard is reviewed at five-year intervals. As the ANSI Standard is revised in the future, the Department intends to review each version, and, if appropriate to make revisions to the Guidelines in accordance with any revisions made to the ANSI Standard. Modifications of the Guidelines, whether or not reflective of changes to the ANSI Standard, will be subject to notice and prior public comment.

Comment. A few commenters requested that the Department republish the ANSI Standard in its entirety in the final Guidelines.

Response. The American National Standards Institute (ANSI) is a private, national organization, and is not connected with the Federal Government. The Department received permission from ANSI to print the ANSI Standard in its entirety, as the time of publication of the proposed guidelines (55 FR 24404–24487), specifically for the purpose of assisting readers of the proposed guidelines in developing timely comments. In the preamble to the proposed guidelines, the Department stated that since it was printing the entire ANSI Standard, as an appendix to the proposed guidelines, the final notice of the Accessibility Guidelines would not include the complete text of the ANSI Standard (55 FR 24371). Copies of the ANSI Standard may be purchased from the American National Standards Institute, 1430 Broadway, New York, NY 10018.

Comment. Another commenter requested that the Department confirm that any ANSI provision not cited in the final Guidelines is not necessary for compliance with the Act.

Response. In the proposed guidelines, the Department stated that: "Where the guidelines rely on sections of the ANSI Standard, the ANSI sections are cited. * * * For those guidelines that differ from the ANSI Standard, recommended specifications are provided" (55 FR 24385). The final Guidelines include this statement, and further state that the ANSI sections not cited in the Guidelines have been determined by the

Federal Register / Vol. 56, No. 44 / Wednesday, March 6, 1991 / Rules and Regulations   9477

Department not to be necessary for compliance with the Act's requirements.

Bias Toward Wheelchair Users

Comment. Two commenters stated that the proposed guidelines were biased toward wheelchair users, and that the Department has erroneously assumed that the elderly and the physically disabled have similar needs. The commenters stated that the physical problems suffered by the elderly often involve arthritic and back problems, which make bending and stooping difficult.

Response. The proposed guidelines, and the final Guidelines, reflect the accessibility requirements contained in the Fair Housing Act. These requirements largely are directed toward individuals with mobility impairments, particularly those who require mobility aids, such as wheelchairs, walkers, or crutches. In two of the Act's accessibility requirements, specific reference is made to wheelchair users. The emphasis of the law and the Guidelines on design and construction standards that are compatible with the needs of wheelchair users is realistic because the requirements for wheelchair access (e.g., wider doorways) are met more easily at the construction stage. (See House Report at 27.) Individuals with nonmobility impairments more easily can be accommodated by later nonstructural adaptations to dwelling units. The Fair Housing Act and the Fair Housing regulations assure the right of these individuals to make such later adaptations. (See section 804(f)(3)(A) of the Act and 24 CFR 100.203 of the regulations. See also discussion of adaptations made to units in this preamble under the heading "Costs of Adaptation" in the section entitled "Discussion of Comments on Related Fair Housing Issues".)

Compliance Problems Due to Lack of Accessibility Guidelines

Comment. A number of commenters from the building industry attributed difficulty in meeting the Act's March 13, 1991 compliance deadline, in part, to the lack of accessibility guidelines. The commenters complained about the time that it has taken the Department to publish proposed guidelines, and the additional time it has taken to publish final Guidelines.

Response. The Department acknowledges that the development and issuance of final Fair Housing Accessibility Guidelines has been a time-consuming process. However, the building industry has not been without guidance on compliance with the Act's

accessibility requirements. The Fair Housing Act identifies the ANSI Standard as providing design standards that would achieve compliance with the Act's accessibility requirements. Additionally, in the preamble to both the proposed and final Fair Housing rule, and in the text of § 100.205, the Department provided examples of how certain of the Act's accessibility requirements may be met. (See 53 FR 45004–45005, 54 FR 3249–3252 (24 CFR Ch. I, Subch. A, App. I, at 583–586 (1990)), 24 CFR 100.205.)

The delay in publication of the final Guidelines has resulted, in part, because of the Department's pledge, at the time of publication of the final Fair Housing regulations, that the public would be provided an opportunity to comment on the Guidelines (54 FR 3251, 24 CFR Ch. I, Subch. A, at 585–586 (1990)). The delay in publication of the final Guidelines also is attributable in part to the Department's effort to develop Guidelines that would (1) ensure that persons with disabilities are afforded the degree of accessibility provided for in the Fair Housing Act, and (2) avoid the imposition of unreasonable requirements on builders.

Comment. Two commenters requested that interim accessibility guidelines should be adopted for projects "caught in the middle", i.e. those projects started before publication of the final Guidelines.

Response. The preamble to the June 15, 1990 proposed guidelines and the August 1, 1990 supplementary notice directly addressed this issue. In both documents, the Department recognized that projects being designed in advance of publication of the Guidelines may not become available for occupancy until after March 13, 1991. The Department advised that efforts to comply with the Option One guidelines, in the design of projects that would be completed before issuance of the final Guidelines, would be considered as evidence of compliance with the Act in connection with the Department's investigation of any complaints. The August 1, 1990 supplementary notice restated the Department's position on compliance with the Act's requirements prior to publication of the final Guidelines, and addressed what "evidence of compliance" will mean in a complaint situation.

Conflict with Historic Preservation Design Codes

Comment. Two commenters expressed concern about a possible conflict between the Act's accessibility requirements and local historic preservation codes (including

compatible design requirements). The commenters stated that their particular concerns are: (1) The conversion of warehouse and commercial space to dwelling units; and (2) new housing construction on vacant lots in historically designated neighborhoods.

Response. Existing facilities that are converted to dwelling units are not subject to the Act's accessibility requirements. Additionally, alteration, rehabilitation or repair of covered multifamily dwellings are not subject to the Act's accessibility requirements. The Act's accessibility requirements only apply to new construction. With respect to new construction in neighborhoods subject to historic codes, the Department believes that the Act's accessibility requirements should not conflict with, or preclude building designs compatible with historic preservation codes.

Conflict with Local Accessibility Codes

Comment. Several commenters inquired about the appropriate course of action to follow when confronted with a conflict between the Act's accessibility requirements and local accessibility requirements.

Response. Section 100.205(i) of the Fair Housing regulations implements section 804(f)(8) of the Act, which provides that the Act's accessibility requirements do not supplant or replace State or local laws that impose higher accessibility standards (53 FR 45005). For accessibility standards, as for other code requirements, the governing principle to follow when Federal and State (or local) codes differ is that the more stringent requirement applies.

This principle is equally applicable when multifamily dwellings are subject to more than one Federal law requiring accessibility for persons with physical disabilities. For example, a multifamily dwelling may be subject both to the Fair Housing Amendments Act and to section 504 of the Rehabilitation Act of 1973. Section 504 requires that 5% of units in a covered multifamily dwelling be fully accessible—thus imposing a stricter accessibility standard for those units than would be imposed by the Fair Housing Act. However, compliance only with the section 504 requirements would not satisfy the requirements of the Fair Housing Act. The remaining units in the covered multifamily dwelling would be required to meet the specific accessibility requirements of the Fair Housing Act.

Comment. One commenter, the Seattle Department of Construction and Land Use, presented an example of how a local accessibility code that is more stringent with respect to some accessibility provisions may interact with the Act's accessibility requirements, where they are more stringent with respect to other provisions. The commenter pointed out that the State of Washington is very hilly, and that the State of Washington's accessibility code requires accessible buildings on sites that would be deemed impractical under the Option One guidelines. The commenter stated that the State of Washington's accessibility code may require installation of a ramp, and that the ramp may then create an accessible entrance for the ground floor, making it subject to the Act's accessibility requirements. The commenter asked that, since the project was not initially subject to the Act's requirements, whether the creation of an accessible ground floor in accordance with the State code provisions would require all units on the ground floor to be made accessible in accordance with the Fair Housing Act. (The State of Washington's accessibility code would require only a percentage of the units to be accessible.)

Response. The answer to the commenter's question is that a nonelevator building with an accessible entrance on an accessible route is required to have the ground floor units designed and constructed in compliance with the Act's accessibility requirements. This response is consistent with the principle that the stricter accessibility requirement applies.

Design Guidelines for Environmental Illness

Comment. Twenty-three (23) commenters advised the Department that many individuals are disabled because of severe allergic reactions to certain chemicals used in construction, and in construction materials. These commenters requested that the Department develop guidelines for constructing or renovating housing that are sensitive to the problems of individuals who suffer from these allergic reactions (commonly referred to as environmental illnesses). These commenters further advised that, as of February 1988, the Social Security Administration lists as a disability "Environmental Illness" (P.O.M.S. Manual No. 24515.065).

Response. The Guidelines developed by the Department are limited to providing guidance relating to the specific accessibility requirements of the Fair Housing Act. As discussed above, under the preamble heading "Bias Toward Wheelchair Users," the Act's requirements primarily are directed to

providing housing that is accessible to individuals with mobility impairments. There is no statutory authority for the Department to create the type of design and construction standards suggested by the commenters.

Design Guidelines for the Hearing and Visually-Impaired

Comment. Several commenters stated that the proposed guidelines failed to provide design features for people with hearing and visual impairments. These commenters stated that visual and auditory design features must be included in the final Guidelines.

Response. As noted in the response to the preceding comment, the Department is limited to providing Guidelines for the specific accessibility requirements of the Act. The Act does not require fully accessible individual dwelling units. For individual dwelling units, the Act requires the following: Doors sufficiently wide to allow passage by handicapped persons in wheelchairs; accessible route into and through the dwelling unit; light switches; electrical outlets, thermostats, and other environmental controls in accessible locations; reinforcements in bathroom walls to allow later installation of grab bars; and usable kitchens and bathrooms such that an individual in a wheelchair can maneuver about the space. To specify visual and auditory design features for individual dwelling units would be to recommend standards beyond those necessary for compliance with the Act. Such features were among those identified in Congressional statements discussing modifications that would be made by occupants.

The Act, however, requires public and common use portions of covered multifamily dwellings to be "readily accessible to and usable by handicapped persons." The more comprehensive accessibility requirement for public and common use areas of dwellings necessitates a more comprehensive accessibility standard for these areas. Accordingly, for public and common use areas, the final Guidelines recommend compliance with the appropriate provisions of the ANSI Standard. The ANSI Standard for public and common use areas specifies certain design features to accommodate people with hearing and visual impairments.

Guidelines as Minimum Requirements

Comment. A number of commenters requested that the Department categorize the final Guidelines as minimum requirements, and not as performance standards, because "recommended" guidelines are less effective in achieving the objectives of

the Act. Another commenter noted that a safe harbor provision becomes a *de facto* minimum requirement, and that it should therefore be referred to as a minimum requirement.

Response. The Department has not categorized the final Guidelines as either performance standards or minimum requirements. The minimum accessibility requirements are contained in the Act. The Guidelines adopted by the Department provide one way in which a builder or developer may achieve compliance with the Act's accessibility requirements. There are other ways to achieve compliance with the Act's accessibility requirements, as for example, full compliance with ANSI A117.1. Given this fact, it would be inappropriate on the part of the Department to constrain designers by presenting the Fair Housing Accessibility Guidelines as minimum requirements. Builders and developers should be free to use any reasonable design that obtains a result consistent with the Act's requirements. Accordingly, the design specifications presented in the final Guidelines are appropriately referred to as "recommended guidelines".

It is true, however, that compliance with the Fair Housing Accessibility Guidelines will provide builders with a safe harbor. Evidence of compliance with the Fair Housing Accessibility Guidelines adopted by this notice shall be a basis for a determination that there is no reasonable cause to believe that a discriminatory housing practice under section 804(f)(3) has occurred or is about to occur in connection with the investigation of complaints filed with the Department relating to covered multifamily dwellings.

National Accessibility Code

Comment. Several commenters stated that there are too many accessibility codes—ANSI, UFAS, and State and local accessibility codes. These commenters requested that the Department work with the individual States to arrive at one national uniform set of accessibility guidelines.

Response. There is no statutory authority to establish one nationally uniform set of accessibility standards. The Department is in agreement with the commenters' basic theme that increased uniformity in accessibility standards is desirable. In furtherance of this objective, the Department has relied upon the ANSI Standard as the design basis for the Fair Housing Accessibility Guidelines. The Department notes that the ANSI Standard also serves as the design basis for the Uniform Federal

Federal Register / Vol. 56, No. 44 / Wednesday, March 6, 1991 / Rules and Regulations   **9479**

Accessibility Standards (UFAS), the Minimum Guidelines and Requirements for Accessible Design (MGRAD) issued by the U.S. Architectural and Transportation Barriers Compliance Board, and many State and local government accessibility codes.

One Set of Design Standards

Comment. A number of commenters objected to the fact that the proposed guidelines included more than one set of design standards. The commenters stated that the final Guidelines should present only one set of design standards so as not to weaken the Act's accessibility requirements.

Response. The inclusion of options for accessibility design in the proposed guidelines was both to encourage a maximum range of public comment, and to illustrate that there may be several ways to achieve compliance with the Act's accessibility requirements. Congress made clear that compliance with the Act's accessibility standards did not require adherence to a single set of design specifications. In section 804(f)(4) of the Act, the Congress stated that compliance with the appropriate requirements of the ANSI Standard suffices to satisfy the accessibility requirements of the Act. In House Report No. 711, the Congress further stated as follows:

However, this section (section 804(f)(4)) is not intended to require that designers follow this standard exclusively, for there may be other local or State standards with which compliance is required or there may be other creative methods of meeting these standards. (House Report at 27)

Similarly, the Department's Guidelines are not the exclusive standard for compliance with the Act's accessibility requirements. Since the Department's Guidelines are a safe harbor, and not minimum requirements, builders and developers may follow alternative standards that achieve compliance with the Act's accessibility requirements. This policy is consistent with the intent of Congress, which was to encourage creativity and flexibility in meeting the requirements of the Act.

Reliance on Preamble to Guidelines

Comment. One commenter asked whether the explanatory information in the background section of the final Guidelines may be relied upon, and deemed to have the same force and effect as the Guidelines themselves.

Response. The Fair Housing Accessibility Guidelines are—as the name indicates—only guidelines, not regulations or minimum requirements. The Guidelines consist of recommended design specifications for compliance

with the specific accessibility requirements of the Fair Housing Act. The final Guidelines provide builders with a safe harbor that, short of specifying all of the provisions of the ANSI Standard, illustrate acceptable methods of compliance with the Act. To the extent that the preamble to the Guidelines provide clarification on certain provisions of the Guidelines, or illustrates additional acceptable methods of compliance with the Act's requirements, the preamble may be relied upon as additional guidance. As noted in the "Summary" portion of this document, the preamble to the Guidelines will be codified in the 1991 edition of the Code of Federal Regulations as Appendix III to the Fair Housing regulations (24 CFR Ch. I, Subch. A, App. III.).

"User Friendly" Guidelines

Comment. A number of commenters criticized the proposed guidelines for being too complicated, too ambiguous, and for requiring reference to a number of different sources. These commenters requested that the final Guidelines be clear, concise and "user friendly". One commenter requested that the final Guidelines use terms that conform to terms used by each of the three major building code organizations: the Building Officials and Code Administrators International, Inc. (BOCA); the International Conference of Building Officials (ICBO), and the Southern Building Code Congress International (SBCCI).

Response. The Department recognizes that the Accessibility Guidelines include several highly technical provisions. In drafting the final Guidelines, the Department has made every effort to explain these provisions as clearly as possible, to use technical and building terms consistent with the terms used by the major building code organizations, to define terms clearly, and to provide additional explanatory information on certain of the provisions of the Guidelines.

2. Section-by-Section Analysis of Final Guidelines

The following presents a section-by-section analysis of the final Guidelines. The text of the final Guidelines is organized into five sections. The first four sections of the Guidelines provide background and explanatory information on the Guidelines. Section 1, the Introduction, describes the purpose, scope and organization of the Guidelines. Section 2 defines relevant terms used. Section 3 reprints the text of 24 CFR 100.205, which implements the Fair Housing Act's accessibility

requirements, and Section 4 describes the application of the Guidelines. Section 5, the final section, presents the design specifications recommended by the Department for meeting the Act's accessibility requirements, as codified in 24 CFR 100.205. Section 5 is subdivided into seven areas, to address each of the seven areas of accessible design required by the Act.

The following section-by-section analysis discusses the comments received on each of the sections of the proposed Option One Guidelines, and the Department's response to these comments. Where no discussion of comments is provided under a section heading, no comments were received on this section.

Section 1. Introduction

Section 1, the Introduction, describes the purpose, scope and organization of the Fair Housing Accessibility Guidelines. This section also clarifies that the accessibility guidelines apply only to the design and construction requirements of 24 CFR 100.205, and do not relieve persons participating in a federal or federally-assisted program or activity from other requirements, such as those required by section 504 of the Rehabilitation Act of 1973 (29 U.S.C. 794), or the Architectural Barriers Act of 1968 (42 U.S.C. 4151–4157). (The design provisions for those laws are found at 24 CFR Part 8 and 24 CFR Part 40, respectively.) Additionally, section 1 explains that only those sections of the ANSI Standard cited in the Guidelines are required for compliance with the accessibility requirements of the Fair Housing Act. Revisions to section 1 reflect the Department's response to the request of several commenters for further clarification on the purpose and scope of the Guidelines.

Section 2. Definitions

This section incorporates appropriate definitions from § 100.201 of the Department's Fair Housing regulations, and provides additional definitions for terms used in the Guidelines. A number of comments were received on the definitions. Clarifications were made to certain definitions, and additional terms were defined. New terms defined in the final Guidelines include: *adaptable, assistive device, ground floor, loft, multistory dwelling unit, single-story dwelling unit,* and *story.* The inclusion of new definitions reflects the comments received, and also reflects new terms introduced by changes to certain of the Option One design specifications. In several instances, the clarifications of existing definitions, or the new terms

9480   Federal Register / Vol. 56, No. 44 / Wednesday, March 6, 1991 / Rules and Regulations

defined, were derived from definitions
of certain terms used by one or more of
the major building code organizations.
Comments on specific definitions are
discussed either below or in that portion
of the preamble under the particular
section heading of the Guidelines in
which these terms appear.

Accessible

Comment. A number of commenters
stated that the Department used the
terms "accessible" and "adaptable"
interchangeably, and requested
clarification of the meaning of each. The
commenters noted that, under several
State building codes, these terms denote
different standards for compliance. The
commenters requested that if the
Department intends these two terms to
have the same meaning, this should be
clearly stated in the final Guidelines,
and, if the terms have different
meanings, "adaptable" should also be
defined.

Response. The Department's use of
the terms "adaptable" and "accessible"
in the preamble to the proposed
guidelines generally reflected Congress'
use of the terms in the text of the Act,
and in the House and Senate conference
reports. However, to respond to
commenters' concerns about the
distinctions between these terms, the
Department has included a definition of
"adaptable dwelling units" to clarify the
meaning of this term, within the context
of the Fair Housing Act. In the final
Guidelines, "adaptable dwelling units",
when used with respect to covered
multifamily dwellings, means dwelling
units that include features of adaptable
design specified in 24 CFR 100.205(c)
(2)–(3).

The Fair Housing Act refers to design
features that include both the minimal
"accessibility" features required to be
built into the unit, and the "adaptable"
feature of reinforcement for bathroom
walls for the future installation of grab
bars. Accordingly, under the Fair
Housing Act, an "adaptable dwelling
unit" is one that meets the minimal
accessibility requirements specified in
the Act (i.e., usable doors, an accessible
route, accessible environmental
controls, and usable kitchens and
bathrooms) and the "adaptable"
structural feature of reinforced
bathroom walls for later installation of
grab bars.

Assistive Device

Comment. Several commenters
requested that we define the phrase
"assistive device."

Response. "Assistive device" means
an aid, tool, or instrument used by a
person with disabilities to assist in

activities of daily living. Examples of
assistive devices include tongs, knob
turners, and oven rack pusher/pullers. A
definition for "assistive device" has
been included in the final Guidelines.

Bathroom

In response to the concern of several
commenters, the Department has
revised the definition of "bathroom" in
the final Guidelines to clarify that a
bathroom includes a "compartmented"
bathroom. A compartmented bathroom
is one in which the bathroom fixtures
are distributed among interconnected
rooms. The fact that bathroom facilities
may be located in interconnecting rooms
does not exempt this type of bathroom
from the Act's accessibility
requirements. This clarification, and
minor editorial changes, were the only
revisions made to the definition of
"bathroom". Other comments on this
term were as follows:

Comment. Several commenters
requested that the Department
reconsider its definition of "bathroom",
to include powder rooms, i.e., rooms
with only a toilet and sink. These
commenters stated that persons with
disabilities should have access to all
bathrooms in their homes, not only full
bathrooms. One commenter believed
that, unless bathroom was redefined to
include single- or two-fixture facilities,
some developers will remove a bathtub
or shower from a proposed second full
bathroom to avoid having to make the
second bathroom accessible. The
commenter suggested that bathroom be
redefined to include any room
containing at least two of the possible
bathroom fixtures (toilet, sink, bathtub
or shower).

Response. In defining "bathroom" to
include a water closet (toilet), lavatory
(sink), and bathtub or shower, the
Department has followed standard
dictionary usage, as well as
Congressional intent. Congressional
statements emphasized that the Act's
accessibility requirements were
expected to have a minimal effect on the
size and design of dwelling units. In a
full-size bathroom, this can be achieved.
To specify space for wheelchair
maneuvering in a powder room would,
in most cases, require enlarging the
room significantly. However, a powder
room would be subject to the Act's
accessibility requirements if the powder
room is the only toilet facility on the
accessible level of a covered multistory
dwelling unit. Additionally, it should be
noted that doors to powder rooms
(regardless of the location of the powder
room), like all doors within dwelling
units, are required by the Act to be wide
enough for wheelchair passage. Some

powder rooms may, in fact, be usable by
persons in wheelchairs.

Comment. One commenter requested
that the final Guidelines provide that a
three-quarters bathroom (water closet,
lavatory and shower) would not be
subject to the accessibility
requirements—specifically, the
requirement for grab bar reinforcement.

Response. The Fair Housing Act
requires reinforcements in bathroom
walls to allow for later installation of
grab bars at toilet, bathtub or shower, if
provided. Accordingly, the Fair Housing
regulations specifically require
reinforcement in bathroom walls to
allow later installation of grab bars
around the shower, where showers are
provided. (See 24 CFR 100.205(c)(3)(iii).)

Building

Comment. One commenter suggested
that the Department use the term
"structure" in lieu of "building". The
commenter stated that, in the building
industry, "building" is defined by
exterior walls and fire walls, and that an
apartment structure of four units could
be subdivided into two separate
buildings of two units each by
inexpensive construction of a firewall.
The commenter suggested that the final
definition of "building" include the
following language: "For the purpose of
the Act, firewall separation does not
define buildings."

Response. The term "building" is the
term used in the Fair Housing Act. The
Department uses this term in the
Guidelines to be consistent with the Act.
With respect to the comment on firewall
separation, the Department believes
that, within the context of the Fair
Housing Act, the more appropriate place
for the language on firewall separation
is in the definition of "covered
multifamily dwellings". Since many
building codes in fact define "building"
by exterior walls and firewalls, a
definition of "building" in the Fair
Housing Accessibility Guidelines that
explicitly excludes firewalls as a means
of identifying a building would place the
Guidelines in conflict with local building
codes. Accordingly, to avoid this
conflict, the Department has clarified
the definition of "covered multifamily
dwelling" (which is discussed below) to
address the issue of firewall separation.

Covered Multifamily Dwellings

The Department has revised the
definition of "covered multifamily
dwellings" to clarify that dwelling units
within a single structure separated by
firewalls do not, for purposes of these
Guidelines, constitute separate
buildings.

Federal Register / Vol. 56, No. 44 / Wednesday, March 6, 1991 / Rules and Regulations **9481**

A number of questions and comments were received on what should, or should not, be considered a covered multifamily dwelling. Several of these comments requested clarification concerning "ground floor dwelling units". These comments generally concluded with a request that the Department define "ground floor" and "ground floor unit". The Department has included a definition of "ground floor" in the final Guidelines. The Department believes that this definition is sufficiently clear to identify ground floor units, and that therefore a separate definition for "ground floor unit" is unnecessary. Specific questions concerning ground floor units are discussed below under the heading "Ground Floor". Comments on other covered multifamily dwellings are as follows:

Comment. (Garden apartments) One commenter requested that the Department clarify whether single family attached dwelling units with all living space on one level (i.e. garden units) fall within the definition of covered multifamily dwellings.

Response. The Fair Housing Act and its regulations clearly define "covered multifamily dwellings" as buildings consisting of four or more dwelling units, if such buildings have one or more elevators, and ground floor dwelling units in other buildings consisting of four or more dwelling units. Garden apartments located in an elevator building of four or more units are subject to the Act's requirements. If the garden apartment is on the ground floor of a nonelevator building consisting of four or more apartments, and if all living space is on one level, then the apartment is subject to the Act's requirements (unless the building is exempt on the basis of site impracticality).

Comment. (Townhouses) Several commenters requested clarification concerning whether townhouses are covered multifamily dwellings.

Response. In the preamble to the Fair Housing regulations, the Department addressed this issue. Using an example of a single structure consisting of five two-story townhouses, the Department stated that such a structure is *not* a covered multifamily dwelling if the building does not have an elevator, because the entire dwelling unit is not on the ground floor. Thus, the first floor of a two-story townhouse in the example is not a ground floor unit, because the entire unit is not on the ground floor. In contrast, a structure consisting of five single-story townhouses would be a covered multifamily dwelling. (See 54 FR 3244; 24

CFR Ch. I, Subch. A, App. I at 575–576 (1990).)

Comment. (Units with basements) One commenter asked whether a unit that contains a basement, which provides additional living space, would be viewed as a townhouse, and therefore exempt from the Act's accessibility requirements. The commenter stated that basements are generally designed with the top of the basement, including the basement entrance, above finished grade, and that basement space cannot be made accessible without installation of an elevator or a lengthy ramp.

Response. If the basement is part of the finished living space of a dwelling unit, then the dwelling unit will be treated as a multistory unit, and application of the Act's accessibility requirements will be determined as provided in the Guidelines for Requirement 4. If the basement space is unfinished, then it would not be considered part of the living space of the unit, and the basement would not be subject to the Act's requirements. Attic space would be treated in the same manner.

Dwelling Unit

"Dwelling unit" is defined as a single unit of residence for a household of one or more persons. The definition provides a list of examples of dwelling units in order to clarify the types of units that may be covered by the Fair Housing Act. The examples include condominiums and apartment units in apartment buildings. Several commenters submitted questions on condominiums, and one commenter requested clarification on whether vacation time-sharing units are subject to the Act's requirements. Their specific comments are as follows:

Comment. (Condominiums) A few commenters requested that condominiums be excluded from covered dwelling units because condominiums are comparable to single family homes. The commenter stated that condominiums do not compete in the rental market, but compete in the sale market with single family homes, which are exempt from the Act's requirements.

Response. The Fair Housing Act requires all covered multifamily dwellings for first occupancy after March 13, 1991 to be designed and constructed in accordance with the Act's accessibility requirements. The Act does not distinguish between dwelling units in covered multifamily dwellings that are for sale, and dwelling units that are for rent. Condominium units in covered multifamily dwellings

must comply with the Act's accessibility requirements.

Comment. (Custom-designed condominium units) Two commenters stated that purchasers of condominium units often request their units to be custom designed. The commenters questioned whether custom-designed units must comply with the Act's accessibility requirements. Another commenter stated that the Department should exempt from compliance those condominium units which are pre-sold, but not yet constructed, and for which owners have expressly requested designs that are incompatible with the Act's accessibility requirements.

Response. The fact that a condominium unit is sold before the completion of construction does not exempt a developer from compliance with the Act's accessibility requirements. The Act imposes affirmative duties on builders and developers to design and construct covered multifamily dwellings for first occupancy after March 13, 1991 in accordance with the Act's accessibility requirements. These requirements are mandatory for covered multifamily dwellings for first occupancy after March 13, 1991, regardless of the ownership status of covered individual dwelling units. Thus, to the extent that the pre-sale *or* post-sale construction included features that are covered by the Act (such as framing for doors in pre-sale "shell" construction), they should be built accordingly.

Comment. (Vacation timeshare units) One commenter questioned whether vacation timeshare units were subject to the Act's requirements. The commenter stated that a timeshare unit may be owned by 2 to 51 individuals, each of whom owns, or has the right to use, the unit for a proportionate period of time equal to his or her ownership.

Response. Vacation timeshare units are subject to the Act's accessibility requirements, when the units are otherwise subject to the accessibility requirements. "Dwelling" is defined in 24 CFR 100.20 as "any building, structure, or portion thereof which is occupied as, or designed or intended for occupancy as, a residence by one or more families, and any vacant land which is offered for sale or lease for the construction or location thereon of any such building, structure or portion thereof". The preamble to the final Fair Housing rule states that the definition of "dwelling" is "broad enough to cover each of the types of dwellings enumerated in the proposed rule: mobile home parks, trailer courts, condominiums, cooperatives, *and time-*

9482 Federal Register / Vol. 56, No. 44 / Wednesday, March 6, 1991 / Rules and Regulations

sharing properties." (Emphasis added.) (See 54 FR 3238, 24 CFR Ch. I, Subch. A, App. I, at 567 (1990).) Accordingly, the fact of vacation timeshare ownership of units in a building does not affect whether the structure is subject to the Act's accessibility requirements.

Entrance

Comment. One commenter requested clarification on whether "entrance" refers to an entry door to a dwelling unit, or an entry door to the building.

Response. As used in the Guidelines, "entrance" refers to an exerior entry door. The definition of "entrance" has been revised in the final Guidelines to clarify this point, and the term "entry" is used instead of "entrance" when referring to the entry into a unit when it is interior to the building.

Ground Floor

As noted above, under the discussion of covered multifamily dwellings, several commenters requested clarification concerning "ground floor" and "ground floor dwelling unit". In response to these comments, the Department has included a definition for "ground floor" in the final Guidelines. The Department has incorporated the definition of "ground floor" found in the Fair Housing regulations (24 CFR 100.201), and has expanded this definition to address specific concerns related to implementation of the Guidelines. In the final Guidelines, "ground floor" is defined as follows:

"Ground floor" means a floor of a building with a building entrance on an accessible route. A building may have one or more ground floors. Where the first floor containing dwelling units in a building is above grade, all units on that floor must be served by a building entrance on an accessible route. This floor will be considered to be a ground floor.

Specific comments concerning ground floor units are as follows:

Comment. (Nonresidential ground floor units) Two commenters advised that, in many urban areas, buildings are constructed without an elevator and with no dwelling units on the ground floor. The ground floor contains either parking, retail shops, restaurants or offices. To bring these buildings into compliance with the Act, one of the commenters recommended that the Department adopt a proposal under consideration by the International Conference of Building Officials (ICBO). The commenter stated that the proposal provides that, in buildings with ground floors occupied by parking and other nonresidential uses, the lowest story containing residential units is considered the ground floor. Another commenter recommended that a

building should be exempt from compliance with the Act's requirements if the ground floor is occupied by a non-residential use (including parking). The commenter stated that if an elevator is to be provided to serve the upper residential floors, then the elevator should also serve the ground floor, and access be provided to all the dwelling units.

Response. The Department believes that the definition of "ground floor unit" incorporated in the final Guidelines addresses the concerns of the commenters.

Comment. (More than one ground floor) One commenter requested guidance on treatment of nonelevator garden apartments (i.e., apartment buildings that generally are built on slopes and contain two stories in the front of the building and three stories in the back). The commenter stated that these buildings arguably may be said to have two ground floors. The commenter requested that the Department clarify that, if a building has more than one ground floor, the developer must make one ground floor accessible—but not both—and the developer may choose which floor to make accessible. Another commenter suggested that, in a garden-type apartment building, the floor served by the primary entrance, and which is located at the parking lot level, is the floor which must be made accessible.

Response. In the preamble to the final Fair Housing rule, the Department addressed the issue of buildings with more than one ground floor. (See 54 3244, 24 CFR Ch. I, Subch. A, App. I at 576 (1990).) The Department stated that if a covered building has more than one floor with a building entrance on an accessible route, then the units on each floor with an accessible building entrance must satisfy the Act's accessibility requirements. (See the discussion of townhouses in nonelevator buildings above.)

Handicap

Comment. Several commenters requested that the Department avoid use of the terms "handicap" and "handicapped persons", and replace them with the terms "disability" and "persons with disabilities".

Response. "Handicap" and "handicapped persons" are the terms used by the Fair Housing Act. These terms are used in Guidelines and regulations to be consistent with the statute.

Principle of Reasonableness and Cost

Comment. Four commenters noted that, in the preamble to the proposed guidelines, the Department indicated

that the Fair Housing Accessibility Guidelines were limited by a "principle of reasonableness and cost". The commenters requested that the Department define this phrase.

Response. In the preamble to the proposed guidelines, the Department stated in relevant part as follows: "These guidelines are intended to provide a safe harbor for compliance with respect to those issues they cover. * * * Where the ANSI Standard is not applicable, the language of the statute itself is the safest guide. The degree of scoping, accessibility, and the like are of course limited by a principle of reasonableness and cost." (55 FR 24371)

In House Report No. 711, the accessibility requirements of the Fair Housing Act were referred to by the Congress as "modest" (House Report at 25), "minimal" and "basic features of adaptability" (House Report at 25). In developing the Fair Housing Accessibility Guidelines, the Department was attentive to the fact that Congress viewed the Act's accessibility requirements as reasonable, and that the Guidelines for these requirements should conform to this "reasonableness" principle—that is, that the Guidelines should provide the level of reasonable accessibility envisioned by Congress, while maintaining the affordability of new multifamily construction. The Department believes that the final Guidelines conform to this principle of reasonableness and cost.

Slope

Comment. One commenter, the Building Officials & Code Administrators International, Inc. (BOCA), requested clarification of the term, "slope". The commenter stated the definition indicates that slope is calculated based on the distance and elevation between two points. The commenter stated that this is adequate when there is a uniform and reasonably consistent change in elevation between point (i.e., one point is at the top of a hill and the other is at the bottom), but the definition does not adequately address land where a valley, gorge, or swale occurs between two points. The commenter stated that the definition also does not adequately address conditions where there is an abrupt change in the rate of slope between the points (i.e. a sharp drop off within a short distance, with the remaining distance being flat or sloped much more gradually).

Response. Slope is measured from ground level at the entrance to all arrival points within 50 feet, and is considered impractical only when it exceeds 10 percent between the entrance and all these points. Since multifamily dwellings typically have an arrival point fairly close to the building, a significant change such as a sharp drop would likely result in an impractical slope. Minor variations, such as a swale, if more than 5 percent, would be easily graded or ramped; a gorge would be bridged or filled, in any event, if it was on an entrance route.

Usable Door

Comment. One commenter stated that a clear definition of "usable door" is required.

Response. The Guidelines for Requirement 3 (usable doors) fully describe what is meant by "usable door" within the meaning of the Act.

Section 3. Fair Housing Act Design and Construction Requirements

This section reprints § 100.205 (Design and Construction Requirements) from the Department's final rule implementing the Fair Housing Act. A reprint of § 100.205 was included to provide easy reference to (1) the Act's accessibility requirements, as codified by § 100.205; and (2) the additional examples of methods of compliance with the Act's requirements that are presented in this regulation.

Section 4. Application of the Guidelines

This section states that the design specifications that comprise the final Guidelines apply to all "covered multifamily dwellings" as defined in Section 2 of the Guidelines. Section 4 also clarifies that the Guidelines, are "recommended" for designing dwellings that comply with the requirements of the Fair Housing Amendments Act of 1988.

Under the discussion of Section 4 in the proposed guidelines, the Department requested comment on the Act's application to dwelling units with design features such as a loft or sunken living room (55 FR 24377). A number of comments were received on this issue. Since the Act's application to units with such features is relevant within the context of an accessible route into and through the dwelling unit, the comments and the Department's response to these comments are discussed in section 5, under the subheading, "Guidelines for Requirement 4".

Section 5. Guidelines

The Guidelines contained in this Section 5 are organized to follow the sequence of requirements as they are presented in the Fair Housing Act and in the regulation implementing these requirements, 24 CFR 100.205. There are

Guidelines for seven requirements: (1) An accessible entrance on an accessible route; (2) accessible and usable public common use areas; (3) doors usable by a person in a wheelchair; (4) accessible route into and through the covered dwelling unit; (5) light switches, electrical outlets and environmental controls in accessible locations; (6) bathroom walls reinforced for grab bars; and (7) usable kitchens and bathrooms.

For each of these seven requirements, the Department adopted the corresponding Option One guidelines, but changes were made to certain of the Option One design specifications. The following discussion describes the Guidelines for each of the seven requirements, and highlights the changes that have been made.

Guidelines for Requirement 1

The Guidelines for Requirement 1 present guidance on designing an accessible entrance on an accessible route, as required by § 100.205(a), and on determining when an accessible entrance is impractical because of terrain or unusual characteristics of the site.

The Department has adopted the Option One guidelines for Requirement 1, with substantial changes to the specifications for determining site impracticality. These changes, and the guidelines that remain unchanged for Requirement 1 are discussed below.

Site Impracticality Determinations. The Guidelines for Requirement 1 begin by presenting criteria for determining when terrain or unusual site characteristics would make an accessible entrance impractical. Section 100.205(a) recognizes that certain sites may have characteristics that make it impractical to provide an accessible route to a multifamily dwelling. This section states that all covered multifamily dwellings shall be designed and constructed to have at least one building entrance on an accessible route unless it is impractical to do so because of the terrain or unusual characteristics of the site.

Comments. The Department received many comments on the site impracticality specifications presented in the proposed guidelines (55 FR 24377–24378). The majority of the members of the disability community who commented on this issue supported the Option One guidelines, and recommended no change. However, other commenters, including a few disability organizations, members of the building industry, State and local government agencies involved in the development and enforcement of accessibility codes, and some of the

major building code organizations, criticized one or more aspects of the Option One and Option Two guidelines for Requirement 1. Specific comments are noted below.

A few commenters suggested that the 10% slope criterion was too low, and easily will be met by a project site having a hilly terrain which could (and typically would) be made more level. These commenters recommended a higher slope criterion ranging anywhere from 12% to 30%. Other commenters stated that the slope criterion for the planned finished grade should not exceed 8.33%. The Congressional sponsors of the Act (U.S. Representatives Edwards, Fish, and Frank) stated that a limited exemption for slopes greater than 10% "was not contemplated by the Act"; but that they believed the Department has the discretion to develop such an exemption if it is "carefully crafted and narrowly tailored".

Several commenters stated that any evaluation of the undisturbed site should be done only on the percentage of land that is buildable. Several commenters stated that the final Guidelines should not require an evaluation of the undisturbed site between the planned entrance and the arrival points—that the only evaluation of the undisturbed site should be the initial threshold slope analysis.

There were a number of questions on arrival points, and requests that these points be more clearly defined. Several commenters presented specific examples of possible problems with the use of arrival points, as specified in the Option One guidelines. A few commenters stated that the individual building analysis should involve a measurement between the entrance and only one designated vehicular or pedestrian arrival point.

Other commenters stated that single buildings on a site should be subject to the same analysis as multiple buildings on a site.

A number of commenters criticized the Option One site impracticality analysis as being too cumbersome and confusing. A number of commenters objected to Option Two's requirement that covered multifamily dwellings with elevators must comply with the Act's accessibility requirements, regardless of site conditions or terrain.

Response. Following careful consideration of these comments, the Department has revised significantly the procedure for determining site impracticality, and its application to covered multifamily dwellings.

For covered multifamily dwellings with elevators, the final Guidelines would not exempt these dwellings from the Act's accessibility requirements. The final Guidelines provide that covered multifamily dwellings with elevators shall be designed and constructed to provide at least one accessible entrance on an accessible route regardless of terrain or unusual characteristics of the site. Every dwelling unit on a floor served by an elevator must be on an accessible route, and must be made accessible in accordance with the Act's requirements for covered dwelling units. The Department has excluded elevator buildings from any exemption from the Act's accessibility requirements because the Department believes that the type of site work that is performed in connection with the construction of a high rise elevator building generally results in a finished grade that would make the building accessible. The Department also notes that the majority of elevator buildings are designed with a primary building entrance and a passenger drop-off area which are easily made accessible to individuals with handicaps. Additionally, many elevator buildings have large, relatively level areas adjacent to the building entrances, which are normally provided for moving vans. These factors lead the Department to conclude that site impracticality considerations should not apply to multifamily elevator buildings.

For covered multifamily dwellings without elevators, the final Guidelines provide two alternative tests for determining site impracticality due to terrain. The first test is an individual building test which involves a two-step process: measurement of the slope of the undisturbed site between the planned entrance and all vehicular or pedestrian arrival points; and measurement of the slope of the planned finished grade between the entrance and all vehicular or pedestrian arrival points. The second test is a site analysis test which involves an analysis of the topography of the existing natural terrain.

A site with a single building, having a common entrance for all units, may be analyzed only under the first test—the individual building test.

All other sites, including a site with a single building having multiple entrances serving individual dwelling units or clusters of dwelling units, may be analyzed either under the first test or the second test. For these sites for which either test is applicable, the final Guidelines provide that regardless of which test is utilized by a builder or developer, at least 20% of the total ground floor units in nonelevator

buildings, on any site, must comply with the Act's accessibility requirements.

The distinctive features of the two tests for determining site impracticality due to terrain, for nonelevator multifamily dwellings, are as follows:

1. *The individual building test.*

a. This test is applicable to all sites.

b. This test eliminates the slope analysis of the entire undisturbed site that was applicable only to multiple building sites, and, concomitantly, the table that specifies the minimum percentage of adaptable units required for every multiple building site. The only analysis for site impracticality will be the individual building analysis. This analysis will be applied to each building regardless of the number of buildings on the site.

c. The individual building analysis has been modified to provide for measurement of the slopes between the planned entrance and all vehicular or pedestrian arrival points within 50 feet of the planned entrance. The analysis further provides that if there are no vehicular or pedestrian arrival points within 50 feet of the planned entrance, then measurement will be made of the slope between the planned entrance and the closest vehicular or pedestrian arrival point. Additionally, the final Guidelines clarify how to measure the slope between the planned entrance and an arrival point.

d. The individual building analysis retains the evaluation of both the undisturbed site and the planned finished grade. Buildings would be exempt only if the slopes of both the original undisturbed site and the planned finished grade exceed 10 percent (1) as measured between the planned entrance and all vehicular or pedestrian arrival points within 50 feet of the planned entrance; or (2) if there are no vehicular or pedestrian arrival points within that 50 foot area, as measured between the planned entrance and the closest vehicular or pedestrian arrival point.

2. *The site analysis test.*

a. This test is only applicable to sites with multiple buildings, or to sites with a single building with multiple entrances.

b. This test involves an analysis of the existing natural terrain (before grading) of the buildable area of the site by topographic survey with 2 foot contour intervals, with slope determination made between each successive contour interval. The accuracy of the slope analysis is to be certified by a professional licensed engineer, landscape architect, architect or surveyor.

c. This test provides that the minimum number of ground floor units to be made accessible on a site must equal the percentage of the total buildable area (excluding floodplains, wetlands, or other restricted use areas) of the undisturbed site that has an existing natural grade of less than 10% slope.

The Department believes that both tests for determining site impracticality due to terrain present enforceable criteria for determining when terrain makes accessibility, as required by the Act, impractical. The Department also believes that by offering a choice of tests, the Department is providing builders and developers with greater flexibility in selecting the approach that is most appropriate, or least burdensome, for their development project, while assuring that accessible units are provided on every site. As noted earlier in this preamble, this policy is consistent with the intent of Congress which was to encourage creativity and flexibility in meeting the Act's requirements, and thus minimize the impact of these requirements on housing affordability.

With respect to determining site impracticality due to unusual characteristics of the site, the test in the final Guidelines is essentially the same as that provided in the Option One guidelines. This test has been modified to limit measurement of the finished grade elevation to that between the entrance and all vehicular or pedestrian arrival points within 50 feet of the planned entrance.

Finally, the final Guidelines for Requirement 1 contemplate that the site tests recommended by the Guidelines will be performed, generally, on "normal" soil. The Department solicits additional public comment only on the issue of the feasibility of the site tests on areas that have difficult soil, such as areas where expansive clay or hard granite is prevalent.

Additional specific comments on the site impracticality determination are as follows:

Comment. One commenter stated that the site impracticality determination seems to suggest that only the most direct path from the pedestrian or vehicular arrival points be used to evaluate the ability to create an accessible route of travel to the building. The commenter stated that it may be possible to use natural or finished contours of the site to provide an accessible route other than a straight-line route.

Response. To be enforceable, the Guidelines must specify where the line is drawn; otherwise it is not possible to

Federal Register / Vol. 56, No. 44 / Wednesday, March 6, 1991 / Rules and Regulations   9485

specify what is "practical". Generally, developers provide relatively direct access from the entrance to the pedestrian and vehicular arrival points. If, in fact, the route as built was accessible, then the building would be expected to have an accessible entrance and otherwise comply with the Act.

Comment. Another commenter stated that the site impracticality determination does not take into account the many building types and unit arrangements. The commenter stated that some buildings have a common entrance with unit entrances off a common corridor, while others have individual, exterior entrances to the units. The commenter stated that if the Department is going to permit exemptions from the Act's requirements caused by terrain, the commenter did not understand why every entrance in a building containing individually-accessed apartments must comply with the Act's requirements, simply because they are in one building.

Response. The final Guidelines recognize (as did the proposed guidelines) the difference in building types. If there is a single entry point serving the entire building (or portions thereof), that entry point is considered the "entrance". If each unit has a separate exterior entrance, then each entrance is to be evaluated for the conditions at that entrance. Thus, a building with four entrances, each serving one of four units, might have only one accessible entrance, depending upon site conditions, or it might have any combination up to four.

Comment. Another commenter stated that the evaluation for unusual characteristics of the site only takes into account floodplains or high hazard coastal areas, and excludes other possible unique and unusual site characteristics.

Response. The provision for unusual characteristics of the site clearly provides that floodplains or high hazard coastal areas are only two examples of unusual site characteristics. The provision states that "unusual site characteristics" includes "sites subject to similar requirements of law or code."

Comment. A number of commenters expressed concern that the site impracticality determination of the Guidelines may conflict with local health, safety, environmental or zoning codes. A principal concern of one of the commenters was that the final Guidelines may require "massive grading" of a site in order to achieve compliance with the Act. The commenter was concerned that such grading may conflict with local laws directed at minimizing environmental

damage, or with zoning codes that severely limit substantial fill activities at a site.

Response. The Department believes that the site impracticality determination adopted in these final Guidelines will not conflict with local safety, health, environmental or zoning codes. The final Guidelines provide, as did the proposed guidelines, that the site planning involves consideration of all State and local requirements to which a site is subject, such as "density constraints, tree-save or wetlands ordinances and other factors impacting development choices" (55 FR 24378), and explicitly accept the site plan that results from balancing these and other factors affecting the development. The Guidelines would not require, for example, that a site be graded in violation of a tree-save ordinance. If, however, access is required based on the final site plan, then installation of a ramp for access, rather than grading, could be necessary in some cases so as not to disturb the trees. Where access is required, the method of providing access, whether grading or a ramp, will be decided by the developer, based on local ordinances and codes, and on business or aesthetic factors. It should be noted that these nonmandatory Guidelines do not purport to preempt conflicting State or local laws. However, where a State or local law contradicts a specification in the Guidelines, a builder must seek other reasonable cost-effective means, consistent with local law, to assure the accessibility of his or her units. The accessibility requirements of the Fair Housing Act remain applicable, and State and local laws must be in accord with those requirements.

Additional Design Specifications for Requirement 1. In addition to the site impracticality determinations, the final Guidelines for Requirement 1 specify that an accessible entrance on an accessible route is practical when (1) there is an elevator connecting the parking area with any floor on which dwelling units are located, and (2) an elevated walkway is planned between a building entrance and a vehicular or pedestrian arrival point, and the planned walkway has a slope no greater than 10 percent. The Guidelines also provide that (i) an accessible entrance that complies with ANSI 4.14, and (2) an accessible route that complies with ANSI 4.3, meets with the accessibility requirements of § 100.205(a). Finally, the Guidelines provide that if the slope of the finished grade between covered multifamily dwellings and a public or common use facility exceeds 8.33%, or where other physical barriers, or legal

restrictions, outside the control of the owner, prevent the installation of an accessible pedestrian route, an acceptable alternative is to provide access via a vehicular route. (These design specifications are unchanged from the proposed Option One guidelines for Requirement 1.)

Comment. Several comments were received on the additional design specifications for Requirement 1. The majority of commenters supported 8.33% as the slope criterion for the finished grade between covered multifamily dwellings and a public or common use facility. A few commenters stated that vehicular access was not an acceptable alternative to pedestrian access. Other commenters stated that the 10% slope criterion for the planned walkway was inconsistent with accessibility requirements that prohibit ramps from having a slope in excess of 8.33%.

Response. With respect to access via a vehicular route, the Department's expectation is that public and common use facilities generally will be on an accessible pedestrian route. The Department, however, recognizes that there may be situations in which an accessible pedestrian route simply is not practical, because of factors beyond the control of the owner. In those situations, vehicular access may be provided. With respect to the 10% slope criterion for planned elevated walkways, this is the criterion for determining whether it is practical to provide an accessible entrance. If the site is determined to be practical, then the slope of the walkway must be reduced to 8.33%.

Guidelines for Requirement 2

The Guidelines for Requirement 2 present design standards that will make public and common use areas readily accessible to and usable by handicapped persons, as required by § 100.205(c)(1).

The Department has adopted the Option One guidelines for Requirement 2, without change. The Guidelines for Requirement 2 identify components of public and common use areas that should be made accessible, reference the section or sections of the ANSI Standard which apply in each case, and describe the appropriate application of the design specifications. In some cases, the Guidelines for Requirement 2 describe variations from the basic ANSI provision that is referenced.

The basic components of public and common use areas covered by the Guidelines include, for example: accessible route(s); protruding objects; ground and floor surface treatments; parking and passenger loading zones;

curb ramps; ramps; stairs; elevator; platform lifts; drinking fountains and water coolers; toilet rooms and bathing facilities, including water closets, toilet rooms and stalls, urinals, lavatories and mirrors, bathtubs, shower stalls, and sinks; seating, tables or work surfaces; places of assembly; common-use spaces and facilities, including swimming pools, playgrounds, entrances, rental offices, lobbies, elevators, mailbox areas, lounges, halls and corridors and the like; and laundry rooms.

Specific comments on the Guidelines for Requirement 2 are as follows:

Comment. A number of comments were received on the various components listed in the Guidelines for Requirement 2, and the accessibility specifications for these components provided by both options One and Two. A few commenters, including the Granite State Independent Living Foundation, submitted detailed comments on the design standards for the listed components of public and common use areas, and, in many cases, recommended specifications different than those provided by either Option One or Option Two.

Response. Following careful consideration of the comments submitted on the design specifications of Requirement 2, the Department has decided not to adopt any of the commenters' proposals for change. The Department believes that application of the appropriate ANSI provisions to each of the basic components of public and common use areas, in the manner specified on the Option One chart, and with the limitations and modifications noted, remains the best approach to meeting the requirements of § 100.205(c)(1) for accessible and usable public and common use areas, both because Congress clearly intended that the ANSI Standard be used where appropriate, and because it is consistent with the Department's support for uniform standards to the greatest degree possible.

Comment. Other commenters requested that the ANSI provisions applicable to certain components in public and common use areas also should be applied to these components when they are part of individual dwelling units (for example, floor surface treatments, carpeting, and work surfaces).

Response. To require such application in individual dwelling units would exceed the requirements imposed by the Fair Housing Act. The Fair Housing Act does not require individual dwelling units to be fully accessible and usable by individuals with handicaps. For individual dwelling units, the Act limits

its requirements to specific features of accessible design.

Comment. A number of commenters indicated confusion concerning when the ANSI standard was applicable to stairs.

Response. Stairs are subject to the ANSI Standard only when they are located along an accessible route not served by an elevator. (Accessibility between the levels served by the stairs or steps would, under such circumstances, be provided by some other means such as a ramp or lift located with the stairs or steps.) For example, a ground floor entry might have three steps up to an elevator lobby, with a ramp located besides the steps. The steps in this case should meet the ANSI specification since they will be used by people with particular disabilities for whom steps are more usable than ramps.

In nonelevator buildings, stairs serving levels above or below the ground floor are not required to meet the ANSI standard, unless they are a part of an accessible route providing access to public or common use areas located on these levels. For example, mailboxes serving a covered multifamily dwelling in a nonelevator building might be located down three steps from the ground floor level, with a ramp located beside the steps. The steps in this case would be required to meet the ANSI specifications.

Comment. Other commenters indicated confusion concerning when handrails are required. A few commenters stated that the installation of handrails limits access to lawn areas.

Response. Handrails are required only on ramps that are on routes required to be accessible. Handrails are not required on any on-grade walks with slopes no greater than 5%. Only on those walks that exceed 5% slope, and that are parts of the required accessible route, would handrails be required. Accordingly, walks from one building containing dwelling units to another, would not be affected even if slopes exceeded 5%, because the Guidelines do not require such walks as part of the accessible route. The Department believes that the benefits provided to persons with mobility-impairments by the installation of handrails on required accessible routes outweigh any limitations on access to lawn areas.

Comment. A number of proposals for revisions were submitted on the final Guidelines for parking and passenger loading zones.

Response. The Department has not adopted any of these proposals. The Department has retained the applicable provisions of the ANSI Standard for

parking space. As noted previously in the preamble, the ANSI Standard is a familiar and widely accepted standard. The Department is reluctant to introduce a new or unfamiliar standard, or to specify parking specifications that exceed the minimal accessibility standards of the Act. However, if a local parking code requires greater accessibility features (e.g. wider aisles) with respect to parking and passenger loading zones, the appropriate provisions of the local code would prevail.

Comment. A number of commenters requested that the final Guidelines for parking specify minimum vertical clearance for garage parking. other commenters suggested that the Department adopt ANSI's vertical height requirement at passenger loading zones as the minimal vertical clearance for garage parking.

Response. No national accessibility standards, including UFAS, require particular vertical clearances in parking garages. The Department did not consider it appropriate to exceed commonly accepted standards by including a minimum vertical clearance in the Fair Housing Accessibility Guidelines, in view of the minimal accessibility requirements of the Fair Housing Act.

Comment. Two commenters stated that parking spaces for condominiums is problematic because the parking spaces are typically deeded in ownership to the unit owner at the time of purchase, and it becomes extremely difficult to arrange for the subsequent provision of accessible parking. one of the commenters recommended that the Guidelines specify that a condominium development have two percent accessible visitor parking, and that these visitor accessible spaces be reassigned to residents with disabilities as needed.

Response. Condominiums subject to the requirements of the Act must provide accessible spaces for two percent of covered units. One approach to the particular situation presented by the commenters would be for condominium documents to include a provision that accessible spaces may be reassigned to residents with disabilities, in exchange for nonaccessible spaces that were initially assigned to units that were later purchased by persons with disabilities.

Comment. Several commenters stated that Option One's requirement of "sufficient accessible facilities" of each type of recreational facility is too vague. The commenters preferred option Two's guidelines on recreational facilities.

Federal Register / Vol. 56, No. 44 / Wednesday, March 6, 1991 / Rules and Regulations 9487

which provides that a minimum of 25% (or at least one of each type) of recreational facilities must be accessible.

Response. The Department decided to retain its more flexible approach to recreational facilities. The final Guidelines specify that where multiple recreational facilities are provided, accessibility is met under § 100.205(c)(1) if sufficient accessible facilities of each type are provided.

Comment. Several commenters suggested that all recreational facilities should be made accessible.

Response. To specify that all recreational facilities should be accessible would exceed the requirements of the Act. Congress stated that the Act did not require every feature and aspect of covered multifamily housing to be made accessible to individuals with handicaps. (See House Report at 26.)

Comment. Several commenters submitted detailed specifications on how various recreational facilities could be made accessible. These comments were submitted in response to the Department's request, in the proposed guidelines, for more specific guidance on making recreational facilities accessible to persons with handicaps (55 FR 24376). The Department specifically requested information about ways to provide access into pools.

Response. The Department appreciates all suggestions on recommended specifications for recreational facilities, and, in particular, for swimming pools. For the present, the Department has decided not to change the specifications for recreational facilities, including swimming pools, as provided by the Option One guidelines, since there are no generally accepted standards covering such facilities. Thus, access to the pool area of a swimming facility is expected, but not specialized features for access into the pool (e.g., hoists, or ramps into the water).

Comment. Several commenters criticized the chart in the Option One guidelines, stating that it was confusing and difficult to follow.

Response. The chart is adapted from ANSI's Table 2 pertaining to basic components for accessible sites, facilities and buildings. The ANSI chart is familiar to persons in the building industry. Accordingly, the Option One chart (and now part of the final Guidelines), which is a more limited version of ANSI's Table 2, is not a novel approach.

Guidelines for Requirement 3

The Guidelines for Requirement 3 present design standards for providing

doors that will be sufficiently wide to allow passage into and within all premises by handicapped persons in wheelchairs (usable doors) as required by § 100.20(c)(2).

The Department has adopted the Option One guidelines for Requirement 3 with minor editorial changes. No changes were made to the design specifications for "usable doors".

The Guidelines provide separate guidance for (1) doors that are part of an accessible route in the public and common use areas of multifamily dwellings, including entry doors to individual dwelling units; and (2) doors within individual dwelling units.

(1) For public and common use areas and entry doors to dwelling units, doors that comply with ANSI 4.13 would meet the requirements of § 100.205(c)(2).

(2) For doors within individual dwelling units, the Department has retained, in the final Guidelines, the design specification that a door with a clear opening of at least 32 inches nominal width when the door is open 90 degrees, as measured between the face of the door and the stop, would meet the requirements of § 100.205(c)(2).

Specific comments on the design specifications presented in the Guidelines for Requirement 3 are as follows:

Minimum Clear Opening

Comment. The issue of minimum clear opening for doors was one of the most widely commented-upon design features of the guidelines. The majority of commenters representing the disability community supported the Option One specification of a minimum clear opening of 32 inches. A few commenters advocated a wider clear opening. U.S. Representatives Edwards, Frank, and Fish expressed their support for the Option One specification on minimum clearance which is consistent with the ANSI Standard.

Commenters from the building industry were almost unanimous in their opposition to a minimum clear opening of 32 inches. Several builders noted that a 32-inch clear opening requires use of 36-inch doors. These commenters stated that a standard 2'10" door (34") provides only a 31¾ inch clear opening. The commenters therefore recommended amending the Guidelines to permit a "nominal" 32 inch clear space, allowing the use of a 2'10" door, which provides a 31¾ inch clear opening. Other commenters stated that, generally, door width should provide a 32-inch clear opening, but that this width can be reduced if sufficient maneuvering space is provided at the door. These commenters supported Option Two's

approach, which provided for clear width to be determined by the clear floor space available for maneuvering on both sides of the door, with the minimum width set at 29¼ inches. (See Option 2 chart and accompanying text at 55 FR 24382.)

Response. The Department considered the recommendations for both wider clear openings, and more narrow clear openings, and decided to maintain the design specification proposed in the Option One guidelines (a clear opening of at least 32 inches nominal width). The clear opening of at least 32 inches nominal width has been the accepted standard for accessibility since the issuance of the original ANSI Standard in 1961. While the Department recognizes that it may be possible to maneuver most wheelchairs through a doorway with a slightly more narrow opening, such doors do not permit ready access on the constant-use basis that is the reality of daily living within a home environment. The Department also recognizes that wider doorways may ensure easier passage for wheelchair users. However, by assuring that the minimum 36-inch hallway and 32-inch clear openings are provided, the Department believes that its recommended opening for doors should accommodate most people with disabilities. In the preamble to the proposed guidelines, the Department stated that the clear width provided by a standard 34-inch door would be acceptable under the Guidelines.

Maneuvering Space at Doors

Comment. Several commenters requested that the final Guidelines incorporate minimum maneuvering clearances at doors, as provided by the ANSI Standard. These commenters stated that maneuvering space on the latch side of the door is as important a feature as minimum door width. Other commenters stated that the maneuvering space was necessary to ensure safe egress in cases of emergency.

Response. The Department has carefully considered these comments, and has declined to adopt this approach. The Department believes that, by adhering to the standard 32-inch clear opening, it is possible to forego other accessibility requirements related to doors (e.g. door closing forces, maneuvering clearances, and hardware) without compromising the Congressional directive requiring doors to be "sufficiently wide to allow passage by handicapped persons in wheelchairs." However, as the Department noted in the preamble to the proposed guidelines, approaches to, and maneuvering spaces at, the exterior side of the entrance door to an individual dwelling unit would be considered part of the public spaces, and therefore would be subject to the appropriate ANSI provisions. (See 55 FR 24380.)

Doors in a Series

Comment. A few commenters expressed concern that the Guidelines did not provide design specification for an entrance that consists of a series of more than one door. The commenters were concerned that, without adequate guidance, a disabled resident or tenant could be trapped between doors.

Response. Doors in a series are not typically part of an individual dwelling unit. Doors in a series generally are used in the entries to buildings, and are therefore part of public spaces. Section 4.13 of the ANSI Standard, which is applicable to doors in public and common use areas, provides design specifications for doors in a series. However, where doors in a series *are* provided as part of a dwelling unit, the Department notes that the requirements of an accessible route into and through the dwelling unit would apply.

Door Hardware

Comment. A few commenters requested that lever hardware be required on doors throughout dwelling units, not only at the entry door to the dwelling unit.

Response. For doors within individual dwelling units, the Fair Housing Act only requires that the doors be sufficiently wide to allow passage by handicapped persons in wheelchairs. Lever hardware is required for entry doors to the building and to individual dwelling units because these doors are part of the public and common use areas, and are, therefore, subject to the ANSI provisions for public and common use areas, which specify lever hardware. Installing lever hardware on doors is the type of adaptation that individual residents can make easily. The ANSI standard also recognizes this point. Under the ANSI Standard, only the entry door into an accessible dwelling unit is required to comply with the requirements for door hardware. (See ANSI section 4.13.9.)

Multiple Usable Entrances

Comment. Several commenters noted that the Guidelines do not provide more than one accessible entrance/exit, and that without a second means of egress, wheelchair users may find themselves in danger in an emergency situation.

Response. As stated previously, the Department is limited to providing Guidelines that are consistent with the accessibility requirements of the Act. The Act requires "an accessible entrance", rather than requiring all entrances to be accessible. However, the requirements for usable doors and an accessible route to exterior spaces such as balconies and decks does respond to this concern.

Guidelines for Requirement 4

The Guidelines for Requirement 4 present design specifications for providing an accessible route into and through the covered dwelling unit, as required by § 100.205(c)(3)(i).

The Department has adopted the Option One guidelines for Requirement 4 with the following changes:

First, the Department has eliminated the specification for maneuvering space if a person in a wheelchair must make a T-turn.

Second, the Department has eliminated the specification for a minimum clear headroom of 80 inches.

Third, and most significantly, the Department has revised the design specifications for "changes in level" within a dwelling unit to include separate design specifications for: (a) single-story dwelling units, including single-story dwelling units with design features such as a loft or a sunken living room; and (b) multistory dwelling units in buildings with elevators.

Fourth, the Department has revised the specifications for changes in level at exterior patios, decks or balconies in certain circumstances, to minimize water damage. For the same reason, the final Guidelines also include separate specifications for changes in level at the primary entry doors of dwelling units in certain circumstances.

Specific comments on the Guidelines for Requirement 4, and the rationale for the changes made, are discussed below.

Minimum Clear Corridor Width

A few commenters from the disability community advocated a minimum clear corridor width of 48 inches. However, the majority of commenters on this issue had no objection to the minimum clear corridor width of 36 inches. The 36-inch minimum clear corridor width, which has been retained, is consistent with the ANSI Standard.

T-turn Maneuvering Space

Comment. Several commenters stated that this design specification was unclear in two respects. First, they stated that it was unclear when it is necessary for a designer to provide space for a T-turn. The commenters stated that it was difficult to envision circumstances where a wheelchair could be pulled into a position traveling forward and then not be capable of backing out. Second, the commenters stated that the two descriptions of the T-turn provided by the Department were contradictory. The commenters stated that the preamble to the proposed guidelines provided one description of the T-turn (55 FR 24380), while Figure 2 of the guideline 4 (55 FR 24392), presented a different description of the T-turn.

Response. The Department has decided to delete the reference to the T-turn dimensions in the Guidelines for Requirement 4. The Guidelines adequately address the accessible route into and through the dwelling unit by the minimum corridor width and door width specifications, given typical apartment layouts. Should a designer find that a unique layout in a particular unit made a T-turn necessary for a wheelchair user, the specifications provided in the ANSI Standard sections referenced for public and common use areas could be used.

Minimum Clear Headroom

Comment. Several commenters from the building industry objected to the specification for a minimum clear headroom of 80 inches. The commenters stated that standard doors provide a height range from 75 to 79 inches, and that an 80-inch specification would considerably increase the cost of each door installed.

Response. The specification for minimum clear headroom of 80 inches was included in the proposed guidelines because it is a specification included in the major accessibility codes. This design specification was not expected to conflict with typical door heights. However, since the principal purpose of the requirement is to restrict obstructions such as overhanging signs in public walkways, the Department has determined that this specification is not needed for accessible routes within individual dwellings units, and has therefore deleted this standard from the final Guidelines for such routes. (The requirement, however, still applies in public and common use spaces.)

Changes in Level within a Dwelling Unit

In the preamble to the proposed guidelines, the Department advised that the Act appears to require that dwelling units with design features such as lofts or with more than one floor in elevator buildings be equipped with internal elevators, chair lifts, or other means of access to the upper levels (55 FR 24377). The Department stated that, although it is not clear that Congress intended this result, the Department's preliminary assessment was that the statute appears

Federal Register / Vol. 56, No. 44 / Wednesday, March 6, 1991 / Rules and Regulations   9489

to offer little flexibility in this regard. The Department noted that several commenters, including the NAHB and the NCCSCI, suggested that units with more than one floor in elevator buildings should be required to comply with the Act's accessibility requirements only on the floor that is served by the building elevator. (This was the position taken by Option Two.) The Department solicited comments on this issue, and received a number of responses opposing the Department's interpretation.

Comment. The commenters opposing the Department's interpretation stated that the Department's interpretation would place an undue burden on developers and needlessly increase housing costs for everyone; defeat the purpose of having multilevel units, which is to provide additional space at a lower cost; eliminate multilevel designs which may be desirable to disabled residents (e.g., to provide living accommodations for live-in attendants); and "create a backlash" against the Accessibility Guidelines.

Response. Following careful consideration of these comments, and a reexamination of the Act and its legislative history, the Department has determined that its previous interpretation of the Act's application to units with changes in level (whether lofts, or additional stories in elevator buildings), which would have required installation of chair lifts or internal elevators in such units, runs contrary to the purpose and intent of the Fair Housing Act, which is to place "modest accessibility requirements on covered multifamily dwellings." (See House Report at 25.)

In House Report No. 711, the Congress repeatedly emphasized that the accessibility requirements of the Fair Housing Act were minimal basic requirements of accessibility.

These modest requirements will be incorporated into the design of new buildings, resulting in features which do not look unusual and will not add significant additional costs. The bill does not require the installation of elevators or 'hospital-like' features, or the renovation of existing units." (House Report at 18)

Accessibility requirements can vary across a wide range. A standard of total accessibility would require that every entrance, doorway, bathroom, parking space, and portion of buildings and grounds be accessible. Many designers and builders have interpreted the term 'accessible' to mean this type of standard. The committee does not intend to impose such a standard. Rather, the committee intends to use a standard of 'adaptable' design, a standard developed in recent years by the building industry and by advocates for handicapped individuals to provide usable housing for handicapped persons without necessarily being significantly different from conventional housing." (House Report at 26)

The Department has determined that a requirement that units with lofts or multiple stories in elevator buildings be equipped with internal elevators, chair lifts, or other means of access to lofts or upper stories would make accessible housing under the Fair Housing Act significantly different from conventional housing, and would be inconsistent with the Act's "modest accessibility requirements". (See House Report at 25.)

The Department also has determined that a requirement that dwelling units with design features, such as sunken living rooms, must provide some means of access, such as ramps or lifts, as submitted in the proposed guidelines (55 FR 24380) is inconsistent with the Act's modest accessibility requirements. Sunken living rooms are not an uncommon design feature. To require a ramp or other means of access to such an area, at the time of construction, would reduce, perhaps significantly, the space provided by the area. The reduced space might interfere with the use and enjoyment of this area by a resident who is not disabled, or whose disability does not require access by means of a ramp or lift. The Department believes that had it maintained in the final Guidelines the access specifications for design features, such as sunken living rooms, as set forth in the proposed guidelines, the final Guidelines would have interfered unduly with a developer's choice of design, or would have eliminated a popular design choice. Accordingly, the final Guidelines provide that access is not required to design features, such as a sunken living room, provided that the area does not have the effect of interrupting the accessible route through the remainder of the unit.

The Department believes that the installation of a ramp or deck in order to make a sunken room accessible is the type of later adaptation that easily can be made by a tenant. The Department, however, does require that design features, such as a split-level entry, which is critical to providing an accessible route into and through the unit, must provide a ramp or other means of access to the accessible route.

In order to comply with the Act's requirement of an accessible route into and through covered dwelling units, the Department has revised the Guidelines for Requirement 4 to provide separate technical guidance for two types of dwelling units: (1) Single-story dwelling units, including single-story dwelling units with design features such as a loft or a sunken living room; and (2) multistory dwelling units in elevator buildings. (Definitions for "single-story dwelling unit," "loft," "multistory dwelling unit" and "story" have been included in section 2 of the final Guidelines.)

"Single-story dwelling unit" is defined as a dwelling unit with all finished living space located on one floor.

"Loft" is defined as an intermediate level between the floor and ceiling of any story, located within a room or rooms of a dwelling.

"Multistory dwelling unit" is defined as a dwelling unit with finished living space located on one floor and the floor or floors immediately above or below it.

"Story" is defined as that portion of a dwelling unit between the upper surface of any floor and the upper surface of the floor next above, or the roof of the unit. Within the context of dwelling units, the terms "story" and "floor" are synonymous.

For single-story dwelling units and multistory dwelling units, the Guidelines for Requirement 4 are as follows:

(1) For single-story dwelling units, the design specifications for changes in level, are the same as proposed in the Option One guidelines. Changes in level within the dwelling unit with heights between ¼ inch and ½ inch are beveled with a slope no greater than 1:2. Changes in level greater than ½ inch (excluding changes in level resulting from design features such as a loft or a sunken living room) must be ramped or must provide other means of access. For example, split-level entries must be ramped or use other means of providing and accessible route into and through the dwelling unit.

For single-story dwelling units with design features such as a loft or a raised or sunken functional area, such as a sunken living room, the Guidelines specify that: (a) access to lofts is not required, provided that all spaces other than the loft are on an accessible route; and (b) design features such as a sunken living room are also exempt from the access specifications, provided that the sunken area does not interrupt the accessible route through the remainder of the unit.

(2) In multistory dwelling units in buildings with elevators, access to the additional story, or stories, is not required, provided that the story of the unit that is served by the building elevator (a) is the primary entry to the unit; (b) complies with Requirements 2 through 7 with respect to the rooms located on the entry/accessible level; and (3) contains a bathroom or powder room which complies with Requirement

7. (As previously noted, multistory units in buildings without elevators are not considered ground floor units, and therefore are exempt.)

The Department believes that the foregoing revisions to the Guidelines for Requirement 4 will provide individuals with handicaps the degree of accessibility intended by the Fair Housing Act, without increasing significantly the cost of multifamily housing.

Comment. Two commenters suggested that the same adaptability requirement that is applied to bathrooms should be applied to dwelling units with more than one story, or with lofts, i.e. that stairs, and the wall along the stairs, contain the appropriate reinforcement to provide for later installation of a wheelchair lift by a disabled resident, if so desired.

Response. The only blocking or wall reinforcement required by the Fair Housing Act is the reinforcement in bathroom walls for later installation of grab bars. As noted earlier in this preamble, the Fair Housing Act does not actually require that features in covered units be "adaptable", except for bathrooms. The adaptable feature is the reinforcement in bathroom walls which allows later installation of grab bars. Accordingly, the Department believes that a specification for reinforcement of the walls along stairs would exceed the Act's requirements, because the necessary reinforcement could vary by type of lift chosen, and more appropriately would be specified and installed as part of the installation of the lift.

Thresholds at Exterior Doors/ Thresholds to Balconies or Decks

Comment. A number of commenters from the building industry objected to the provision of the Option One guidelines that specified that an exterior deck, balcony, patio, or similar surface may be no more than ¾ inch below the adjacent threshold. Several commenters stated that, in many situations, this height is unworkable for balconies and decks because of waterproofing and safety concerns. This was a particular concern among commenters from the South Florida building industry, who stated that the ¾" height is ineffective for upper floors of high rise buildings in a coastal environment and invites water control problems. Others noted that the suggestion of a wooden decking insert, or the specification of a ¾ inch maximum change in level, in general, might conflict with fire codes.

Response. In response to these concerns, and mindful that Congress did not intend the accessibility requirements of the Act to override the need to protect

the physical integrity of multifamily housing, the Department has included two additional provisions for changes in level at thresholds leading to certain exterior surfaces, as a protective measure against possible water damage. The final Guidelines provide that exterior deck, patio or balcony surfaces should be no more than ½ inch below the floor level of the interior of the dwelling unit, unless they are constructed of impervious material such as concrete, brick or flagstone. In such case, the surface should be no more than 4 inches below the floor level of the interior dwelling unit, unless the local code requires a lower drop. Additionally, the final Guidelines provide that at the primary entry doors to dwelling units with direct exterior access, outside landing surfaces constructed of impervious materials such as concrete, brick, or flagstone should be no more than ½ inch below the floor level of the interior of the dwelling unit. The Guidelines further provide that the finished surface of this area, located immediately outside the entry door, may be sloped for drainage, but the sloping may be no more than ⅛ inch per foot.

In response to commenters' concern that the Guidelines for an accessible route to balconies and decks may conflict with certain building codes that require higher thresholds, or balconies or decks lower than the ¾ inch specified by the Guidelines, the Department notes that the Guidelines are "recommended" design specifications, not building code "requirements". Accordingly, the Guidelines cannot preempt State or local law. However, the builder confronted with local requirements that thwart the particular means of providing accessibility suggested by the Guidelines is under a duty to take reasonable steps to provide for accessibility by other means consistent with local law constraints and considerations of cost-effectiveness, in order to provide dwelling units that meet the specific accessibility requirements of the Fair Housing Act.

Guidelines for Requirement 5

The Guidelines for Requirement 5 present design specifications for providing dwelling units that contain light switches, electrical outlets, thermostats, and other environmental controls in accessible locations, as required by § 100.205(c)(2)(ii).

The Department has adopted the Option One guidelines for Requirement 5 with minor technical changes. The final Guidelines clarify that to be in an accessible location within the meaning of the Act, the maximum height for an

environmental control, for which reach is over an obstruction, is 44 inches for forward approach (as was proposed in the Option One guidelines), or 46 inches for side approach, provided that the obstruction is no more than 24 inches in depth. The inclusion of this additional specification for side approach is consistent with the comparable provisions in the ANSI standard.

Specific comments on the Guidelines for Requirement 5 are as follows:

Comments. Three comments stated that lowered thermostats could pose a safety hazard for children. However, the majority of comments requested clarification as to what is meant by "other environmental controls". Several commenters from the disability community requested that circuit breakers be categorized as environmental controls. Other commenters asked whether light and fan switches on range hoods fall within the category of light switches and environmental controls.

Response. With regard to concerns about lowered thermostats, the Act specifically identifies "thermostats" as one of the controls that must be in accessible locations, and the mounting heights specified in the Guidelines are necessary for an accessible location. The only other environmental controls covered by the Guidelines for Requirement 5 would be heating, air conditioning or ventilation controls (e.g., ceiling fan controls). The Department interprets the Act's requirement of placing environmental controls in accessible locations as referring to those environmental controls that are used by residents or tenants on a daily or regular basis. Circuit breakers do not fall into this category, and therefore are not subject to accessible location specifications. Light and fan switches on range hoods are appliance controls and therefore are not covered by the Act.

Comment. Other commenters asked whether light switches and electrical outlets in the inside corners of kitchen counter areas, and floor outlets are permissible?

Response. Light switches and electrical outlets in the inside corners of kitchen counters, and floor outlets, are permissible, if they are not the only light switches and electrical outlets provided for the area.

Comment. Another commenter pointed out that some electrical outlets that are installed specifically to serve individual appliances, such as refrigerators or microwave ovens, cannot realistically be mounted in an accessible location.

Federal Register / Vol. 56, No. 44 / Wednesday, March 6, 1991 / Rules and Regulations   **9491**

Response. Electrical outlets installed to serve individual appliances, such as refrigerators or built-in microwave ovens, may be mounted in non-accessible locations. These are not the type of electrical outlets which a disabled renter or tenant would need access to on a regular or frequent basis.

Comment. One commenter stated that Figure 3 in the proposed guidelines (Figure 2 in the final Guidelines) specifies a reach requirement more stringent than the ANSI Standard.

Response. The ANSI Standard presents reach ranges for both forward and side approaches for two situations: (1) unobstructed; and (2) over an obstruction. The proposed guidelines specified only the heights for forward reach, because those heights also are usable in side approach. The diagram in Figure 2 (formerly Figure 3) showing forward reach is identical to that of Figure 5 in the ANSI Standard. The ANSI Standard also includes a figure (Figure 6) for side reach that permits higher placement. The reach range for forward approach was the only one referenced in the proposed guidelines for use in the dwelling unit, because it was considered simpler and easier to use a single specification that would work in all situations. The reach range for forward approach has been retained in the final Guidelines for situations where there is no built-in obstruction in order to assure usability when the unit was furnished. However, the final Guidelines have added the specification for side reach over a built-in obstruction that is consistent with the ANSI requirement, and that permits placement two inches higher than forward reach.

Guidelines for Requirement 6

The Guidelines for Requirement 6 present design standards for installation of reinforcement in bathroom walls to allow for later installation of grab bars around the toilet, tub, shower stall and shower seat where such facilities are provided, as required by § 100.205(c)(3)(iii).

The Department adopted the Option One guidelines for Requirement 6 with two modifications. First, the final Guidelines provide that a powder room is subject to the requirement for reinforced walls for grab bars when the powder room is the only toilet facility located on the accessible level of a covered multistory dwelling unit. Second, the final Guidelines further clarify that reinforced bathroom walls will meet the accessibility requirement of § 100.205(c)(3)(iii), if reinforced areas are provided at least at those points where grab bars will be mounted.

Specific comments on this guideline were as follows:

Comment. A number of commenters requested that the Department specify the dimensions for grab bar reinforcement, and suggested that grab bar reinforcing material run horizontally throughout the entire length of the space given for grab bars, as provided by the ANSI Standard. These commenters stated that if this type of reinforcement was required, residents could locate more easily the studs for future grab bar installation, and have flexibility in the placement of grab bars for optimal use, and safety in bathrooms. One commenter noted that many grab bars are of such a length that they require an intermediate fastener, but the proposed standard does not permit intermediate fastening. Two commenters recommended that the final Guidelines follow ANSI and UFAS Standards for requirements for mounting grab bars. One commenter recommended the installation of panels of plywood behind bathroom walls because this would provide greater flexibility in the installation of grab bars.

Response. The illustrations of grab bar wall reinforcement accompanying the Guidelines for Requirement 6 are intended only to show where reinforcement for grab bars is needed. The illustrations are not intended to prescribe how the reinforcing should be provided, or that the bathtub or shower is required to be surrounded by three walls of reinforcement. The additional language added to the Guidelines is to clarify that the Act's accessibility requirement for grab bar reinforcement is met if reinforced areas are provided, at a minimum, at those points where grab bars will be mounted. The Department recognizes that reinforcing for grab bars may be accomplished in a variety of ways, such as by providing plywood panels in the areas illustrated, or by installing vertical reinforcement (in the form of double studs, for example) at the points noted on the figures accompanying the Guidelines.

Comment. Several commenters stated that the final Guidelines should incorporate Option Two's specification of reinforcement for shower seats when shower stalls are provided.

Response. The Fair Housing Act only requires reinforcement for later installation of grab bars. The Act does not cover reinforcement for shower seats; rather, it mentions shower seats (if provided) as an area where grab bar reinforcement would be needed. However, as will be discussed more fully in the following section concerning the Guidelines for Requirement 7

(Usable Bathrooms), reinforcement for shower seats would provide adaptability to increase usability of shower stalls, and is a design option available to builders and developers in designing "usable" bathrooms.

Comment. One commenter recommended that the final Guidelines incorporate Option Two's specification that prefabricated tub/shower enclosures would have to be fabricated with reinforcement for grab bar enclosures.

Response. The Department did not incorporate this specification in the final Guidelines. The Department believes that it is inappropriate to specify product design. A builder should have the flexibility to choose how reinforcement for grab bars will be provided.

Comment. Two commenters stated that half-baths should also contain grab-bar reinforcements.

Response. Half-baths are not considered "bathrooms", as this term is commonly used, and, therefore are not subject to the bathroom wall reinforcement requirement, unless a half-bath facility is the only restroom facility on the accessible level of a covered multistory dwelling unit.

Comment. One commenter requested that the final Guidelines incorporate language clearly to specify that the builder's responsibility is limited solely to wall reinforcement, and later installation is the responsibility of the resident or tenant.

Response. It is unnecessary to incorporate the suggested language in the final Guidelines. The Guidelines for Requirement 6 are solely directed to reinforcement. No guidelines are provided for the actual installation of grab bars. Accordingly, there should be no confusion on this issue.

Guidelines for Requirement 7

The Guidelines for Requirement 7 present design specifications for providing usable kitchens and bathrooms such that an individual in a wheelchair can maneuver about the space, as required by § 100.205(c)(3)(iv).

For usable kitchens, the Department adopted the Option One guidelines with one change. The Department has eliminated the specification that controls for ranges and cooktops be placed so that reaching across burners is not required.

For usable bathrooms, the final Guidelines provide two alternative sets of design specifications. The Fair Housing Act requires that an accessible or "usable" bathroom is one which provides sufficient space for an individual in a wheelchair to maneuver about. The two sets of specifications provide different approaches as to how compliance with this maneuvering space requirement may be accomplished. The first set of specifications also includes size dimensions for shower stalls, but only when a shower stall is the only bathing facility provided in a dwelling unit. Additionally, either set of specifications is applicable to powder rooms, when a powder room is the only restroom facility on the accessible level of a covered multistory dwelling unit.

With the exception of the inclusion of shower stall specifications, the first set of "usable bathroom" specifications remain the same as the Option One guidelines for usable bathrooms. The second set of "usable bathroom" specifications provide somewhat greater accessibility than the first set, but would be applicable only to one bathroom in a dwelling unit that has two or more bathrooms. The second set of specifications include clear space specifications for bathrooms with in-swinging doors and for bathrooms with outswinging doors. This second set of specifications also provides that toilets must be located in a manner that permits a grab bar to be installed on one side of the fixture, and provides specifications on the installation of vanities and lavatories.

To meet the Act's requirements for usable bathrooms, the final Guidelines provide that (1) in a dwelling unit with a single bathroom, either set of specifications may be used; and (2) in a dwelling unit with more than one bathroom, all bathrooms in the unit must comply with the first set of specifications, or, alternatively, at least one bathroom must comply with the second set of specifications, and all other bathrooms must be on an accessible route, and must have a usable entry door in accordance with the guidelines for Requirements 3 and 4. However, in multistory dwelling units, only those bathrooms on the accessible level are subject to the Act's requirements for usable bathrooms. Where a powder room is the only restroom facility provided on the accessible level of a multistory dwelling unit, the powder room must meet either the first set of specifications or the second set of specifications. All bathrooms and powder rooms that are subject to Requirement 7, must have reinforcements for grab bars as provided in the Guideline for Requirement 8.

In developing the final Guidelines for the usable bathroom requirement, the Department recognized that the Option One guidelines for usable bathrooms

presented the minimum specifications necessary to meet the Act's requirements. Accordingly, the Department believes that it is appropriate to provide a second set of specifications which provide somewhat different accessibility accommodations than the Option One guidelines. The Department believes that by offering two sets of specifications for usable bathrooms, the Department is providing builders and developers with more development choices in designing dwelling units that contain more than one bathroom, and it is providing individuals and families with more housing options. Builders and developers may design all bathrooms to meet the minimal specifications of the first set of specifications, or they may design only one bathroom to meet the somewhat greater accessibility specifications of the second set. Regardless of which set of usable bathroom specifications is selected by a builder or developer, all doors to bathrooms and powder rooms must meet the minimum door width specifications of Requirement 3.

The following presents a discussion of the specific comments received on usable kitchens and usable bathrooms.

Controls for Ranges and Cooktops

Comment. A few commenters stated that the Department lacks authority under the Fair Housing Act to impose design standards on appliances. The commenter stated that standards that specify certain design features for appliances in individual dwelling units exceed the scope of the Department's statutory authority. Other commenters objected to front range controls as a safety hazard for children. Commenters from the disability community were strongly supportive of this design specification.

Response. With respect to usable kitchens, the Act solely requires that kitchens have sufficient space such that an individual in a wheelchair can maneuver about. Accordingly, a specification that controls for ranges and cooktops be located so that they can be used without reaching across burners is not consistent with the Act's requirement for usable kitchens.

In the proposed guidelines, the Option One guidelines for usable kitchens specified that controls should be located so as to be usable without reaching across burners. As the preamble to the proposed guidelines noted, many standard styles of ranges and cooktops meeting this specification (other than those with front controls) are available on the market. However, in reviewing the entire rulemaking history on the

design and constructions requirements, the Department has concluded that the requirements of the Fair Housing Act did not cover any appliance controls. Accordingly, this specification was not included in the final Guidelines.

Maneuvering Space, Adjustable Cabinetry, Fixtures and Plumbing

Comment. A number of commenters from the disability community stated that it was important that the Guidelines for both kitchens and bathrooms specify a five-foot turning radius; adjustable cabinetry, and fixture controls that comply with the appropriate provisions of the ANSI Standard.

Response. The legislative history of the Fair Housing Act clearly indicates that Congress did not envision usable kitchens and bathrooms to be designed in accordance with the specifications suggested by the commenters. In House Report No. 711, the Congress stated as follows:

The fourth feature is that kitchens and bathrooms be usable such that an individual in a wheelchair can maneuver about the space. This provision is carefully worded to provide a living environment usable by all. Design of standard sized kitchens and bathrooms can be done in such a way as to assure usability by persons with disabilities without necessarily increasing the size of space. The Committee intends that such space be usable by handicapped persons, but this does not necessarily require that a turning radius be provided in every situation. This provision also does not require that fixtures, cabinetry or plumbing be of such design as to be adjustable. (House Report at 27)

Accordingly, the Department is unable to adopt any of the proposals suggested by the commenters. The Act's requirement for usable kitchens and bathrooms only specifies maneuverability for wheelchair users, and this maneuverability does not require the specification advocated by the commenters. (See previous discussion of this issue in the preamble to the proposed Fair Housing regulations at 53 FR 45005.)

Comment. Two commenters requested clarification concerning what is meant by "sufficient maneuvering space". One of the commenters recommended that this term be defined to include "such space as shall permit a person in a wheelchair to use the features and appliances of a room without having to leave the room to obtain an approach to an appliance, work surface, or cabinet".

Response. The Guidelines for Requirement 7 (usable kitchens and bathrooms) describe what constitutes sufficient maneuvering space in the

Federal Register / Vol. 56, No. 44 / Wednesday, March 6, 1991 / Rules and Regulations   **9493**

kitchen and the bathroom. Additionally, the preamble to the proposed guidelines explicitly states that sufficient maneuvering space for kitchens does not require a wheelchair turning radius (55 FR 24381). As noted in response to the preceding comment, a wheelchair turning radius also is not required for either usable kitchens or usable bathrooms. The Guidelines for usable bathroom state that sufficient maneuvering space is provided within the bathroom for a person using a wheelchair or other assistive device to enter and close the door, use the fixtures, reopen the door and exit. This specification was not changed in the final Guidelines.

Kitchen Work Surfaces

Comment. One commenter stated that "Element 12" in the chart accompanying the Guidelines for Requirement 2 (public and common use areas) seems to require a portion of the kitchen counters to be accessible since they are work surfaces. This commenter stated that if this interpretation is correct then it should be made clear in the Guidelines.

Response. The commenter's interpretation is not correct. The chart accompanying the Guidelines for Requirement 2 is only applicable to the public and common use areas, not to individual dwelling units.

Showers

Comments. Several commenters requested that the final Guidelines provide dimensions on the appropriate width and height of showers and shower doors. Another commenter asked whether showers were required to comply with dimensions specified by the ANSI Standard.

Response. The final Guidelines for usable bathrooms (the first set of specifications) specify size dimensions for shower stalls in only one situation— when the shower stall is the only bathing facility provided in a covered dwelling unit. The Department believes that, where a shower stall is the only bathing facility provided, size specification for the shower stall is consistent with the Act's requirement for usable bathrooms. However, if a shower stall is not the only bathing facility provided in the dwelling unit, then the only specification for showers, appropriate under the Act, concerns reinforced walls in showers. (The titles under the illustrations (figures) related to showers in the final Guidelines for Requirement 6 have been revised to make it clear that the figures are specifying only the different areas required to be reinforced in showers of

different sizes, not the required sizes of the shower stalls.)

In-swinging Bathroom Doors

Comment. One commenter stated that in-swinging bathroom doors generally are problematic, unless the bathroom is unusually large. The commenter noted that an in-swinging door makes it extremely difficult to enter and exit. The commenter recommended that in-swinging doors be prohibited unless there is sufficient internal bathroom space, exclusive of the swing of the door, which allows either a five foot turning radius or two mutually exclusive 30″ x 48″ wheelchair spaces. Another commenter stated that in-swinging bathroom doors create a serious obstacle for the wheelchair user.

Response. The Department declines to prohibit in-swinging bathroom doors. Adjusting an in-swinging door to swing out is the type of later adaptation that can be made fairly easily by a resident or tenant. Once a minimum door width is provided, a tenant who finds a bathroom not readily usable can have the door rehung as an outswinging door. Note, however, that the second set of guidelines for usable bathrooms specifies clear space for bathrooms with in-swinging doors.

Bathroom Design Illustrations

Comment. A number of commenters from the disability community stated that two of the six bathroom drawings in the preamble to the proposed guidelines (numbers 4 and 6 at 55 FR 24374–24375) did not allow for a parallel approach to the tub. These commenters requested that these drawings be removed from the final Guidelines. Other commenters stated that the Department's bathroom design illustrations at 55 FR 24374–24375 are not consistent with the Figure 8 bathroom design illustrations at 55 FR 24401.

Response. While a parallel approach to the tub would provide somewhat greater accessibility, the Department believes that to indicate, through the Guidelines, that a parallel approach to the tub is necessary to meet the Act's requirements, exceeds the Fair Housing Act's minimal design expectations for bathrooms. Accordingly, the first set of specifications for usable bathrooms does not specify a parallel approach to the tub. However, the second set of specifications provides for a clear access aisle adjacent to the tub that would permit a parallel approach to the tub. Either method would meet the Act's requirements. With respect to the comments on the bathroom design illustrations, these illustrations have been revised to make the clear floor

space requirements more readily understood. The illustrations are adapted from ANSI A117.1.

Number of Accessible Bathrooms

Comment. A number of comments were received on how many bathrooms in a dwelling unit should be subject to the Act's "usable" bathroom requirement. Many commenters recommended that all full bathrooms be made accessible. Other commenters recommended that only one full bathroom be required to be made accessible. A few commenters recommended that half-baths/powder rooms also be subject to the Act's requirement.

Response. In House Report No. 711, the Congress distinguished between "total accessibility" and the level of accessibility required by the Fair Housing Act. The report referred to standards requiring every aspect or portion of buildings to be totally accessible, and pointed out that this was not the level of accessibility required by the Act. The final Guidelines for bathrooms are consistent with the Act's usable bathroom requirement, and provide the level of accessibility intended by Congress. As discussed previously in this preamble, the final Guidelines for usable bathrooms provide two sets of specifications. The second set of specifications provides somewhat greater accessibility than the first set of specifications. In view of this fact, the final Guidelines provide that in a dwelling unit with a single bathroom, the bathroom may be designed in accordance with either set of specifications—the first set or the second set. However, in a dwelling unit with more than one bathroom, all bathrooms in the unit must comply with the first set of specifications, or a minimum of one bathroom must comply with the second set of specifications, and all other bathrooms must be on an accessible route, and must have a usable entry door in accordance with the guidelines for Requirements 3 and 4. Additionally, the final Guidelines provide that a powder room must comply with the Act's usable bathroom requirements when the powder room is the only restroom facility provided on the accessible level of a multistory dwelling unit.

3. Discussion of Comments on Related Fair Housing Issues Compliance Deadline

Section 100.205 of the Fair Housing regulations incorporates the Act's design and construction requirements, including the requirement that multifamily dwellings for first occupancy after March 13, 1991 be designed and constructed in accordance with the Act's accessibility requirements. Section 100.205(a) provides that covered multifamily dwellings shall be deemed to be designed and constructed for first occupancy on or before March 13, 1991 (and, therefore, exempt from Act's accessibility requirements), if they are occupied by that date, or if the last building permit or renewal thereof for the covered multifamily dwellings is issued by a State, County, or local government on or before January 13, 1990.

Comment. The Department received a number of comments on the March 13, 1991 compliance deadline, and on methods of achieving compliance. Many commenters objected to the March 13, 1991 compliance deadline on the basis that this deadline was unreasonable. Several commenters from the building industry stated that, in many cases, design plans for buildings now under construction were submitted over two years ago, and it would be very expensive to make changes to buildings near completion. Other commenters stated that it is unreasonable to impose additional requirements on a substantially completed project that unexpectedly has been delayed for occupancy beyond the March 13, 1991 effective date.

Response. Section 804(f)(3)(C) of the Fair Housing Act states that the design and construction standards will be applied to covered multifamily dwelling units for first occupancy after the date that is 30 months after the date of enactment of the Fair Housing Amendments Act. The Fair Housing Act was enacted on September 13, 1988. The date that is 30 months from that date is March 13, 1991. Accordingly, the inclusion of a March 13, 1991 compliance date in § 100.205 is a codification of the Act's compliance deadline. The Department has no authority to change that date. Only Congress may extend the March 13, 1991 deadline.

The Department, however, has been attentive to the concerns of the building industry, and has addressed these concerns, to the extent that it could, in prior published documents. In the preamble to the final Fair Housing rule, the Department addressed the objections of the building industry to the Department's reliance on "actual occupancy" as the sole basis for determining "first occupancy". (See 54 FR 3251; 24 CFR Ch. I, Subch. A, App. I at 585 (1990).) Commenters to the

proposed Fair Housing rule, like the commenters to the proposed guidelines, argued that coverage of the design and construction requirements must be determinable at the beginning of planning and development, and that projects delayed by unplanned and uncontrollable events (labor strikes, Acts of God, etc.) should not be subject to the Act.

In order to accommodate the "legitimate concerns on the part of the building industry" the Department expanded § 100.205 of the final rule to provide that covered multifamily dwellings would be deemed to be for first occupancy if the last building permit or renewal thereof was issued on or before January 13, 1990. A date of fourteen months before the March 13, 1991 deadline was selected because the median construction time for multifamily housing projects of all sizes was determined to be fourteen months, based on data provided by the Marshall Valuation Service.

More recently, the Department addressed similar concerns of the building industry in the preamble to the proposed accessibility guidelines. In the June 15, 1990 publication, the Department recognized that projects designed in advance of the publication of the final Guidelines, may not become available for first occupancy until after March 13, 1991. To provide some guidance, the Department stated in the June 15, 1990 notice that compliance with the Option One guidelines would be considered as evidence of compliance with the Act, in projects designed before the issuance of the final Guidelines. The Department restated its position on this issue in a supplementary notice published in the Federal Register on August 1, 1990 (55 FR 31131). The specific circumstances under which the Department would consider compliance with the Option One guidelines as compliance with the accessibility requirements of the Act were more fully addressed in the August 1, 1990 notice.

Comment. A number of commenters requested extending the date of issuance of the last building permit from January 13, 1990 to some other date, such as June 15, 1990, the date of publication of the proposed guidelines; August 1, 1990, the date of publication of the supplementary notice; or today's date, the date publication of the final Guidelines.

Response. The date of January 13, 1990 was not randomly selected by the Department. This date was selected because it was fourteen months before the compliance deadline of March 13, 1991. As previously noted in this

preamble, fourteen months was found to represent a reasonable median construction time for multifamily housing projects of all sizes, based on data contained in the Marshall Valuation Service. Builders have been on notice since January 23, 1989—the publication date of the final Fair Housing rule, that undertaking construction after January 13, 1990 without adequate attention to accessibility considerations would be at the builder's risk.

Comment. One commenter requested that the applicable building permit be the "primary" building permit for a particular building. Other commenters inquired about the status of building permits that are issued in stages, or about small modifications to building plans during construction which necessitate a reissued building permit.

Response. Following publication of the proposed Fair Housing regulation, and the many comments received at that time from the building industry expressing concern that "actual occupancy" was the only standard for determining "first occupancy", the Department gave careful consideration to the steps and stages involved in the building process. On the basis of this study, the Department determined that an appropriate standard to determine "first occupancy", other than actual occupancy, would be issuance of the last building permit on or before January 13, 1990. This additional standard was added to the final Fair Housing Act regulation. The Department believes that, aside from actual occupancy, issuance of the last building permit remains the appropriate standard.

Compliance Determinations by State and Local Jurisdictions

Comment. A few commenters questioned the role of States and units of local government in determining compliance with the Act's accessibility requirements. The commenters noted that (1) § 100.205(g) encourages States and units of general local government to include, in their existing procedures for the review and approval of newly constructed covered multifamily dwellings, determinations as to whether the design and construction of such dwellings are consistent with the Act's accessibility requirements; but (2) § 100.205(h) provides that determinations of compliance or noncompliance by a State or a unit of general local government are not conclusive in enforcement proceedings under the Fair Housing Act. These commenters stated that, unless determinations of compliance or

Federal Register / Vol. 56, No. 44 / Wednesday, March 6, 1991 / Rules and Regulations   **9495**

noncompliance by a State or unit of general local government are deemed to be conclusive, local jurisdictions will be discouraged from performing compliance reviews because they will not be able to provide a building permit applicant with a sense of finality that proposed design plans are in compliance with the Act.

Response. Sections 100.205 (g) and (h) of the Fair Housing regulations implement sections 804(f)(5) (B) and (C), and section 804(f)(6)(b) of the Fair Housing Act. The language of §§ 100.205 (g) and (h) is taken directly from these statutory provisions. The Congress, not the Department, made the decision that determinations of compliance or noncompliance with the Act by a State or unit of general local government shall not be conclusive in enforcement proceedings. The Department, however, agrees with the position taken in the statute. The Department believes that it would be inappropriate to accord particular "weight" to determinations made by a wide variety of State and local government agencies involving a new civil rights law, without first having the benefit of some experience reviewing the accuracy of the determinations made by State and local authorities under the Fair Housing Act.

Comment. Two commenters stated that local building departments, especially those in smaller urban areas and in rural areas, do not have the manpower or expert knowledge to assure a proper determination of compliance, particularly in "close call" situations. The commenters recommended that liability for any infractions exclude local building departments unless the Department is willing to provide qualified personnel from its local field office to attend staff reviews of every building permit request.

Response. The Department is reluctant to assume that State and local jurisdictions, by performing compliance reviews, will subject themselves to liability under the Fair Housing Act, particularly in light of section 804(f)(5)(C) of the Act, which encourages States and localities to make reviews for compliance with the statute; and the implicit recognition, under Section 804(f)(6)(B), that these reviews may not be correct.

Comment. With reference to a violation of the Act's requirements, several commenters questioned how violations of the Act would be determined, and what the penalty would be for a violation. The commenters asked whether a builder would be cited, and fined, for each violation per building, or for each violation per unit.

Response. If it is determined that a violation of the Act has occurred, a Federal District Court or an administrative law judge (ALJ) has the authority to award actual damages, including damages for humiliation and emotional distress; punitive damages (in court) or civil penalties (in ALJ proceedings); injunctive relief; attorneys fees (except to the United States); and any other equitable relief that may be considered appropriate. Whether a violation will be found for each violation per building, for each violation per unit, or on any other basis, is properly left to the courts and the ALJs.

Enforcement Mechanisms

In the proposed guidelines, the Department solicited public comment on effective enforcement mechanisms (55 FR 24383–24384). Specifically, the Department requested comment on the effectiveness of: annual surveys to assess the number of projects developed with accessible buildings; recordkeeping requirements; and a "second opinion" by an independent, licensed architect or engineer on the site impracticality issue. The Department stated that comments on these proposals would be considered in connection with forthcoming amendments to the Fair Housing regulation.

The Department appreciates all comments submitted on the proposed enforcement mechanisms, and the suggestions offered on other possible enforcement mechanisms, such as a preconstruction review process, certification by a licensed architect, engineer or other building professional that a project is in compliance with the Act, and certification of local accessibility codes by the Department. All these comments will be considered in connection with future amendments to the Fair Housing Act regulation.

First Occupancy

Comment. A number of commenters requested clarification of the determination of "first occupancy" after March 13, 1991. A few commenters referred to the Act's first occupancy requirement as that of "ready for occupancy" by March 13, 1991.

Response. The phrase "ready for occupancy" does not correctly describe the standard contained in the Fair Housing Act. The Act states that covered multifamily dwellings subject to the Act's accessibility requirements are those that are "for first occupancy" after March 13, 1991. The standard, "first occupancy," is based on actual occupancy of the covered multifamily dwelling, or on issuance of the last building permit, or building permit

renewal, on or before January 13, 1990. Where an individual is relying on a claim that a building was actually occupied on March 13, 1991, the Department, in making a determination of reasonable cause, will consider each situation on a case-by-case basis. As long as one dwelling unit in a covered multifamily dwelling is occupied, the one occupied dwelling unit is sufficient to meet the requirements for actual occupancy. However, the question of whether the occupancy was in compliance with State and local law (e.g., pursuant to a local occupancy permit, where one is required) will be a crucial factor in determining whether first occupancy has been achieved.

Comment. Several commenters requested clarification of "first occupancy", with respect to projects involving several buildings, or projects with extended build-out terms, such as planned communities with completion dates 5 to 10 years into the future.

Response. "First occupancy" is determined on a building-by-building basis, *not* on a project-by-project basis. For a project that involves several buildings, one building in the project could be built without reference to the accessibility requirements, while a building constructed next door might have to comply with the Act's requirements. The fact that one or more buildings in a multiple building project were occupied on March 13, 1991 will not be sufficient to afford an exemption from the Act's requirements for other buildings in the same project that are developed at a later time.

Costs of Adaptation

Comment. A few commenters requested clarification on who incurs the cost of making a unit adaptable for a disabled tenant.

Response. All costs associated with incorporating the new design and construction requirements of the Fair Housing Act are borne by the builder. There are, of course, situations where a tenant may need to make modifications to the dwelling unit which are necessary to make the unit accessible for that person's particular type of disability. The tenant would incur the cost of this type of modification—whether or not the dwelling unit is part of a multifamily dwelling exempt from the Act's accessibility requirements. For dwellings subject to the statute's accessibility requirements, the tenant's costs would be limited to those modifications that were not covered by the Act's design and construction requirements. (For example, the tenant would pay for the cost of purchasing and installing grab bars.) For dwellings not subject to the accessibility requirements, the tenant would pay the cost of all modifications necessary to meet his or her needs. (Using the grab bar example, the tenant would pay both the cost of buying and installing the grab bars and the costs associated with adding bathroom wall reinforcement.)

Section 100.203 of the Fair Housing regulations provides that discrimination includes a refusal to permit, at the expense of a handicapped person, reasonable modifications of existing premises occupied or to be occupied by that person, if modifications are necessary to afford the person full enjoyment of the premises. In the case of a rental, the landlord may reasonably condition permission for a modification on the renter's agreeing to restore the interior of the unit to the condition that existed before its modification— reasonable wear and tear excepted. This regulatory section provides examples of reasonable modifications that a tenant may make to existing premises. The examples include bathroom wall reinforcement. In House Report No. 711, the Congress provided additional examples of reasonable modifications that could be made to existing premises by persons with disabilities:

For example, persons who have a hearing disability could install a flashing light in order to 'see' that someone is ringing the doorbell. Elderly individuals with severe arthritis may need to replace the doorknobs with lever handles. A person in a wheelchair may need to install fold-back hinges in order to be able to go through a door or may need to build a ramp to enter the unit. Any modifications protected under this section [section 804(f)(3)(A)] must be reasonable and must be made at the expense of the individual with handicaps. (House Report at 25)

Reasonable Modification

Comment. One commenter requested clarification concerning what is meant by "reasonable modification".

Response. What constitutes "reasonable modification" is discussed to some extent in the preceding section, "Costs of Adaptation", and also was discussed extensively in the preambles to both the proposed and final Fair Housing rules. (See 53 FR 45002–45003, 54 FR 3247–3248; 24 CFR Ch. I, Subch. A, App. I at 580–583 (1990).) Additionally, examples of reasonable modifications are provided in 24 CFR 100.203(c).

Scope of Coverage

Comment. A number of comments were received on the issue of which types of dwelling units should be subject to the Act's accessibility requirements, and the number or percentage of

dwelling units that must comply with the Act's requirements.

Response. The Department lacks the authority to adopt any of the proposals recommended by the commenters. The type of multifamily dwelling subject to the Fair Housing Act's accessibility requirements, and the number of individual dwelling units that must be made accessible were established by the Congress, not the Department. The Fair Housing Act defines "covered multifamily dwelling" to mean buildings consisting of four or more units if such buildings have one or more elevators; and ground floor units in other buildings consisting of four or more units." (See Section 804(f)(7) of the Act.) The Fair Housing Act requires that covered multifamily dwellings for first occupancy after March 13, 1991 be designed and constructed in accordance with the Act's accessibility requirements. The Act does not permit only a percentage of units in covered multifamily dwellings to be designed in accordance with the Act's requirements, nor does the Department have the authority so to provide by regulation.

VI. Other Matters

Codification of Guidelines. In order to assure the availability of the Guidelines, and the preamble to the Guidelines, to interested persons in the future, the Department has decided to codify both documents. The Guidelines will be codified in the 1991 edition of the Code of Federal Regulations as appendix II to the Fair Housing regulations (i.e., 24 CFR Ch. I, Subch. A, App. II), and the preamble to the Guidelines will be codified as appendix III (i.e., 24 CFR Ch. I, Subch. A, App. III).

Regulatory Impact Analysis. A Preliminary Impact Analysis was published in the **Federal Register** on September 7, 1990 (55 FR 37072–37129). A Final Regulatory Impact Analysis is available for public inspection during regular business hours in the Office of the Rules Docket Clerk, room 10276, Department of Housing and Urban Development, 451 Seventh Street, SW., Washington, DC 20410–0500.

Environmental Impact. A Finding of No Significant Impact with respect to the environment has been made in accordance with HUD regulations at 24 CFR part 50, which implement section 102(2)(C) of the National Environmental Policy Act of 1969. The Finding of No Significant Impact is available for public inspection during regular business hours in the Office of the Rules Docket Clerk, Office of the General Counsel, Department of Housing and Urban Development, room 10276, 451 Seventh Street, SW., Washington, DC 20410– 0500.

Executive Order 12606, The Family. The General Counsel, as the Designated Official under Executive Order No. 12606, The Family, has determined that this notice will likely have a significant beneficial impact on family formation, maintenance or well-being. Housing designed in accordance with the Guidelines will offer more housing choices for families with members who have disabilities. Housing designed in accordance with the Guidelines also may be beneficial to families that do not have members with disabilities. For example, accessible building entrances, as required by the Act and implemented by the Guidelines, may benefit parents with children in strollers, and also allow residents and visitors the convenience of using luggage or shopping carts easily. Additionally, with the aging of the population, and the increase in incidence of disability that accompanies aging, significant numbers of people will be able to remain in units designed in accordance with the Guidelines as the aging process advances. Compliance with these Guidelines may also increase the costs of developing a multifamily building, and, thus, may increase the cost of renting or purchasing homes. Such costs could negatively affect families' ability to obtain housing. However, the Department believes that the benefits provided to families by housing that is in compliance with the Fair Housing Amendments Act outweigh the possible increased costs of housing.

Executive Order 12611, Federalism. The General Counsel, as the Designated Official under section 6(a) of Executive Order No. 12611, Federalism, has determined that this notice does not involve the preemption of State law by Federal statute or regulation and does not have federalism implications. The Guidelines only are recommended design specifications, not legal requirements. Accordingly, the Guidelines do not preempt State or local laws that address the same issues covered by the Guidelines.

Dated: February 27, 1991.

Gordon H. Mansfield,

Assistant Secretary for Fair Housing and Equal Opportunity.

Accordingly, the Department adds the Fair Housing Accessibility Guidelines as Appendix II and the text of the preamble to these final guidelines beginning at the heading "Adoption of Final Guidelines" and ending before "VI. Other Matters" as appendix III to 24 CFR, ch. I, subchapter A to read as follows:

Appendix II to Ch. I, subchapter A—Fair Housing Accessibility Guidelines

BILLING CODE 4210-28-M

Federal Register / Vol. 56, No. 44 / Wednesday, March 6, 1991 / Rules and Regulations 9497

U.S. Department of Housing and Urban Development
Office of Fair Housing and Urban Development

Fair Housing Accessibility Guidelines

Design Guidelines for Accessible/Adaptable Dwellings

Issued by the Department of Housing and Urban Development

NOTE: This is a reprint of the final Fair Housing Accessibility Guidelines published in the Federal Register on March 6, 1991, Vol. 56, No. 44, pages 9472-9515. This reprint incorporates corrections to the final Guidelines which were published in the Federal Register on June 24, 1991.

9498   Federal Register / Vol. 56, No. 44 / Wednesday, March 6, 1991 / Rules and Regulations

Contents

Federal Register / Vol. 56, No. 44 / Wednesday, March 6, 1991 / Rules and Regulations   9499

Fair Housing Accessibility Guidelines

Section 1. Introduction

Authority

Section 804(f)(5)(C) of the Fair Housing Amendments Act of 1988 directs the Secretary of the Department of Housing and Urban Development to provide technical assistance to States, local governments, and other persons in implementing the accessibility requirements of the Fair Housing Act. These guidelines are issued under this statutory authority.

Purpose

The purpose of these guidelines is to provide technical guidance on designing dwelling units as required by the Fair Housing Amendments Act of 1988 (Fair Housing Act). These guidelines are not mandatory, nor do they prescribe specific requirements which must be met, and which, if not met, would constitute unlawful discrimination under the Fair Housing Act. Builders and developers may choose to depart from these guidelines and seek alternate ways to demonstrate that they have met the requirements of the Fair Housing Act. These guidelines are intended to provide a safe harbor for compliance with the accessibility requirements of the Fair Housing Act.

Scope

These guidelines apply only to the design and construction requirements of 24 CFR 100.205. Compliance with these guidelines do not relieve persons participating in a Federal or Federally-assisted program or activity from other requirements, such as those required by section 504 of the Rehabilitation Act of 1973 (29 U.S.C. 794) and the Architectural Barriers Act of 1968 (42 U.S.C. 4151-4157). Accessible design requirements for Section 504 are found at 24 CFR Part 8. Accessible design requirements for the Architectural Barriers Act are found at 24 CFR Part 40.

Organization of Guidelines

The design guidelines are incorporated in Section 5 of this document. Each guideline cites the appropriate paragraph of HUD's regulation at 24 CFR 100.205; quotes from the regulation to identify the required design features, and states recommended specifications for each design feature.

Generally, these guidelines rely on the American National Standards Institute (ANSI) A117.1-1986, American National Standard for Buildings and Facilities—Providing Accessibility and Usability for Physically Handicapped People (ANSI Standard). Where the guidelines rely on sections of the ANSI Standard, the ANSI sections are cited. Only those sections of the ANSI Standard cited in the guidelines are recommended for compliance with 24 CFR 100.205. For those guidelines that

differ from the ANSI Standard, recommended specifications are provided. The texts of cited ANSI sections are not reproduced in the guidelines. The complete text of the 1986 version of the ANSI A117.1 Standard may be purchased from the American National Standards Institute, 1430 Broadway, New York, NY 10018.

Section 2. Definitions

As used in these Guidelines:

"Accessible", when used with respect to the public and common use areas of a building containing covered multifamily dwellings, means that the public or common use areas of the building can be approached, entered, and used by individuals with physical handicaps. The phrase "readily accessible to and usable by" is synonymous with accessible. A public or common use area that complies with the appropriate requirements of ANSI A117.1-1986, a comparable standard or these guidelines is "accessible" within the meaning of this paragraph.

"Accessible route" means a continuous unobstructed path connecting accessible elements and spaces in a building or within a site that can be negotiated by a person with a severe disability using a wheelchair, and that is also safe for and usable by people with other disabilities. Interior accessible routes may include corridors, floors, ramps, elevators and lifts. Exterior accessible routes may include parking access aisles, curb ramps, walks, ramps and lifts. A route that complies with the appropriate requirements of ANSI A117.1-1986, a comparable standard, or Section 5, Requirement 1 of these guidelines is an "accessible route". In the circumstances described in Section 5, Requirements 1 and 2, "accessible route" may include access via a vehicular route.

"Adaptable dwelling units", when used with respect to covered multifamily dwellings, means dwelling units that include the features of adaptable design specified in 24 CFR 100.205(c) (2)-(3).

"ANSI A117.1-1986" means the 1986 edition of the American National Standard for buildings and facilities providing accessibility and usability for physically handicapped people.

"Assistive device" means an aid, tool, or instrument used by a person with disabilities to assist in activities of daily living. Examples of assistive devices include tongs, knob-turners, and oven-rack pusher/pullers.

"Bathroom" means a bathroom which includes a water closet (toilet), lavatory (sink), and bathtub or shower. It does not include single-fixture facilities or those with only a water closet and lavatory. It does include a compartmented bathroom. A

9500 **Federal Register** / Vol. 56, No. 44 / Wednesday, March 6, 1991 / Rules and Regulations

compartmented bathroom is one in which the fixtures are distributed among interconnected rooms. A compartmented bathroom is considered a single unit and is subject to the Act's requirements for bathrooms.

"Building" means a structure, facility or portion thereof that contains or serves one or more dwelling units.

"Building entrance on an accessible route" means an accessible entrance to a building that is connected by an accessible route to public transportation stops, to parking or passenger loading zones, or to public streets or sidewalks, if available. A building entrance that complies with ANSI A117.1-1986 (see Section 5, Requirement 1 of these guidelines) or a comparable standard complies with the requirements of this paragraph.

"Clear" means unobstructed.

"Common use areas" means rooms, spaces or elements inside or outside of a building that are made available for the use of residents of a building or the guests thereof. These areas include hallways, lounges, lobbies, laundry rooms, refuse rooms, mail rooms, recreational areas and passageways among and between buildings. See Section 5, Requirement 2 of these guidelines.

"Controlled substance" means any drug or other substance, or immediate precursor included in the definition in Section 102 of the Controlled Substances Act (21 U.S.C. 802).

"Covered multifamily dwellings" or "covered multifamily dwellings subject to the Fair Housing Amendments" means buildings consisting of four or more dwelling units if such buildings have one or more elevators; and ground floor dwelling units in other buildings consisting of four or more dwelling units. Dwelling units within a single structure separated by firewalls do not constitute separate buildings.

"Dwelling unit" means a single unit of residence for a household of one or more persons. Examples of dwelling units covered by these guidelines include: condominiums; an apartment unit within an apartment building; and other types of dwellings in which sleeping accommodations are provided but toileting or cooking facilities are shared by occupants of more than one room or portion of the dwelling. Examples of the latter include dormitory rooms and sleeping accommodations in shelters intended for occupancy as a residence for homeless persons.

"Entrance" means any exterior access point to a building or portion of a building used by residents for the purpose of entering. For purposes of these guidelines, an "entrance" does not include a door to a loading dock or a door used primarily as a service entrance, even if nonhandicapped residents occasionally use that door to enter.

"Finished grade" means the ground surface of the site after all construction, levelling, grading, and development has been completed.

"Ground floor" means a floor of a building with a building entrance on an accessible route. A building may have one or more ground floors. Where the first floor containing dwelling units in a building is above grade, all units on that floor must be served by a building entrance on an accessible route. This floor will be considered to be a ground floor.

"Handicap" means, with respect to a person, a physical or mental impairment which substantially limits one or more major life activities; a record of such an impairment; or being regarded as having such an impairment. This term does not include current, illegal use of or addiction to a controlled substance. For purposes of these guidelines, an individual shall not be considered to have a handicap solely because that individual is a transvestite.

As used in this definition:

(a) "Physical or mental impairment" includes:
   (1) Any physiological disorder or condition, cosmetic disfigurement, or anatomical loss affecting one or more of the following body systems: Neurological; musculoskeletal; special sense organs; respiratory, including speech organs; cardiovascular; reproductive; digestive; genito-urinary; hemic and lymphatic; skin; and endocrine; or
   (2) Any mental or psychological disorder, such as mental retardation, organic brain syndrome, emotional or mental illness, and specific learning disabilities. The term "physical or mental impairment" includes, but is not limited to, such diseases and conditions as orthopedic, visual, speech and hearing impairments, cerebral palsy, autism, epilepsy, muscular dystrophy, multiple sclerosis, cancer, heart disease, diabetes, Human Immunodeficiency Virus infection, mental retardation, emotional illness, drug addiction (other than addiction caused by current, illegal use of a controlled substance) and alcoholism. These guidelines are designed to make units accessible or adaptable for people with physical handicaps.

(b) "Major life activities" means functions such as caring for one's self, performing manual tasks, walking, seeing, hearing, speaking, breathing, learning and working.

(c) "Has a record of such an impairment" means has a history of, or has been misclassified as having, a mental or physical impairment that substantially limits one or more major life activities.

(d) "Is regarded as having an impairment" means:
   (1) Has a physical or mental impairment that does not substantially limit one or more major life activities but that is treated by another person as constituting such a limitation;
   (2) Has a physical or mental impairment that substantially limits one or more major life activities only as a result of the attitudes of others toward such impairment; or
   (3) Has none of the impairments defined in paragraph (a) of this definition but is treated by another person as having such an impairment.

"Loft" means an intermediate level between the floor and ceiling of any story, located within a room or rooms of a dwelling.

"Multistory dwelling unit" means a dwelling unit with finished living space located on one floor and the floor or floors immediately above or below it.

Federal Register / Vol. 56, No. 44 / Wednesday, March 6, 1991 / Rules and Regulations   **9501**

"Public use areas" means interior or exterior rooms or spaces of a building that are made available to the general public. Public use may be provided at a building that is privately or publicly owned.

"Single-story dwelling unit" means a dwelling unit with all finished living space located on one floor.

"Site" means a parcel of land bounded by a property line or a designated portion of a public right of way.

"Slope" means the relative steepness of the land between two points and is calculated as follows: The distance and elevation between the two points (e.g., an entrance and a passenger loading zone) are determined from a topographical map. The difference in elevation is divided by the distance and that fraction is multiplied by 100 to obtain a percentage slope figure. For example, if a principal entrance is ten feet from a passenger loading zone, and the principal entrance is raised one foot higher than the passenger loading zone, then the slope is $1/10 \times 100 = 10\%$.

"Story" means that portion of a dwelling unit between the upper surface of any floor and the upper surface of the floor next above, or the roof of the unit. Within the context of dwelling units, the terms "story" and "floor" are synonymous.

"Undisturbed site" means the site before any construction, levelling, grading, or development associated with the current project.

"Vehicular or pedestrian arrival points" means public or resident parking areas, public transportation stops, passenger loading zones, and public streets or sidewalks.

"Vehicular route" means a route intended for vehicular traffic, such as a street, driveway or parking lot.

Section 3.   Fair Housing Act Design and Construction Requirements

The regulations issued by the Department at 24 CFR 100.205 state:

§ 100.205   Design and construction requirements.

(a) Covered multifamily dwellings for first occupancy after March 13, 1991 shall be designed and constructed to have at least one building entrance on an accessible route unless it is impractical to do so because of the terrain or unusual characteristics of the site. For purposes of this section, a covered multifamily dwelling shall be deemed to be designed and constructed for first occupancy on or before March 13, 1991 if they are occupied by that date or if the last building permit or renewal thereof for the covered multifamily dwellings is issued by a State, County or local government on or before January 13, 1990. The burden of establishing impracticality because of terrain or unusual site characteristics is on the person or persons who designed or constructed the housing facility.

(b) The application of paragraph (a) of this section may be illustrated by the following examples:

Example (1): A real estate developer plans to construct six covered multifamily dwelling units on a site with a hilly terrain. Because of the terrain, it will be necessary to climb a long and steep stairway in order to enter the dwellings. Since there is no practical way to provide an accessible route to any of the dwellings, one need not be provided.

Example (2): A real estate developer plans to construct a building consisting of 10 units of multifamily housing on a waterfront site that floods frequently. Because of this unusual characteristic of the site, the builder plans to construct the building on stilts. It is customary for housing in the geographic area where the site is located to be built on stilts. The housing may lawfully be constructed on the proposed site on stilts even though this means that there will be no practical way to provide an accessible route to the building entrance.

Example (3): A real estate developer plans to construct a multifamily housing facility on a particular site. The developer would like the facility to be built on the site to contain as many units as possible. Because of the configuration and terrain of the site, it is possible to construct a building with 105 units on the site provided the site does not have an accessible route leading to the building entrance. It is also possible to construct a building on the site with an accessible route leading to the building entrance. However, such a building would have no more than 100 dwelling units. The building to be constructed on the site must have a building entrance on an accessible route because it is not impractical to provide such an entrance because of the terrain or unusual characteristics of the site.

(c) All covered multifamily dwellings for first occupancy after March 13, 1991 with a building entrance on an accessible route shall be designed and constructed in such a manner that—

(1) The public and common use areas are readily accessible to and usable by handicapped persons;

(2) All the doors designed to allow passage into and within all premises are sufficiently wide to allow passage by handicapped persons in wheelchairs; and

(3) All premises within covered multifamily dwelling units contain the following features of adaptable design:

(i) An accessible route into and through the covered dwelling unit;

(ii) Light switches, electrical outlets, thermostats, and other environmental controls in accessible locations;

(iii) Reinforcements in bathroom walls to allow later installation of grab bars around the toilet, tub, shower, stall and shower seat, where such facilities are provided; and

(iv) Usable kitchens and bathrooms such that an individual in a wheelchair can maneuver about the space.

(d) The application of paragraph (c) of this section may be illustrated by the following examples:

Example (1): A developer plans to construct a 100 unit condominium apartment building with one elevator. In accordance with paragraph (a), the building has at least one accessible route leading to an accessible entrance. All 100 units are covered multifamily dwelling units and they all must be designed and constructed so that they comply with the accessibility requirements of paragraph (c) of this section.

Example (2): A developer plans to construct 30 garden apartments in a three story building. The building will not have an elevator. The building will have one accessible entrance which will be on the first floor. Since the building does not have an elevator, only the "ground floor" units are covered multifamily units. The "ground floor" is the first floor because that is the floor that has an accessible entrance. All of the dwelling units on the first floor must meet the accessibility requirements of paragraph (c) of this section and must have access to at least one of each type of public or common use area available for residents in the building.

(e) Compliance with the appropriate requirements of ANSI A117.1–1986 suffices to satisfy the requirements of paragraph (c)(3) of this section.

(f) Compliance with a duly enacted law of a State or unit of general local government that includes the requirements of paragraphs (a) and (c) of this section satisfies the requirements of paragraphs (a) and (c) of this section.

(g)(1) It is the policy of HUD to encourage States and units of general local government to include, in their existing procedures for the review and approval of newly constructed covered multifamily dwellings, determinations as to whether the design and construction of such dwellings are consistent with paragraphs (a) and (c) of this section.

(2) A State or unit of general local government may review and approve newly constructed multifamily dwellings for the purpose of making determinations as to whether the requirements of paragraphs (a) and (c) of this section are met.

(h) Determinations of compliance or noncompliance by a State or a unit of general local government under paragraph (f) or (g) of this section are not conclusive in enforcement proceedings under the Fair Housing Amendments Act.

(i) This subpart does not invalidate or limit any law of a State or political subdivision of a State that requires dwellings to be designed and constructed in a manner that affords handicapped persons greater access than is required by this subpart.

Federal Register / Vol. 56, No. 44 / Wednesday, March 6, 1991 / Rules and Regulations **9503**

Section 4.   Application of the Guidelines

The design specifications (guidelines) presented in Section 5 apply to new construction of "covered multifamily dwellings", as defined in Section 2. These guidelines are recommended for designing dwellings that comply with the requirements of the Fair Housing Amendments Act of 1988.

Section 5.   Guidelines

Requirement 1. Accessible building entrance on an accessible route.

Under section 100.205(a), covered multifamily dwellings shall be designed and constructed to have at least one building entrance on an accessible route, unless it is impractical to do so because of terrain or unusual characteristics of the site.

Guideline

(1) Building entrance. Each building on a site shall have at least one building entrance on an accessible route unless prohibited by the terrain, as provided in paragraphs (2)(a)(i) or (2)(a)(ii), or unusual characteristics of the site, as provided in paragraph (2)(b). This guideline applies both to a single building on a site and to multiple buildings on a site.

   (a) Separate ground floor unit entrances. When a ground floor unit of a building has a separate entrance, each such ground floor unit shall be served by an accessible route, except for any unit where the terrain or unusual characteristics of the site prohibit the provision of an accessible route to the entrance of that unit.

   (b) Multiple entrances. Only one entrance is required to be accessible to any one ground floor of a building, except in cases where an individual dwelling unit has a separate exterior entrance, or where the building contains clusters of dwelling units, with each cluster sharing a different exterior entrance. In these cases, more than one entrance may be required to be accessible, as determined by analysis of the site. In every case, the accessible entrance should be on an accessible route to the covered dwelling units it serves.

(2) Site impracticality. Covered multifamily dwellings with elevators shall be designed and constructed to provide at least one accessible entrance on an accessible route, regardless of terrain or unusual characteristics of the site. Covered multifamily dwellings without elevators shall be designed and constructed to provide at least one accessible entrance on an accessible route unless terrain or unusual characteristics of the site are such that the following conditions are found to exist:

   (a) Site impracticality due to terrain. There are two alternative tests for determining site impracticality due to terrain: the individual building test provided in paragraph (i), or the site analysis test provided in paragraph (ii). These tests may be used as follows.

A site with a single building having a common entrance for all units may be analyzed only as described in paragraph (i).

All other sites, including a site with a single building having multiple entrances serving either individual dwelling units or clusters of dwelling units, may be analyzed using the methodology in either paragraph (i) or paragraph (ii). For these sites for which either test is applicable, regardless of which test is selected, at least 20% of the total ground floor units in nonelevator buildings, on any site, must comply with the guidelines.

   (i)   Individual building test. It is impractical to provide an accessible entrance served by an accessible route when the terrain of the site is such that:

     (A) the slopes of the undisturbed site measured between the planned entrance and all vehicular or pedestrian arrival points within 50 feet of the planned entrance exceed 10 percent; and

     (B) the slopes of the planned finished grade measured between the entrance and all vehicular or pedestrian arrival points within 50 feet of the planned entrance also exceed 10 percent.

If there are no vehicular or pedestrian arrival points within 50 feet of the planned entrance, the slope for the purposes of this paragraph (i) will be measured to the closest vehicular or pedestrian arrival point.

For purposes of these guidelines, vehicular or pedestrian arrival points include public or resident parking areas; public transportation stops; passenger loading zones; and public streets or sidewalks. To determine site impracticality, the slope would be measured at ground level from the point of the planned entrance on a straight line to (i) each vehicular or pedestrian arrival point that is within 50 feet of the planned entrance, or (ii) if there are no vehicular or pedestrian arrival points within that specified area, the vehicular or pedestrian arrival point closest to the planned entrance. In the case of sidewalks, the closest point to the entrance will be where a public sidewalk entering the site intersects with the sidewalk to the entrance. In the case of resident parking areas, the closest point to the planned entrance will be measured from the entry point to the parking area that is located closest to the planned entrance.

   (ii) Site analysis test. Alternatively, for a site having multiple buildings, or a site with a single building with multiple entrances, impracticality of providing an accessible entrance served by an accessible route can be established by the following steps:

(A) The percentage of the total buildable area of the undisturbed site with a natural grade less than 10% slope shall be calculated. The analysis of the existing slope (before grading) shall be done on a topographic survey with two foot (2') contour intervals with slope determination made between each successive interval. The accuracy of the slope analysis shall be certified by a professional licensed engineer, landscape architect, architect or surveyor.

(B) To determine the practicality of providing accessibility to planned multifamily dwellings based on the topography of the existing natural terrain, the minimum percentage of ground floor units to be made accessible should equal the percentage of the total buildable area (not including floodplains, wetlands, or other restricted use areas) of the undisturbed site that has an existing natural grade of less than 10% slope.

(C) In addition to the percentage established in paragraph (B), all ground floor units in a building, or ground floor units served by a particular entrance, shall be made accessible if the entrance to the units is on an accessible route, defined as a walkway with a slope between the planned entrance and a pedestrian or vehicular arrival point that is no greater than 8.33%

(b) Site impracticality due to unusual characteristics. Unusual characteristics include sites located in a federally-designated floodplain or coastal high-hazard area and sites subject to other similar requirements of law or code that the lowest floor or the lowest structural member of the lowest floor must be raised to a specified level at or above the base flood elevation. An accessible route to a building entrance is impractical due to unusual characteristics of the site when:

(i) the unusual site characteristics result in a difference in finished grade elevation exceeding 30 inches and 10 percent measured between an entrance and all vehicular or pedestrian arrival points within 50 feet of the planned entrance; or

(ii) if there are no vehicular or pedestrian arrival points within 50 feet of the planned entrance, the unusual characteristics result in a difference in finished grade elevation exceeding 30 inches and 10 percent measured between an entrance and the closest vehicular or pedestrian arrival point.

(3) Exceptions to site impracticality . Regardless of site considerations described in paragraphs (1) and (2), an accessible entrance on an accessible route is practical when:

(a) There is an elevator connecting the parking area with the dwelling units on a ground floor. (In this case, those dwelling units on the ground floor served by an elevator, and at least one of each type of public and common use areas, would be subject to these guidelines.) However:

(i) Where a building elevator is provided only as a means of creating an accessible route to dwelling units on a ground floor, the building is not considered an elevator building for purposes of these guidelines; hence, only the ground floor dwelling units would be covered.

(ii) If the building elevator is provided as a means of access to dwelling units other than dwelling units on a ground floor, then the building is an elevator building which is a covered multifamily dwelling, and the elevator in that building must provide accessibility to all dwelling units in the building, regardless of the slope of the natural terrain; or

(b) An elevated walkway is planned between a building entrance and a vehicular or pedestrian arrival point and the planned walkway has a slope no greater than 10 percent.

(4) Accessible entrance. An entrance that complies with ANSI 4.14 meets section 100.205(a).

(5) Accessible route. An accessible route that complies with ANSI 4.3 would meet section 100.205(a). If the slope of the finished grade between covered multifamily dwellings and a public or common use facility (including parking) exceeds 8.33%, or where other physical barriers (natural or manmade) or legal restrictions, all of which are outside the control of the owner, prevent the installation of an accessible pedestrian route, an acceptable alternative is to provide access via a vehicular route, so long as necessary site provisions such as parking spaces and curb ramps are provided at the public or common use facility.

Requirement 2. Accessible and usable public and common use areas.

Section 100.205(c)(1) provides that covered multifamily dwellings with a building entrance on an accessible route shall be designed in such a manner that the public and common use areas are readily accessible to and usable by handicapped persons.

Guideline

The following chart identifies the public and common use areas that should be made accessible, cites the appropriate section of the ANSI Standard, and describes the appropriate application of the specifications, including modifications to the referenced Standard.

Federal Register / Vol. 56, No. 44 / Wednesday, March 6, 1991 / Rules and Regulations **9505**

BASIC COMPONENTS FOR ACCESSIBLE AND USABLE PUBLIC AND COMMON USE AREAS OR FACILITIES

Accessible element or space	ANSI A117.1 section	Application
1. Accessible route(s)	4.3	Within the boundary of the site: (a) From public transportation stops, accessible parking spaces, accessible passenger loading zones, and public streets or sidewalks to accessible building entrances (subject to site considerations described in section 5). (b) Connecting accessible buildings, facilities, elements and spaces that are on the same site. On-grade walks or paths between separate buildings with covered multifamily dwellings, while not required, should be accessible unless the slope of finish grade exceeds 8.33% at any point along the route. Handrails are not required on these accessible walks. (c) Connecting accessible building or facility entrances with accessible spaces and elements within the building or facility, including adaptable dwelling units. (d) Where site or legal constraints prevent a route accessible to wheelchair users between covered multifamily dwellings and public or common-use facilities elsewhere on the site, an acceptable alternative is the provision of access via a vehicular route so long as there is accessible parking on an accessible route to at least 2% of covered dwelling units, and necessary site provisions such as parking and curb cuts are available at the public or common use facility.
2. Protruding objects	4.4	Accessible routes or maneuvering space including, but not limited to halls, corridors, passageways, or aisles.
3. Ground and floor surface treatments	4.5	Accessible routes, rooms, and spaces, including floors, walks, ramps, stairs, and curb ramps.
4. Parking and passenger-loading zones	4.6	If provided at the site, designated accessible parking at the dwelling unit on request of residents with handicaps, on the same terms and with the full range of choices (e.g., surface parking or garage) that are provided for other residents of the project, with accessible parking on a route accessible to wheelchairs for at least 2% of the covered dwelling units; accessible visitor parking sufficient to provide access to grade-level entrances of covered multifamily dwellings; and accessible parking at facilities (e.g., swimming pools) that serve accessible buildings.
5. Curb ramps	4.7	Accessible routes crossing curbs.
6. Ramps	4.8	Accessible routes with slopes greater than 1:20.
7. Stairs	4.9	Stairs on accessible routes connecting levels not connected by an elevator.
8. Elevator	4.10	If provided.
9. Platform lift	4.11	May be used in lieu of an elevator or ramp under certain conditions.
10. Drinking fountains and water coolers	4.15	Fifty percent of fountains and coolers on each floor, or at least one, if provided in the facility or at the site.
11. Toilet rooms and bathing facilities (including water closets, toilet rooms and stalls, urinals, lavatories and mirrors, bathtubs, shower stalls, and sinks.)	4.22	Where provided in public-use and common-use facilities, at least one of each fixture provided per room.
12. Seating, tables, or work surfaces	4.30	If provided in accessible spaces, at least one of each type provided.
13. Places of assembly	4.31	If provided in the facility or at the site.
14. Common-use spaces and facilities (including swimming pools, playgrounds, entrances, rental offices, lobbies, elevators, mailbox areas, lounges, halls and corridors, and the like.)	4.1 through 4.30	If provided in the facility or at the site: (a) Where multiple recreational facilities (e.g., tennis courts) are provided sufficient accessible facilities of each type to assure equitable opportunity for use by persons with handicaps. (b) Where practical, access to all or a portion of nature trails and jogging paths.
15. Laundry rooms	4.32.6	If provided in the facility or at the site, at least one of each type of appliance provided in each laundry area, except that laundry rooms serving covered multifamily dwellings would not be required to have front-loading washers in order to meet the requirements of § 100.205(c)(1). (Where front loading washers are not provided, management will be expected to provide assistive devices on request if necessary to permit a resident to use a top loading washer.)

160 APPENDIX A

Requirement 3. Usable doors.

Section 100.205(c)(2) provides that covered multifamily dwellings with a building entrance on an accessible route shall be designed in such a manner that all the doors designed to allow passage into and within all premises are sufficiently wide to allow passage by handicapped persons in wheelchairs.

Guideline

Section 100.205(c)(2) would apply to doors that are a part of an accessible route in the public and common use areas of multifamily dwellings and to doors into and within individual dwelling units.

(1) On accessible routes in public and common use areas, and for primary entry doors to covered units, doors that comply with ANSI 4.13 would meet this requirement.

(2) Within individual dwelling units, doors intended for user passage through the unit which have a clear opening of at least 32 inches nominal width when the door is open 90 degrees, measured between the face of the door and the stop, would meet this requirement. (See Fig. 1 (a), (b), and (c).) Openings more than 24 inches in depth are not considered doorways. (See Fig. 1 (d).)

Note:
A 34-inch door, hung in the standard manner, provides an acceptable nominal 32-inch clear opening. This door can be adapted to provide a wider opening by using offset hinges, by removing lower portions of the door stop, or both. Pocket or sliding doors are acceptable doors in covered dwelling units and have the added advantage of not impinging on clear floor space in small rooms. The nominal 32-inch clear opening provided by a standard six-foot sliding patio door assembly is acceptable.

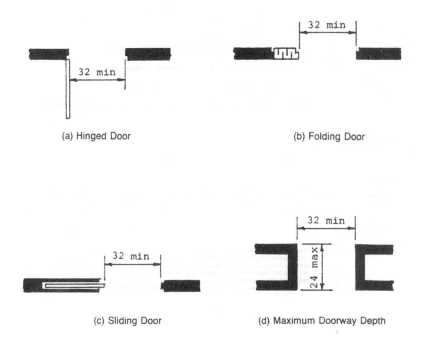

(a) Hinged Door

(b) Folding Door

(c) Sliding Door

(d) Maximum Doorway Depth

Fig. 1 Clear Doorway Width and Depth

Requirement 4. Accessible route into and through the covered dwelling unit.

Section 100.205(c)(3)(i) provides that all covered multifamily dwellings with a building entrance on an accessible route shall be designed and constructed in such a manner that all premises within covered multifamily dwelling units contain an accessible route into and through the covered dwelling unit.

Guideline

Accessible routes into and through dwelling units would meet section 100.205(c)(3)(i) if:

(1) A minimum clear width of 36 inches is provided.

(2) In single-story dwelling units, changes in level within the dwelling unit with heights between 1/4 inch and 1/2 inch are beveled with a slope no greater than 1:2. Except for design features, such as a loft or an area on a different level within a room (e.g., a sunken living room), changes in level greater than 1/2 inch are ramped or have other means of access. Where a single story dwelling unit has special design features, all portions of the single-story unit, except the loft or the sunken or raised area, are on an accessible route; and

   (a) In single-story dwelling units with lofts, all spaces other than the loft are on an accessible route.

   (b) Design features such as sunken or raised functional areas do not interrupt the accessible route through the remainder of the dwelling unit.

(3) In multistory dwelling units in buildings with elevators, the story of the unit that is served by the building elevator (a) is the primary entry to the unit, (b) complies with Requirements 2 through 7 with respect to the rooms located on the entry/accessible floor; and (c) contains a bathroom or powder room which complies with Requirement 7. (Note: multistory dwelling units in non-elevator buildings are not covered dwelling units because, in such cases, there is no ground floor unit.)

(4) Except as provided in paragraphs (5) and (6) below, thresholds at exterior doors, including sliding door tracks, are no higher than 3/4 inch. Thresholds and changes in level at these locations are beveled with a slope no greater than 1:2.

(5) Exterior deck, patio, or balcony surfaces are no more than 1/2 inch below the floor level of the interior of the dwelling unit, unless they are constructed of impervious material such as concrete, brick or flagstone. In such case, the surface is no more than 4 inches below the floor level of the interior of the dwelling unit, or lower if required by local building code.

(6) At the primary entry door to dwelling units with direct exterior access, outside landing surfaces constructed of impervious materials such as concrete, brick or flagstone, are no more than 1/2 inch below the floor level of the interior of the dwelling unit. The finished surface of this area that is located immediately outside the entry may be sloped, up to 1/8 inch per foot (12 inches), for drainage.

Requirement 5. Light switches, electrical outlets, thermostats and other environmental controls in accessible locations.

Section 100.205(c)(3)(ii) requires that all covered multifamily dwellings with a building entrance on an accessible route shall be designed and constructed in such a manner that all premises within covered multifamily dwelling units contain light switches, electrical outlets, thermostats, and other environmental controls in accessible locations.

Guideline

Light switches, electrical outlets, thermostats and other environmental controls would meet section 100.205(c)(3)(ii) if operable parts of the controls are located no higher than 48 inches, and no lower than 15 inches, above the floor. If the reach is over an obstruction (for example, an overhanging shelf) between 20 and 25 inches in depth, the maximum height is reduced to 44 inches for forward approach; or 46 inches for side approach, provided the obstruction (for example, a kitchen base cabinet) is no more than 24 inches in depth. Obstructions should not extend more than 25 inches from the wall beneath a control. (See Fig.2.)

Note

Controls or outlets that do not satisfy these specifications are acceptable provided that comparable controls or outlets (i.e., that perform the same functions) are provided within the same area and are accessible, in accordance with this guideline for Requirement 5.

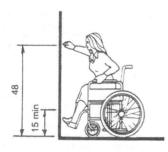

(a) Forward Reach Limit

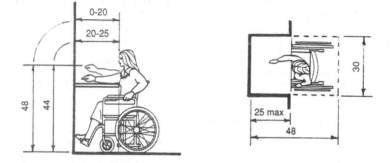

NOTE: Clear knee space should be as deep as the reach distance.

(b) Maximum Forward Reach
Over an Obstruction

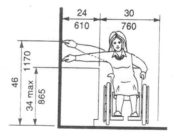

(c) Maximum Side Reach Over Obstruction

Fig. 2 Reach Ranges

Federal Register / Vol. 56, No. 44 / Wednesday, March 6, 1991 / Rules and Regulations   **9509**

Requirement 6. Reinforced walls for grab bars.

Section 100.205(c)(3)(iii) requires that covered multifamily dwellings with a building entrance on an accessible route shall be designed and constructed in such a manner that all premises within covered multifamily dwelling units contain reinforcements in bathroom walls to allow later installation of grab bars around toilet, tub, shower stall and shower seat, where such facilities are provided.

Guideline

Reinforced bathroom walls to allow later installation of grab bars around the toilet, tub, shower stall and shower seat, where such facilities are provided, would meet section 100.205(c)(3)(iii) if reinforced areas are provided at least at those points where grab bars will be mounted. (For example, see Figs. 3, 4 and 5.) Where the toilet is not placed adjacent to a side wall, the bathroom would comply if provision was made for installation of floor mounted, foldaway or similar alternative grab bars. Where the powder room (a room with a toilet and sink) is the only toilet facility located on an accessible level of a multistory dwelling unit, it must comply with this requirement for reinforced walls for grab bars.

Note:

Installation of bathtubs is not limited by the illustrative figures; a tub may have shelves or benches at either end; or a tub may be installed without surrounding walls, if there is provision for alternative mounting of grab bars. For example, a sunken tub placed away from walls could have reinforced areas for installation of floor-mounted grab bars. The same principle applies to shower stalls -- e.g., glass-walled stalls could be planned to allow floor-mounted grab bars to be installed later.

Reinforcement for grab bars may be provided in a variety of ways (for example, by plywood or wood blocking) so long as the necessary reinforcement is placed so as to permit later installation of appropriate grab bars.

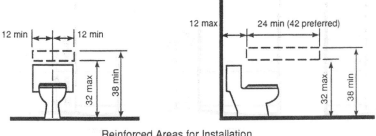

Reinforced Areas for Installation
of Grab Bars

Fig. 3 Water Closets in Adaptable Bathrooms

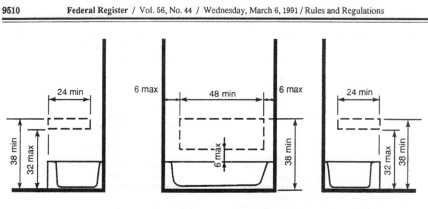

Fig. 4 Location of Grab Bar Reinforcements
for Adaptable Bathtubs

NOTE: The areas outlined in dashed lines represent locations for future installation
of grab bars for typical fixture configurations.

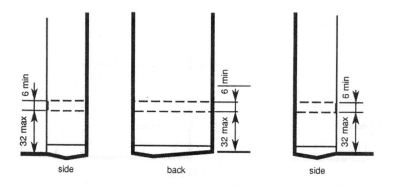

Fig. 5 Location of Grab Bar Reinforcements for Adaptable Showers

NOTE: The areas outlined in dashed lines represent locations for future
installation of grab bars.

Federal Register / Vol. 56, No. 44 / Wednesday, March 6, 1991 / Rules and Regulations **9511**

Requirement 7. Usable kitchens and bathrooms.

Section 100.205(c)(3)(iv) requires that covered multifamily dwellings with a building entrance on an accessible route shall be designed and constructed in such a manner that all premises within covered multifamily dwelling units contain usable kitchens and bathrooms such that an individual in a wheelchair can maneuver about the space.

Guideline

(1) Usable kitchens. Usable kitchens would meet section 100.205(c)(3)(iv) if:

(a) A clear floor space at least 30 inches by 48 inches that allows a parallel approach by a person in a wheelchair is provided at the range or cooktop and sink, and either a parallel or forward approach is provided at oven, dish washer, refrigerator/freezer or trash compactor. (See Fig. 6)

(b) Clearance between counters and all opposing base cabinets, countertops, appliances or walls is at least 40 inches.

(c) In U-shaped kitchens with sink or range or cooktop at the base of the "U", a 60-inch turning radius is provided to allow parallel approach, or base cabinets are removable at that location to allow knee space for a forward approach.

(2) Usable bathrooms. To meet the requirements of section 100.205(c)(3)(iv) either:

All bathrooms in the dwelling unit comply with the provisions of paragraph (a); or

At least one bathroom in the dwelling unit complies with the provisions of paragraph (b), and all other bathrooms and powder rooms within the dwelling unit must be on an accessible route with usable entry doors in accordance with the guidelines for Requirements 3 and 4.

However, in multistory dwelling units, only those bathrooms on the accessible level are subject to the requirements of section 100.205(c)(3)(iv). Where a powder room is the only facility provided on the accessible level of a multistory dwelling unit, the powder room must comply with provisions of paragraph (a) or paragraph (b). Powder rooms that are subject to the requirements of section 100.205(c)(3)(iv) must have reinforcements for grab bars as provided in the guideline for Requirement 6.

(a) Bathrooms that have reinforced walls for grab bars (see Requirement 6) would meet section 100.205(c)(3)(iv) if:

(i) Sufficient maneuvering space is provided within the bathroom for a person using a wheelchair or other mobility aid to enter and close the door, use the fixtures, reopen the door and exit. Doors may swing into the clear floor space provided at any fixture if the maneuvering space is provided. Maneuvering spaces may include any kneespace or toespace available below bathroom fixtures.

(ii) Clear floor space is provided at fixtures as shown in Fig. 7 (a), (b), (c) and (d). Clear floor space at fixtures may overlap.

(iii) If the shower stall is the only bathing facility provided in the covered dwelling unit, the shower stall measures at least 36 inches x 36 inches.

Note:
Cabinets under lavatories are acceptable provided the bathroom has space to allow a parallel approach by a person in a wheelchair; if parallel approach is not possible within the space, any cabinets provided would have to be removable to afford the necessary knee clearance for forward approach.

(b) Bathrooms that have reinforced walls for grab bars (see Requirement 6) would meet section 100.205(c)(3)(iv) if:

(i) Where the door swings into the bathroom, there is a clear space (approximately, 2' 6" by 4'0") within the room to position a wheelchair or other mobility aid clear of the path of the door as it is closed and to permit use of fixtures. This clear space can include any kneespace and toespace available below bathroom fixtures.

(ii) Where the door swings out, a clear space is provided within the bathroom for a person using a wheelchair or other mobility aid to position the wheelchair such that the person is allowed use of fixtures. There also shall be clear space to allow persons using wheelchairs to reopen the door to exit.

(iii) When both tub and shower fixtures are provided in the bathroom, at least one is made accessible. When two or more lavatories in a bathroom are provided, at least one is made accessible.

(iv) Toilets are located within bathrooms in a manner that permit a grab bar to be installed on one side of the fixture. In locations where toilets are adjacent to walls or bathtubs, the center line of the fixture is a minimum of 1'6" from the obstacle. The other (non-grab bar) side of the toilet fixture is a minimum of 1'3" from the finished surface of adjoining walls, vanities or from the edge of a lavatory. (See Figure 7(a).)

(v) Vanities and lavatories are installed with the centerline of the fixture a minimum of 1'3" horizontally from an adjoining wall or fixture. The top of the fixture rim is a maximum height of 2'10" above the finished floor. If kneespace is provided below the vanity, the bottom of the apron is at least 2'3" above the floor. If provided, full kneespace (for front approach) is at least 1'5" deep. (See Figure 7(c).)

(vi) Bathtubs and tub/showers located in the bathroom provide a clear access aisle adjacent to the lavatory that is at least 2'6" wide and extends for a length of 4'0" (measured from the foot of the bathtub). (See Figure 8.)

(vii) Stall showers in the bathroom may be of any size or configuration. A minimum clear floor space 2'6" wide by 4'0" should be available outside the stall. (See Figure 7(d).) If the shower stall is the only bathing facility provided in the covered dwelling unit, or on the accessible level of a covered multistory unit, and measures a nominal 36 x 36, the shower stall must have reinforcing to allow for installation of an optional wall hung bench seat.

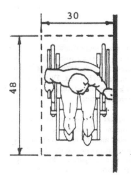

(a) Parallel Approach

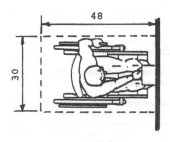

(b) Forward Approach

Fig. 6 Minimum Clear Floor Space for Wheelchairs

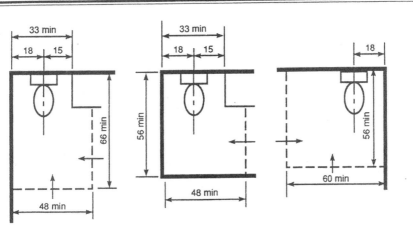

(a) Clear Floor Space for Water Closets

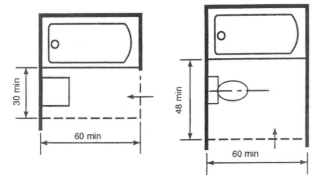

(b) Clear Floor Space at Bathtubs

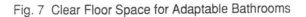

Fig. 7 Clear Floor Space for Adaptable Bathrooms

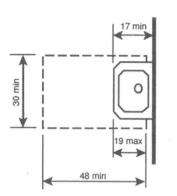

Lavatory With Knee Space

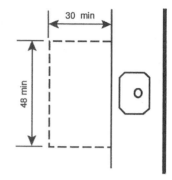

Lavatory Without Knee Space

(c) Clear Floor Space at Lavatories

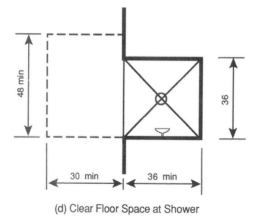

(d) Clear Floor Space at Shower

Federal Register / Vol. 56, No. 44 / Wednesday, March 6, 1991 / Rules and Regulations **9515**

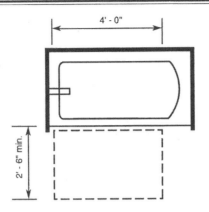

Fig. 8 Alternative Specification – Clear Floor Space at Bathtub

NOTE: Clear floor space beside tub may overlap with clear floor space
beneath adjacent fixtures.

**Appendix III to Ch. I, Subchapter A—
Preamble to Final Housing Accessibility
Guidelines (Published March 6, 1991).**

[FR Doc. 91–5228 Filed 3–5–91; 8:45 am]

BILLING CODE 4210–28–M

BILLING CODE 4210–28–C

APPENDIX B

Tuesday
June 28, 1994

Part III

Department of Housing and Urban Development

Office of the Assistant Secretary for Fair Housing and Equal Opportunity

24 CFR Ch. I
Fair Housing: Accessibility Guidelines; Questions and Answers; Supplement to Notice

33362   **Federal Register** / Vol. 59, No. 123 / Tuesday, June 28, 1994 / Rules and Regulations

DEPARTMENT OF HOUSING AND URBAN DEVELOPMENT

Office of the Assistant Secretary for Fair Housing and Equal Opportunity

24 CFR Chapter I

[Docket No. N–94–2011; FR–2665–N–09]

Supplement to Notice of Fair Housing Accessibility Guidelines: Questions and Answers About the Guidelines

AGENCY: Office of the Assistant Secretary for Fair Housing and Equal Opportunity, HUD.

ACTION: Supplement to notice of fair housing accessibility guidelines.

SUMMARY: On March 6, 1991, the Department published final Fair Housing Accessibility Guidelines (Guidelines) to provide builders and developers with technical guidance on how to comply with the accessibility requirements of the Fair Housing Amendments Act of 1988 (Fair Housing Act) that are applicable to certain multifamily dwellings designed and constructed for first occupancy after March 13, 1991. Since publication of the Guidelines, the Department has received many questions regarding the applicability of the technical specifications set forth in the Guidelines to certain types of new multifamily dwellings and certain types of units within covered multifamily dwellings. The Department also has received several questions concerning the types of new multifamily dwellings that are subject to the design and construction requirements of the Fair Housing Act.

This document reproduces the questions that have been most frequently asked by members of the public, and the Department's answers to these questions. The Department believes that the issues addressed by these questions and answers may be of interest and assistance to other members of the public who must comply with the design and construction requirements of the Fair Housing Act.

EFFECTIVE DATE: June 28, 1994.

FOR FURTHER INFORMATION CONTACT: Judith Keeler, Director, Office of Program Compliance and Disability Rights. For technical questions regarding this notice, contact Office of Fair Housing and Equal Opportunity, room 5112, Department of Housing and Urban Development, 451 Seventh Street, Washington, DC 20410, telephone 202–708–2618 (voice), 202–708–1734 TTY; for copies of this notice contact the Fair Housing Information Clearinghouse at 1–800–795–7915 (this is a toll-free

number), or 1–800–483–2209 (this is a toll-free TTY number).

SUPPLEMENTARY INFORMATION:

Background

The Fair Housing Amendments Act of 1988 (Pub.L. 100–430, approved September 13, 1988) (the Fair Housing Amendments Act) amended title VIII of the Civil Rights Act of 1968 (Fair Housing Act or Act) to add prohibitions against discrimination in housing on the basis of disability and familial status. The Fair Housing Amendments Act also made it unlawful to design and construct certain multifamily dwellings for first occupancy after March 13, 1991, in a manner that makes them inaccessible to persons with disabilities, and established design and construction requirements to make these dwellings readily accessible to and usable by persons with disabilities.[1] Section 100.205 of the Department's regulations at 24 CFR part 100 implements the Fair Housing Act's design and construction requirements (also referred to as accessibility requirements).

On March 6, 1991 (56 FR 9472), the Department published final Fair Housing Accessibility Guidelines (Guidelines) to provide builders and developers with technical guidance on how to comply with the accessibility requirements of the Fair Housing Act. (The Guidelines are codified at 24 CFR Ch.I, Subch.A., App. II. The preamble to the Guidelines is codified at 24 CFR Ch.I, Subch.A., App.III.) The Guidelines are organized to follow the sequence of requirements as they are presented in the Fair Housing Act and in 24 CFR 100.205. The Guidelines provide technical guidance on the following seven requirements:

Requirement 1. Accessible building entrance on an accessible route.
Requirement 2. Accessible common and public use areas.
Requirement 3. Usable doors (usable by a person in a wheelchair).
Requirement 4. Accessible route into and through the dwelling unit.
Requirement 5. Light switches, electrical outlets, thermostats and other environmental controls in accessible locations.
Requirement 6. Reinforced walls for grab bars.
Requirement 7. Usable kitchens and bathrooms.

The design specifications presented in the Guidelines are recommended guidelines only. Builders and

[1] Although this notice uses the terms "disability" and "disabilities," the terms used in the Fair Housing Amendments Act are "handicap" and "handicaps."

developers may choose to depart from these guidelines and seek alternate ways to demonstrate that they have met the requirements of the Fair Housing Act. The Fair Housing Act and the Department's implementing regulation provides, for example, for use of the appropriate requirements of the ANSI A117.1 standard. However, adherence to the Guidelines does constitute a safe harbor in the Department's administrative enforcement process for compliance with the Fair Housing Act's design and construction requirements.

Since publication of the Guidelines, the Department has received many questions regarding applicability of the design specifications to certain types of new multifamily dwellings and to certain types of interior housing designs. The Department also has received several questions concerning the types of new multifamily dwellings that are subject to compliance with the design and construction requirements of the Fair Housing Act. Given the wide variety in the types of multifamily dwellings and the types of dwelling units, and the continual introduction into the housing market of new building and interior designs, it was not possible for the Department to prepare accessibility guidelines that would address every housing type or housing design. Although the Guidelines cannot address every housing design, it is the Department's intention to assist the public in complying with the design and construction requirements of the Fair Housing Act through workshops and seminars, telephone assistance, written replies to written inquiries, and through the publication of documents such as this one. The Department has contracted for the preparation of a design manual that will further explain and illustrate the Fair Housing Act Accessibility Guidelines.

The questions and answers set forth in this notice address the issues most frequently raised by the public with respect to types of multifamily dwellings subject to the design and construction requirements of the Fair Housing Act, and the technical specifications contained in the Guidelines.

The question and answer format is divided into two sections. Section 1, entitled "Dwellings Subject to the New Construction Requirements of the Fair Housing Act" addresses the issues raised in connection with the types of multifamily dwellings (including portions of such dwellings) constructed for first occupancy after March 13, 1991 that must comply with the Act's design and construction requirements. Section

Federal Register / Vol. 59, No. 123 / Tuesday, June 28, 1994 / Rules and Regulations   **33363**

2, entitled "Accessibility Guidelines," addresses the issues raised in connection with the design and construction specifications set forth in the Guidelines.

Dated: March 23, 1994.

Roberta Achtenberg,

Assistant Secretary for Fair Housing and Equal Opportunity.

Accordingly, the Department adds the "Questions and Answers about the Fair Housing Accessibility Guidelines" as Appendix IV to 24 CFR Chapter I, Subchapter A to read as follows:

U.S. Department of Housing and Urban Development
Office of the Assistant Secretary for
Fair Housing and Equal Opportunity

Supplement to Notice of Fair Housing Accessibility Guidelines: Questions and Answers about the Guidelines

---

24 CFR Ch.I

Appendix IV to Subchapter A—

Note: This is a reprint of the Supplement to Notice of Fair Housing Accessibility Guidelines: Questions and Answers About the Guidelines published in the Federal Register on June 28, 1994, Vol. 59, No. 123, pages 33362-33368.

Questions and Answers about the Fair Housing Accessibility Guidelines

Introduction

On March 6, 1991 (56 FR 9472), the Department published final Fair Housing Accessibility Guidelines (Guidelines). (The Guidelines are codified at 24 CFR Ch. I, Subch. A, App. II.) The Guidelines provide builders and developers with technical guidance on how to comply with the accessibility requirements of the Fair Housing Amendments Act of 1988 (Fair Housing Act) that are applicable to certain multifamily dwellings designed and constructed for first occupancy after March 13, 1991. Since publication of the Guidelines, the Department has received many questions regarding the applicability of the technical specifications set forth in the Guidelines to certain types of new multifamily dwellings and certain types of units within covered multifamily dwellings. The Department also has received several questions concerning the types of new multifamily dwellings that are subject to the design and construction requirements of the Fair Housing Act.

The questions and answers contained in this document address some of the issues most frequently raised by the public with respect to the types of multifamily dwellings subject to the design and construction requirements of the Fair Housing Act, and the technical specifications contained in the Guidelines.

The issues addressed in this document are addressed only with respect to the application of the Fair Housing Act and the Guidelines to dwellings which are "covered multifamily dwellings" under the Fair Housing Act. Certain of these dwellings, as well as certain public and common use areas of such dwellings, may also be covered by various other laws, such as section 504 of the Rehabilitation Act of 1973 (29 U.S.C. 794); the Architectural Barriers Act of 1968 (42 U.S.C. 4151-4157); and the Americans with Disabilities Act of 1990 (42 U.S.C. 12101-12213).

Section 504 applies to programs and activities receiving federal financial assistance. The Department's regulations for section 504 are found at 24 CFR part 8.

The Architectural Barriers Act applies to certain buildings financed in whole or in part with federal funds. The Department's regulations for the Architectural Barriers Act are found at 24 CFR parts 40 and 41.

The Americans with Disabilities Act (ADA) is a broad civil rights law guaranteeing equal opportunity for individuals with disabilities in employment, public accommodations, transportation, State and local government services, and telecommunications. The Department of Justice is the lead federal agency for implementation of the ADA and should be contacted for copies of relevant ADA regulations.

The Department has received a number of questions regarding applicability of the ADA to residential housing, particularly with respect to title III of the ADA, which addresses accessibility requirements for public accommodations. The Department has been asked, in particular, if public and common use areas of residential housing are covered by title III of the ADA. Strictly residential facilities are not considered places of public accommodation and therefore would not be subject to title III of the ADA, nor would amenities provided for the exclusive use of residents and their guests. However, common areas that function as one of the ADA's twelve categories of places of public accommodation within residential facilities are considered places of public accommodation if they are open to persons other than residents and their guests. Rental offices and sales office for residential housing, for example, are by their nature open to the public, and are places of public accommodation and must comply with the ADA requirements in addition to all applicable requirements of the Fair Housing Act. As stated above, the remainder of this notice addresses issues most frequently raised by the public with respect to the types of multifamily dwellings subject to the design and construction requirements of the Fair Housing Act, and the technical specifications contained in the Guidelines.

Section 1: Dwellings Subject to the New Construction Requirements of the Fair Housing Act.

The issues addressed in this section concern the types of multifamily dwellings (or portions of such dwellings) designed and constructed for first occupancy after March 13, 1991 that must comply with the design and construction requirements of the Fair Housing Act.

1. Townhouses

(a) Q. Are townhouses in non-elevator buildings which have individual exterior entrances required to be accessible?
A. Yes, if they are single-story townhouses.   If they are multistory townhouses, accessibility is not required. (See the discussion of townhouses in the preamble to the Guidelines under "Section 2--Definitions [Covered Multifamily Dwellings]" at 56 FR 9481, March 6, 1991, or 24 CFR Ch. I, Subch. A, App. III.)

(b) Q. Does the Fair Housing Act cover four one-story dwelling units that share common walls and have individual entrances?
A. Yes. The Fair Housing Act applies to all units in buildings consisting of four or more dwelling units if such buildings have one or more elevators; and ground floor dwelling units in other buildings consisting of four or more dwelling units. This would include one-story homes, sometimes called "single-story townhouses," "villas," or "patio apartments," regardless of ownership, even though such homes may not be considered multifamily dwellings under various building codes.

(c) Q. What if the single-story dwelling units are separated by firewalls?
A. The Fair Housing Act would still apply. The Guidelines define covered multifamily dwellings to include buildings having four or more units within a single structure separated by firewalls.

2. Commercial Space

Q. If a building includes three residential dwelling units and one or more commercial spaces, is the building a "covered multifamily dwelling" under the Fair Housing Act?
A. No. Covered multifamily dwellings are buildings consisting of four or more dwelling units, if such buildings have one or more elevators; and ground floor dwelling units in other buildings consisting of four or more dwelling units. Commercial space does not meet the definition of "dwelling unit." Note, however, that title III of the ADA applies to public accommodations and commercial facilities, therefore an independent determination should be made regarding applicability of the ADA to the commercial space in such a building (see the introduction to these questions and answers, which provides some background on the ADA).

3. Condominiums

(a) Q. Are condominiums covered by the Fair Housing Act?
A. Yes. Condominiums in covered multifamily dwellings are covered by the Fair Housing Act. The Fair Housing Act makes no distinctions based on ownership.

(b) Q. If a condominium is pre-sold as a shell and the interior is designed and constructed by the buyer, are the Guidelines applicable?
A. Yes. The Fair Housing Act applies to design and construction of covered multifamily dwellings, regardless of whether the person doing the design and construction is an architect, builder, or private individual. (See discussion of condominiums in the preamble to Guidelines under "Section 2--Definitions [Dwelling Units]" at 56 FR 9481, March 6, 1991, or 24 CFR Ch. I, Subch. A, App. III.)

3

4. Additions

(a) **Q.** If an owner adds four or more dwelling units to an existing building, are those units covered by the Fair Housing Act?
A. Yes, provided that the units constitute a new addition to the building and not substantial rehabilitation of existing units.

(b) **Q.** What if new public and common use spaces are also being added?
A. If new public and common use areas or buildings are also added, they are required to be accessible.

(c) **Q.** If the only new construction is an addition consisting of four or more dwelling units, would the existing public and common use spaces have to be made accessible?
A. No, existing public and common use areas would not have to be made accessible. The Fair Housing Act applies to new construction of covered multifamily dwellings. (See section 804(f)(3)(C)(i) of the Act.) Existing public and common use facilities are not newly constructed portions of covered multifamily dwellings. However, reasonable modifications to the existing public and common use areas to provide access would have to be allowed, and the Americans with Disabilities Act (ADA) may apply to certain public and common use areas. An independent determination should be made regarding applicability of the ADA. (See the introduction to these questions and answers, which provides some background on the ADA.)

5. Units Over Parking

(a) **Q.** Plans for a three-story building consist of a common parking area with assigned stalls on grade as the first story, and two stories of single-story dwelling units stacked over the parking. All of the stories above the parking level are to be accessed by stairways. There are no elevators planned to be in the building. Would the first story of single-story dwelling units over the parking level be required to be accessible?
A. Yes. The Guidelines adopt and amplify the definition of "ground floor" found in HUD's regulation implementing the Fair Housing Act (see 24 CFR 100.201) to indicate that ". . .where the first floor containing dwelling units is above grade, all units on that floor must be served by a building entrance on an accessible route. This floor will be considered to be a ground floor." (See definition of "ground floor" in the Guidelines at 24 CFR Ch. I, Subch. A, App. II, Section 2.) Where no dwelling units in a covered multifamily dwelling are located on grade, the first floor with dwelling units will be considered to be a ground floor, and must be served by a building entrance on an accessible route. However, the definition of "ground floor" does not require that there be more than one ground floor.

(b) **Q.** If a building design contains a mix of single-story flats on grade and single-story flats located above grade over a public parking area, do the flats over the parking area have to be accessible?
A. No. In the example in the above question, because some single-story flats are situated on grade, these flats would be the ground floor dwelling units and would be required to be accessible. The definition of ground floor in the Guidelines states, in part, that "ground floor means a floor of a building with a building entrance on an accessible route. A building may have one or more ground floors. . ." Thus, the definition includes situations where the design plan is such that more than one floor of a building may be accessed by means of an accessible route (for an example, see Question 6, which follows). There is no requirement in the Department's regulations implementing the Fair Housing Act that there be more than one ground floor.

6. More Than One Ground Floor

Q. If a two or three story building is to be constructed on a slope, such that the lowest story can be accessed on grade on one side of the building and the second story can be accessed on grade on the other side of the building, do the dwelling units on both the first and second stories have to be made accessible?

A. Yes. By defining "ground floor" to be any floor of a building with an accessible entrance on an accessible route, the Fair Housing Act regulations recognize that certain buildings, based on the site and the design plan, have more than one story which can be accessed at or near grade. In such cases, if more than one story can be designed to have an accessible entrance on an accessible route, then all such stories should be so designed. Each story becomes a ground floor and the dwelling units on that story must meet the accessibility requirements of the Act. (See the discussion on this issue in Question 12 of this document.)

7. Continuing Care Facilities

Q. Do the new construction requirements of the Fair Housing Act apply to continuing care facilities which incorporate housing, health care and other types of services?

A. The new construction requirements of the Fair Housing Act would apply to continuing care facilities if the facility includes at least one building with four or more dwelling units. Whether a facility is a "dwelling" under the Act depends on whether the facility is to be used as a residence for more than a brief period of time. As a result, the operation of each continuing care facility must be examined on a case-by-case basis to determine whether it contains dwellings. Factors that the Department will consider in making such an examination include, but are not limited to: (1) the length of time persons stay in the project; (2) whether policies are in effect at the project that are designed and intended to encourage or discourage occupants from forming an expectation and intent to continue to occupy space at the project; and (3) the nature of the services provided by or at the project.

8. Evidence of First Occupancy

Q. The Fair Housing Act applies to covered multifamily dwellings built for first occupancy after March 13, 1991. What is acceptable evidence of "first occupancy"?

A. The determination of first occupancy is made on a building by building basis. The Fair Housing Act regulations provide that "covered multifamily dwellings shall be deemed to be designed and constructed for first occupancy on or before March 13, 1991 (and therefore exempt from the Act's accessibility requirements) if they are occupied by that date or if the last building permit or renewal thereof for the covered multifamily dwellings is issued by a State, county or local government on or before June 15, 1990."

For buildings that did not obtain the final building permit on or before June 15, 1990, proof of the date of first occupancy consists of (1) a certificate of occupancy, and (2) a showing that at least one dwelling unit in the building actually was occupied by March 13, 1991. For example, a tenant has signed a lease and has taken possession of a unit. The tenant need not have moved into the unit, but the tenant must have taken possession so that, if desired, he or she could have moved into the building by March 13, 1991. For dwelling units that were for sale, this means that the new owner had completed settlement and taken possession of the dwelling unit by March 13, 1991. Once again, the new owner need not have moved in, but the owner must have been in possession of the unit and able to move in, if desired, on or before March 13, 1991. A certificate of occupancy alone would not be an acceptable means of establishing first occupancy, and units offered for sale, but not sold, would not meet the test for first occupancy.

9. Converted Buildings

Q. If a building was used previously for a nonresidential purpose, such as a warehouse, office building, or school, and is being converted to a multifamily dwelling, must the building meet the requirements of the Fair Housing Act?

A. No, the Fair Housing Act applies to "covered multifamily dwellings for first occupancy after" March 13, 1991, and the Fair Housing Act regulation defines "first occupancy" as "a building that has never before been used for any purpose." (See 24 CFR 100.201, for the definition of "first occupancy," and also 24 CFR Ch. I, Subch. A, App. I.)

Section 2: Accessibility Guidelines.

The issues addressed in this section concern the technical specifications set forth in the Fair Housing Accessibility Guidelines.

Requirement 1 -- Accessible Entrance on an Accessible Route

10. Accessible Routes to Garages

(a) **Q.** Is it necessary to have an accessible path of travel from a subterranean garage to single-story covered multifamily dwellings built on top of the garage?

A. Yes. The Fair Housing Act requires that there be an accessible building entrance on an accessible route. To satisfy Requirement 1 of the Guidelines, there would have to be an accessible route leading to grade level entrances serving the single-story dwelling units from a public street or sidewalk or other pedestrian arrival point. The below grade parking garage is a public and common use facility. Therefore, there must also be an accessible route from this parking area to the covered dwelling units. This may be provided either by a properly sloped ramp leading from the below grade parking to grade level, or by means of an elevator from the parking garage to the dwelling units.

(b) **Q.** Does the route leading from inside a private attached garage to the dwelling unit have to be accessible?

A. No. Under Requirement 1 of the Guidelines, there must be an accessible entrance to the dwelling unit on an accessible route. However, this route and entrance need not originate inside the garage. Most units with attached garages have a separate main entry, and this would be the entrance required to be accessible. Thus, if there were one or two steps inside the garage leading into the unit, there would be no requirement to put a ramp in place of the steps. However, the door connecting the garage and dwelling unit would have to meet the requirements for usable doors.

11. Site Impracticality Tests

(a) **Q.** Under the individual building test, how is the second step of the test performed, which involves measuring the slope of the finished grade between the entrance and applicable arrival points?

A. The slope is measured at ground level from the entrance to the top of the pavement of all vehicular and pedestrian arrival points within 50 feet of the planned entrance, or, if there are none within 50 feet, the vehicular or pedestrian arrival point closest to the planned entrance.

(b) **Q.** Under the individual building test, at what point of the planned entrance is the measurement taken?

A. On a horizontal plane, the center of each individual doorway should be the point of measurement when measuring to an arrival point, whether the doorway is an entrance door to the building or an entrance door to a unit.

(c) **Q.** The site analysis test calls for a calculation of the percentage of the buildable areas having slopes of less than 10 percent. What is the definition of "buildable areas"?

A. The "buildable area" is any area of the lot or site where a building can be located in compliance with applicable codes and zoning regulations.

12. Second Ground Floors

(a) **Q.** The Department's regulation for the Fair Housing Act provides that there can be more than one ground floor in a covered multifamily dwelling (such as a three-story building built on a slope with three stories at and above grade in front and two stories at grade in back). How is the individual building test performed for additional stories, to determine if those stories must also be treated as "ground floors"?

A. For purposes of determining whether a non-elevator building has more than one ground floor, the point of measurement for additional ground floors, after the first ground floor has been established, is at the center of the entrance (building entrance for buildings with one or more common entrance and each dwelling unit entrance for buildings with separate ground floor unit entrances) at floor level for that story.

(b) **Q.** What happens if a builder deliberately manipulates the grade so that a second story, which also might have been treated as a ground floor, requires steps?

A. Deliberate manipulation of the height of the finished floor level to avoid the requirements of the Fair Housing Act would serve as a basis for the Department to determine that there is reasonable cause to believe that a discriminatory housing practice has occurred.

Requirement 2 -- Public and Common Use Areas

13. No Covered Dwellings

Q. Are the public and common use areas of a newly constructed development that consists entirely of buildings having four or more multistory townhouses, with no elevators, required to be accessible?

A. No. The Fair Housing Act applies only to new construction of covered multifamily dwellings. Multistory townhouses, provided that they meet the definition of "multistory" in the Guide-

lines, are not covered multifamily dwellings if the building does not have an elevator. (See discussion of townhouses in the preamble to the Guidelines under "Section 2--Definitions [Covered Multifamily Dwellings]" at 56 FR 9481, March 6, 1991, or 24 CFR Ch. I, Subch. A, App. III.) If there are no covered multifamily dwellings on a site, then the public and common use areas of the site are not required to be accessible. However, the Americans with Disabilities Act (ADA) may apply to certain public and common use areas. Again, an independent determination should be made regarding applicability of the ADA. (See the introduction to these questions and answers, which provides some background on the ADA.)

14. Parking Spaces and Garages

(a) **Q.** How many resident parking spaces must be made accessible at the time of construction?

A. The Guidelines provide that a minimum of two percent of the parking spaces serving covered dwelling units be made accessible and located on an accessible route to wheelchair users. Also, if a resident requests an accessible space, additional accessible parking spaces would be necessary if the two percent are already reserved.

(b) **Q.** If both open and covered parking spaces are provided, how many of each type must be accessible?

A. The Guidelines require that accessible parking be provided for residents with disabilities on the same terms and with the full range of choices, e.g., surface parking or garage, that are provided for other residents of the project. Thus, if a project provides different types of parking such as surface parking, garage, or covered spaces, some of each must be made accessible. While the total parking spaces required to be accessible is only two percent, at least one space for each type of parking should be made accessible even if this number exceeds two percent.

(c) **Q.** If a project having covered multifamily dwellings provides parking garages where there are several individual garages grouped together either in a separate area of the building (such as at one end of the building, or in a detached building), for assignment or rental to residents, are there any requirements for the inside dimensions of these individual parking garages?

A. Yes. These garages would be public and common use space, even though the individual garages may be assigned to a particular dwelling unit. Therefore, at least two percent of the garages should be at least 14' 2" wide and the vehicular door should be at least 10'-0" wide.

(d) **Q.** If a covered multifamily dwelling has a below grade common use parking garage, is there a requirement for a vertical clearance to allow vans to park?

A. This issue was addressed in the preamble to the Guidelines, but continues to be a frequently asked question. (See the preamble to the Guidelines under the discussion of "Section 5--Guidelines for Requirement 2" at 56 FR 9486, March 6, 1991, or 24 CFR Ch. I, Subch. A, App. III.) In response to comments from the public that the Guidelines for parking specify minimum vertical clearance for garage parking, the Department responded: No national accessibility standards, including UFAS, require particular vertical clearances in parking garages. The Department did not consider it appropriate to exceed commonly accepted standards by including a minimum vertical clearance in the Fair Housing Accessibility Guidelines, in view of the minimal accessibility requirements of the Fair Housing Act.

Since the Guidelines refer to ANSI A117.1 1986 for the standards to follow for public and common use areas, and since the ANSI does not include a vertical clearance for garage parking, the Guidelines likewise do not. (Note: UFAS is the Uniform Federal Accessibility Standard.)

15. Public Telephones

Q. If a covered multifamily dwelling has public telephones in the lobby, what are the requirements for accessibility for these telephones?

A. The requirements governing public telephones are found in Item #14, "Common use spaces and facilities," in the chart under Requirement 2 of the Guidelines. While the chart does not address the quantity of accessible public telephones, at a minimum, at least one accessible telephone per bank of telephones would be required. The specifications at ANSI 4.29 would apply.

Requirement 3 -- Usable Doors

16. Required Width

Q. Will a standard hung 32-inch door provide sufficient clear width to meet the requirements of the Fair Housing Act?

A. No, a 32-inch door would not provide a sufficient clear opening to meet the requirement for usable doors. A notation in the Guidelines for Requirement 3 indicates that a 34-inch door, hung in the standard manner, provides an acceptable nominal 32-inch clear opening.

17. Maneuvering Clearances and Hardware

Q. Is it correct that only the exterior side of the main entry door of covered multifamily dwellings must meet the ANSI requirements?

A. Yes. The exterior side of the main entry door is part of the public and common use areas and therefore must meet ANSI A117.1 1986 specifications for doors. These specifications include necessary maneuvering clearances and accessible door hardware. The interior of the main entry door is part of the dwelling unit and only needs to meet the requirements for usable doors within the dwelling intended for user passage, i.e., at least 32 inches nominal clear width, with no requirements for maneuvering clearances and hardware. (See 56 FR 9487-9488, March 6, 1991, or 24 CFR Ch. I, Subch. A, App. III.)

18. Doors to Inaccessible Areas

Q. Is it necessary to provide usable doors when the door leads to an area of the dwelling that is not accessible, such as the door leading down to an unfinished basement, or the door connecting a single-story dwelling with an attached garage? (In the latter case, there is a separate entrance door to the unit which is accessible.)

A. Yes. Within the dwelling unit, doors intended for user passage through the unit must meet the requirements for usable doors. Such doors would have to provide at least 32 inches nominal clear width when the door is open 90 degrees, measured between the face of the door and the stop. This will ensure that, if a wheelchair user occupying the dwelling unit chooses to modify the unit to provide accessibility to these areas, such as installing a ramp from the dwelling unit into the garage, the door will be sufficiently wide to allow passage. It also will allow passage for people using walkers or crutches.

Requirement 4 -- Accessible Route Into and Through the Unit

19. Sliding Door

Q. If a sliding door track has a threshold of 3/4", does this trigger requirements for ramps?

A. No. The Guidelines at Requirement 4 provide that thresholds at doors, including sliding door tracks, may be no higher than 3/4" and must be beveled with a slope no greater than 1:2.

20. Private Attached Garages

(a) **Q.** If a covered multifamily dwelling has an individual, private garage which is attached to and serves only that dwelling,

does the garage have to be accessible in terms of width and length?

A. Garages attached to and which serve only one covered multifamily dwelling are part of that dwelling unit, and are not covered by Requirement 2 of the Guidelines, which addresses accessible and usable public and common use space. Because such individual garages attached to and serving only one covered multifamily dwelling typically are not finished living space, the garage is not required to be accessible in terms of width or length. The answer to this question should be distinguished from the answer to Question 14(c). Question 14(c) addresses parking garages where there are several garages or stalls located together, either in a separate, detached building, or in a central area of the building, such as at one end. These types of garages are not attached to, and do not serve, only one unit and are therefore considered public and common use garages.

21. Split-Level Entry

Q. Is a dwelling unit that has a split entry foyer, with the foyer and living room on an accessible route and the remainder of the unit down two steps, required to be accessible if it is a ground floor unit in a covered multifamily dwelling?

A. Yes. Under Requirement 4, there must be an accessible route into and through the dwelling unit. This would preclude a split level foyer, unless a properly sloped ramp can be provided.

Requirement 5 -- Environmental Controls

22. Range Hood Fans

Q. Must the switches on range hood kitchen ventilation fans be in accessible locations?

A. No. Kitchen ventilation fans located on a range hood are considered to be part of the appliance. The Fair Housing Act has no requirements for appliances in the interiors of dwelling units, or the switches that operate them. (See "Guidelines for Requirement 5" and "Controls for Ranges and Cooktops" at 56 FR 9490 and 9492, March 6, 1991, or 24 CFR Ch. I, Subch. A, App. III.)

Requirement 6 -- Reinforced Walls for Grab Bars

23. Type of Reinforcement

Q. What type of reinforcement should be used to reinforce bathroom walls for the later installation of grab bars?
A. The Guidelines do not prescribe the type of material to use or method of providing reinforcement for bathroom walls. The Guidelines recognize that grab bar reinforcing may be accomplished in a variety of ways, such as by providing plywood panels in the areas illustrated in the Guidelines under Requirement 6, or by installing vertical reinforcement in the form of double studs at the points noted on the figures in the Guidelines. The builder/owners should maintain records that reflect the placement of the reinforcing material, for later reference by a resident who wishes to install a grab bar.

24. Type of Grab Bar

Q. What types of grab bars should the reinforcement be designed to accommodate and what types may be used if the builder elects to install grab bars in some units at the time of construction?
A. The Guidelines do not prescribe the type of product for grab bars, or the structural strength for grab bars. The Guidelines only state that the necessary reinforcement must be placed "so as to permit later installation of appropriate grab bars." (Emphasis added.) In determining what is an appropriate grab bar, builders are encouraged to look to the 1986 ANSI A117.1 standard, the standard cited in the Fair Housing Act. Builders also may follow State or local standards in planning for or selecting appropriate grab bars.

Requirement 7 -- Usable Kitchens and Bathrooms

25. Counters and Vanities

Q. It appears from Figure 2(c) of the Guidelines (under Requirement 5) that there is a 34 inch height requirement for kitchen counters and vanities. Is this true?
A. No. Requirement 7 addresses the requirement for usable kitchens and bathrooms so that a person in a wheelchair can maneuver about the space. The legislative history of the Fair Housing Act makes it clear that the Congress intended that the Act affect ability to maneuver within the space of the kitchen and bathroom, but not to require fixtures, cabinetry or plumbing of adjustable design. Figure 2(c) of the Guidelines is illustrating the maximum side reach range over an obstruction. Because the picture was taken directly from the ANSI A117.1 1986 standard, the diagram also shows the height of the obstruction, which, in this picture, is a countertop. This 34 inch height, however, should not be regarded as a requirement.

26. Showers

Q. Is a parallel approach required at the shower, as shown in Figure 7(d) of the Guidelines?
A. Yes. For a 36" x 36" shower, as shown in Figure 7(d), a person in a wheelchair would typically add a wall hung seat. Thus the parallel approach as shown in Figure 7(d) is essential in order to be able to transfer from the wheelchair to the shower seat.

27. Tub Controls

Q. Do the Guidelines set any requirements for the type or location of bathtub controls?
A. No, except where the specifications in Requirement 7(2)(b) are used. In that case, while the type of control is not

specified, the control must be located as shown in Figure 8 of the Guidelines.

28. Paragraph (b) Bathrooms

Q. If an architect or builder chooses to follow the bathroom specifications in Requirement 7, Guideline 2, paragraph (b), where at least one bathroom is designed to comply with the provisions of paragraph (b), are the other bathrooms in the dwelling unit required to have reinforced walls for grab bars?

A. Yes. Requirement 6 of the Guidelines requires reinforced walls in bathrooms for later installation of grab bars. Even though Requirement 6 was not repeated under Requirement 7--Guideline 2, it is a separate requirement which must be met in all bathrooms. The same would be true for other Requirements in the Guidelines, such as Requirement 5, which applies to usable light switches, electrical outlets, thermostats and other environmental controls; Requirement 4 for accessible route; and Requirement 3 for usable doors.

29. Bathroom Clear Floor Space

Q. Is it acceptable to design a bathroom with an in-swinging 2'10" door which can be retrofitted to swing out in order to provide the necessary clear floor space in the bathroom?

A. No. The requirements in the Guidelines must be included at the time of construction. Thus, for a bathroom, there must be sufficient maneuvering space and clear floor space so that a person using a wheelchair or other mobility aid can enter and close the door, use the fixtures and exit.

30. Lavatories

Q. Would it be acceptable to use removable base cabinets beneath a wall-hung

lavatory where a parallel approach is not possible?

A. Yes. The space under and around the cabinet should be finished prior to installation. For example, the tile or other floor finish must extend under the removable base cabinet.

31. Wing Walls

Q. Can a water closet (toilet) be located in an alcove with a wing wall?

A. Yes, as long as the necessary clear floor space shown in Figure 7(a) is provided. This would mean that the wing wall could not extend beyond the front edge of a lavatory located on the other side of the wall from the water closet.

32. Penalties

Q. What types of penalties or monetary damages will be assessed if covered multifamily dwellings are found not to be in compliance with the Fair Housing Act?

A. Under the Fair Housing Act, if an administrative law judge finds that a respondent has engaged in or is about to engage in a discriminatory housing practice, the administrative law judge will order appropriate relief. Such relief may include actual and compensatory damages, injunctive or other equitable relief, attorney's fees and costs, and may also include civil penalties ranging from $10,000 for the first offense to $50,000 for repeated offenses. In addition, in the case of buildings which have been completed, structural changes could be ordered, and an escrow fund might be required to finance future changes.

Further, a Federal district court judge can order similar relief plus punitive damages as well as civil penalties for up to $100,000 in an action brought by a private individual or by the U.S. Department of Justice.

Index